ANCIENT HISTORY: KEY THEMES AND APPROACHES

Ancient History: Key Themes and Approaches is a sourcebook of writings on ancient history. In over 500 extracts from a wide range of secondary sources, it opens up the most important, stimulating and provocative arguments by modern writers on the subject, and as such constitutes an invaluable reference source. The first section deals with different aspects of life in the ancient world, such as democracy, imperialism, slavery and sexuality, while the second section covers the ideas of key ancient historians and other writers on classical antiquity. Overall, this unique book offers an invaluable introduction to the most important ideas, theories and controversies in ancient history, and a thought-provoking survey of the range of views and approaches to the subject.

ROUTLEDGE KEY GUIDES

ANCIENT HISTORY: KEY THEMES AND APPROACHES

Neville Morley

London and New York

First published 2000
by Routledge
11 New Fetter Lane, London EC4P 4EE

Simultaneously published in the USA and Canada
by Routledge
29 West 35th Street, New York, NY 10001

Routledge is an imprint of the Taylor & Francis Group

© 2000 Neville Morley

Typeset in Bembo by Keystroke, Jacaranda Lodge, Wolverhampton
Printed and bound in Great Britain by MPG Books Ltd, Bodmin

British Library Cataloguing in Publication Data
A catalogue record for this book is available from the British Library

Library of Congress Cataloging in Publication Data
Morley, Neville.
Ancient history : key themes and approaches / Neville Morley.
p. cm. – (Routledge key guides)
Includes bibliographical references and indexes.
ISBN 0–415–16508–3 (alk. paper) – ISBN 0–415–16509–1 (pbk. : alk. paper)
1. History, Ancient. 2. History, Ancient–Historiography. I. Title. II. Series.

D56.M659 2000
930–dc21   99–047074

ISBN 0–415–16509–1 (pbk)
ISBN 0–415–16508–3 (hbk)

For my grandparents

CONTENTS

PREFACE

How do you 'do' ancient history? How do you go about trying to discover what it was like in the ancient world? The obvious answer is that you should concentrate on analysing the ancient evidence, the texts, pots, coins, etc. that have survived from antiquity until today. These are the 'traces' which the past has left in the present; these are what historians use to support their reconstructions of what the past was like. If you study ancient history at university you are likely to be given lectures on 'The Use of Sources'. You will probably also be encouraged to make use of sourcebooks, collections of extracts from the key texts relating to a particular subject, when these are available.

However, the fact is that most practising ancient historians don't actually spend all their time studying such 'primary' sources; they are more often concerned with studying the arguments of other historians. At the same time as they develop and modify their interpretations by examining the ancient evidence, historians are also making sense of that evidence by relating it to their overall interpretation – and that interpretation is often based on or developed in opposition to those of other historians.[1] On a more practical level, if someone has already collected all (or almost all) the evidence, it makes sense to start with their work rather than starting from scratch. It certainly makes sense to get some idea of what other people have thought on the subject to help you develop your own ideas. If you are investigating, say, the reason(s) for the fall of the Roman republic, no-one is expecting you to start by reading the entire works of Cicero, Caesar, Sallust, Cassius Dio and the rest; rather, you should concentrate first of all on the *secondary* literature, the writings of modern historians, analysing and evaluating their different interpretations of the evidence. It is just as important to have a clear idea of the key issues about which these historians argue as it is to be familiar with the evidence they use.

This book is a kind of sourcebook, a collection of extracts from key texts, but of secondary rather than primary sources. It contains an assortment of quotations – important, definitive, stimulating and/or provocative – taken from modern writers discussing different aspects of ancient history. The first section offers quotations on key themes and debates in the subject, arranged by topic (e.g. democracy, imperialism, religion, war). The second section covers the ideas of some 'key' ancient historians and other writers on classical antiquity, past and present; both their ideas about the nature of the ancient world and more especially their ideas on the theory, methodology and purpose of ancient history – basically, how historians *ought* to go about studying the ancient world.

It is entirely impossible for a book like this to be definitive. I have no doubt that everyone who reads it will at some point feel that there are significant gaps; vitally important topics omitted, key writers neglected and crucial quotes ignored for no good reason. Inevitably, this is a very personal selection. Even if I had the space to include everything I wanted to, not everyone would agree with my choice of what was worth including. I have tried to cover as wide a range of topics and historians as possible, but in the end these are simply the subjects that I think are important (you will notice a certain bias towards economic and social history and against the more traditional 'biographical' approach to history), and the writers whom I find stimulating or entertaining. This should serve as a reminder that *all* historians are, consciously or unconsciously, equally selective in their choice of evidence on which to base their interpretations. As far as this volume is concerned, I can only hope that you will find something useful here more often that not.

How, then, might you use this book? Simply reading through the quotes relating to a particular topic should provide you with an introduction to some of the key issues, debates and problems, and to the range of ideas which different historians have put forward. This should help you in your critical reading of the secondary literature, by providing a certain amount of context. If you already have some idea of the main argument of a book (incidentally, another way of getting this information is to read reviews in journals like *Classical Review*, *Journal of Roman Studies* and *Journal of Hellenic Studies*), it's easier to focus on analysing how the writer develops her arguments, the criteria used for the selection of evidence and the way in which the evidence is interpreted. Equally importantly, you can get an idea of how the book responds to or has been criticised in the writings of other historians, and how it fits into the wider debate on the subject.

You might also want to make use of some of these quotes when discussing the views of other historians, or if you want to support your argument by calling on the authority of another historian. However, there are two important things which you should note. First, you should always acknowledge your sources; make it clear that you're quoting someone else, not giving your own views (failure to do so is plagiarism, a serious offence in any sort of academic work). Second, remember that quotations shouldn't be left to 'speak for themselves'; quite simply, they don't. Quotations need to be analysed and interpreted as much as any other piece of evidence does, and above all they must be read critically. It should be clear that many of the writers quoted here disagree violently about what the ancient world was like and how we should study it. Many of these quotes flatly contradict one another, or are at any rate incompatible; some are even 'booby-trapped', either examples of what people once thought but no-one believes any longer, or quite simply bizarre. It isn't going to look very impressive if you include such quotes without remarking on these problems.

A final note to lecturers, tutors and the like, who will, I suspect, be far less convinced than students and other general readers of the merits of this collection, and far more aware of its omissions, deficiencies and eccentricities. If nothing else, I myself have found this to be a wonderful source of material for setting essay and exam questions along the lines of 'Provocative statement by well-known historian': Discuss.

Note

1 For a more detailed discussion of the ways that historians 'do' history, including the process of selecting and interpreting evidence, you might want to look at E.H. Carr, *What is History?* (London, 2nd edn 1987), Keith Jenkins, *Re-Thinking History* (London, 1991) or Neville Morley, *Writing Ancient History* (London, 1999).

ACKNOWLEDGEMENTS

Full publication details, including copyright notices where publishers have asked for them to be included, are given after each quotation. Where a particular work is quoted twice or more in a section, full details are given after the first quotation.

While the publisher has made every effort to contact all copyright holders, if any have been inadvertently omitted the publisher will be pleased to make the necessary arrangements at the first opportunity.

The author would like to thank all the publishers who responded promptly and helpfully to permissions requests, and all the historians who agreed for their work to be quoted.

I would also like to thank Anne and the rest of my family for their constant support and encouragement; Onno van Nijf, for getting me involved in this project in the first place and for much invaluable bibliographical assistance; Charles Martindale; Roger Thorp at Routledge; Monika Smith for assistance with translations; the libraries of Bristol and Lampeter and the Inter-Library Loans service.

Part 1

KEY THEMES AND DEBATES

ADMINISTRATION

See also STATE

Government without bureaucracy. **1**
Title of chapter in Peter Garnsey & Richard Saller, *The Roman Empire: economy, society, culture*, London, Duckworth, and Berkeley and Los Angeles, University of California Press, 1987, p. 20. Copyright © 1987 Peter Garnsey and Richard Saller.

Tax rates could be low principally because the services offered by **2** the Roman administration were rudimentary. By this I do not mean to underestimate the benefits of Roman peace, prosperity and justice – although they have often been exaggerated. One telling index is the extremely sparse presence of élite administrators in the provinces outside Italy. Contrast, for example, the Roman empire with the Chinese. In the second century A.D., to govern a population estimated at 50–60 million people, there were only about 150 senatorial and equestrian administrators in the Roman provinces, that is one élite administrator for every 350,000–400,000 persons. In southern China, in the twelfth century, with a population of a similar size, there were 4,000 gentry officials working in about 1,000 administrative areas outside the capital (compared with forty-five Roman provinces), that is one Chinese élite administrator for roughly every 15,000 people. The scale of difference outweighs any quibbles about the difficulties of comparison.
Keith Hopkins, 'Taxes and trade in the Roman Empire (200 B.C.–A.D. 400)', *Journal of Roman Studies*, 70 (1980), pp. 120–1.

The Romans did not normally garrison cities or appoint high **3** commissioners with power of constitutional control or nominate to the important magistracies. Instead they so arranged the constitution of the cities that the power rested with the wealthier classes ... Having established in power persons likely to watch over her interests, Rome left them in practice with a fairly free hand.
A.H.M. Jones, *The Greek City from Alexander to Justinian*, Oxford, OUP, 1940, pp. 120–1.

AGRICULTURE

See also PEASANTS

1   None of this can be translated into quantitative terms . . . We must
    therefore rest content with the vague but sure proposition that most
    people in the ancient world lived off the land, in one fashion or
    another, and that they themselves recognized the land to be the
    fountainhead of all good, material and moral.
    M.I. Finley, *The Ancient Economy*, London, Hogarth Press, 2nd edn 1985,
    p. 97.

2   All Greek cities were fundamentally dependent upon their country-
    side, but there was enormous variation in the particular land-forms
    available to individual cities . . . The variety of the countryside and
    the rigours of the climate imposed different conditions in different
    places and demanded different agricultural strategies. These strategies
    enabled the country to be highly productive, but not reliably so. Both
    the form and the success of the strategies directly affected the nature
    and structure of society and hence the course of much of military and
    political history.
    Robin Osborne, *Classical Landscape with Figures: the ancient Greek city and its
    countryside*, London, George Philip, 1987, p. 27.

3   What we call land is an element of nature inextricably woven with
    man's institutions. Traditionally, land and labor are not separated; labor
    forms part of life, land remains part of nature, life and nature form an
    articulate whole. Land is thus tied up with the organization of kinship,
    neighborhood, craft, and creed – with tribe and temple, village, gild,
    and church.
    Karl Polanyi, *The Great Transformation: the political and economic origins of our
    time*, Boston, Beacon Press, 1944, p. 178.

4   The economic basis of Greek and Roman civilisation in the first
    millennium BC was provided by a new and more productive
    agricultural system, permitting human population growth. What was
    new about it was not that there was any great technological progress –
    a false perspective – but that a whole range of new crops, especially the
    olive, vine and the modern types of wheat, besides a whole host of
    other plants of lesser significance, either were domesticated or else
    enormously expanded their geographical range.
    Robert Sallares, *The Ecology of the Ancient Greek World*, London, Duckworth,
    and Ithaca, Cornell University Press, 1991, p. 14.

5   Most descriptions of traditional Mediterranean farming recognize the
    influence of two distinctive features of the Mediterranean natural

environment – climate and relief. The climate of the coastal lowlands, where most human settlement is concentrated, is characterized by an alternation between mild winters and hot summers and by a winter rainfall regime. Annual crops like wheat take advantage of the mild winters to complete their growth cycle by early summer, while perennial crops like the olive are adapted to surviving the summer drought. The relief is heavily broken, such that the plains and hills of the lowlands usually lie within days, if not hours, of high mountains which are snow-bound in winter but cool and well-watered in summer. The flocks of sheep and goats which overwinter in the lowlands can thus escape the summer drought by moving to the high pastures of the mountains and there are 'transhumant' pastoral communities which undertake such a pattern of twice-yearly movement between lowland and mountain throughout the Mediterranean.

Paul Halstead, 'Traditional and ancient rural economy in Mediterranean Europe: plus ça change?', *Journal of Hellenic Studies*, 107 (1987), p. 77.

The sparse contemporary sources mention the biennial system alternating between fallow and crop; systematical growing of specialized fodder plants does not appear to have been commonly practised, and consequently animal farming on a greater scale has been limited to special ecological niches. More generally speaking, Eric Wolf has contrasted 'mixed farming' or 'balanced livestock and crop-raising' with the so-called 'Mediterranean ecotype', which fits fairly well with the picture to which our analysis leads us.   **6**

Signe Isager & Jens Erik Skydsgaard, *Ancient Greek Agriculture: an introduction*, London and New York, Routledge, 1992, p. 108.

The catch of the situation is that animals compete with people for scarce resources. A small peasant could increase his labour productivity by using work animals, but would thereby make his family's labour redundant. A decent standard of living and a high population density are mutually exclusive in this case. To have enough land to own a plough and oxen must therefore have been one of the most distinctive elements of social differentiation within the peasantry.   **7**

Wim Jongman, 'Adding it up', in C.R. Whittaker (ed.), *Pastoral Economies in Classical Antiquity*, Cambridge, Cambridge Philological Society, 1988, p. 211.

The Roman agricultural writers do not describe just one type of agricultural system. To state this does not mean only that they discuss vineyards as well as oliveyards and cereal cultivation, but that in a discussion of each such topic, they recognize different systems of   **8** cultivation. Thereby the complexity of the Roman rural economy and agriculture is revealed.

M.S. Spurr, *Arable Cultivation in Roman Italy*, London, Society for the Promotion of Roman Studies, 1986, p. 117.

9   In the Roman period the type of husbandry practised on the large farm and the smallholding had much in common. Ultimately the explanation of this lies in the fact that the Romans in Italy were not alien conquerors imposing exotic ideas upon a subjugated population: rather their strong military and political power was built upon an indigenous agricultural and pastoral tradition. The owner of the villa was drawing upon a fund of knowledge and practice built up by generations of small farmers.

Joan M. Frayn, *Subsistence Farming in Roman Italy*, Sussex and London, Centaur Press, 1979, p. 148.

ALEXANDER THE GREAT

1   Alexander was in most things a Macedonian through and through, only in part a Greek by blood and education, and primarily a man of war whose genius is seen mostly clearly on the field of battle.

N.G.L. Hammond, *Alexander the Great: king, commander and statesman*, London, Chatto & Windus, 1980, p. v.

2   In Alexander it is tempting to see the romantic's complex nature for the first time in Greek history. There are the small details, his sudden response to a show of nobility, his respect for women, his appreciation of eastern customs, his extreme fondness for his dog and especially his horse.

Robin Lane Fox, *Alexander the Great*, London, Allen Lane, 1973, p. 497. Reproduced with permission of Curtis Brown Ltd, London, on behalf of Robin Lane Fox. Copyright © Robin Lane Fox 1973.

3   In brief, he had many of the qualities of the noble savage.

Hammond, *Alexander the Great*, p. 270.

4   Alexander was fortunate in his death. His fame could hardly have increased; but it might perhaps have been diminished. For he died with the real task yet before him. He had made war as few have made it; it remained to be seen if he could make peace.

W.W. Tarn, *Alexander the Great*, Cambridge, CUP, 1948, p. 121.

The king's name and image were invoked as his conquests were **5** renounced and dismembered. The debate over legitimacy lasted a mere generation. After that Alexander was a symbol and nothing else. For subsequent ages he typified the world conqueror, and his territorial acquisitions were a standing inspiration and challenge to successive dynasts.

A.B. Bosworth, *Conquest and Empire: the reign of Alexander the Great*, Cambridge, CUP, 1988, p. 181.

Determined to astound contemporaries and awe future generations **6** with his unique *arete*, Alexander exploited mankind and god with relentless perseverance. In the process, his *hybris* offended a deity capable of revealing and expiating mortal deficiencies with artful brutality. Dionysus chose wine as the vehicle through which he would unveil and magnify the defects of a brilliant man who was spiritually blind.

John Maxwell O'Brien, *Alexander the Great: the invisible enemy*, London and New York, Routledge, 1992, pp. 229–30.

Alexander the Great partly conquered Greece, and then Asia; *therefore* **7** he was filled with a *lust* for conquest. He acted from lust for fame and conquest, and the proof that these were his motives is that his actions brought him fame. What schoolmaster has not demonstrated of Alexander the Great or Julius Caesar that they were impelled by such passions and were therefore immoral characters? – from which it at once follows that the schoolmaster himself is a more admirable man than they were, because he does not have such passions (the proof being that he does not conquer Asia or vanquish Darius and Porus, but simply lives and lets live). These psychologists are particularly apt to dwell on the private idiosyncrasies of the great figures of history. Man must eat and drink; he has relationships with friends and acquaintances, and has feelings and momentary outbursts of emotion. The great men of history also had such idiosyncrasies; they ate and drank, and preferred this course to another and that wine to another (or to water). 'No man is a hero to his valet de chambre' is a well known saying. I have added – and Goethe repeated it two years later – 'not because the former is not a hero, but because the latter is a valet'.

G.W.F. Hegel, *Lectures on the Philosophy of World History: Introduction* [1840], trans. H.B. Nisbet, Cambridge, CUP, 1975, pp. 87–8.

8 I shall call this third subdivision, 'autobiographical documents in the guise of scholarly books.' The genre should not be unfamiliar. Most Alexander books belong to it.

William M. Calder III, 'Ecce Homo: the autobiographical in Wilamovitz' scholarly writings', in Calder, *Men in their Books: studies in the modern history of classical scholarship*, J.P. Harris & R.S. Smith (eds), Hildesheim, Zürich and New York, Georg Olms, 1998, p. 33.

ARCHAEOLOGY

1 It is self-evident that the potential contribution of archaeology to history is, in a rough way, inversely proportional to the quantity and quality of the available written sources.

M.I. Finley, 'Archaeology and history', in *The Use and Abuse of History*, London, Chatto & Windus, 1975, p. 93.

2 The expression of archaeological results may call for nicely written historical narrative but this is a matter of choosing one particular vehicle to convey results obtained by quite alien methods. The danger of historical narrative as a vehicle for archaeological results is that it pleases by virtue of its smooth coverage and apparent finality, whilst the data on which it is based are never comprehensive, never capable of supporting but one interpretation and rest upon complex probabilities. Archaeological data are not historical data and consequently archaeology is not history.

David Clarke, *Analytical Archaeology*, London, Methuen, 1968, p. 12.

3 Classical archaeology, a subject dominated for some time past by various kinds of positivism, has in the process succumbed to a form of 'positivist fallacy'. The fallacy consists in making archaeological prominence and historical importance into almost interchangeable terms; in equating what is observable with what is significant.

Anthony M. Snodgrass, *An Archaeology of Greece: the present state and future scope of a discipline*, Berkeley, Los Angeles and London, University of California Press, 1987, pp. 37–8.

4 Classical archaeology is, of course, saturated in historical texts (ancient histories old and new, and literatures from antiquity), but there is a striking absence of archaeologically derived historical narratives. They are simply not the sort of thing that serious academic Classical archaeologists write.

Michael Shanks, *Classical Archaeology of Greece: experiences of the discipline*, London, Routledge, 1996, p. 95.

[Greek archaeologists] tied themselves more to classical philology than **5** to world archaeology. Two forces were decisive in shaping the discipline. The first was the need to prevent archaeological data from challenging the Hellenist charter of 'Western Civilisation'; the second was the archaeologists' attempt to achieve high status by matching the highest standards of scientific archaeological method while remaining classicists . . . I argue that the current sense of 'crisis' has been misrepresented as a conflict between theoretical and traditional archaeology, or even between young and old. In fact it is just one part of the general collapse of intellectuals' attempts to define what 'the West' is and should be. Archaeologists of Greece had neutralised their material to protect a set of beliefs which gave prestige to classical studies; now that these beliefs are crumbling, they are left defending nothing.

Ian Morris, 'Introduction', in Morris (ed.), *Classical Greece: ancient histories and modern archaeologies*, Cambridge, CUP, 1994, p. 3.

ARCHITECTURE

See also ART

The Greek was incurious about construction *qua* construction. He **1** found, in the column and the lintel, means perfectly adequate to realize his ideal of high unattainable beauty, and he was content. The Romans, who for a time were satisfied with these simple methods, became impatient of the constructive limitation of the post and lintel. They wanted to cover in great spaces, and to leave the floor unencumbered; and concentrating on this they arrived at the arch, the vault, and the dome, and so became the greatest builders of the world. To them, the orders were a mere appendage of decoration, which they never properly appreciated, of which they mistook the intention, adopted the worst elements, and often enough made a gross misuse. The Greeks took another line. They adopted the column and lintel once for all as the only possible method of construction, and devoted all their labours to the incessant refinement of this type, eliminating the unessential, arriving by constant selection at the most perfect expression of their purpose, and their purpose was not that of the Roman and the modern architect, mainly utilitarian, it was directed entirely to the aesthetic appeal, the appeal to the emotions through beauty of line, of form, and in a less degree of colour.

Sir Reginald Bloomfield, 'Architecture', in R.W. Livingstone (ed.), *The Legacy of Greece*, Oxford, OUP, 1923, pp. 405–6.

2　Now what has happened in the five-and-a-half centuries between the Parthenon and the Pantheon? Bluntly, architecture has been turned inside-out. Philosophy and religion and politics have combined to alter the shape of the world and man's relationship to it. The world has ceased to be a collection of disjected phenomena, expressed politically by a scatter of city-states; it has become a coherent cosmos, expressed politically by an empire. Its encompassing vault finds a proper symbol in the Pantheon, which stands for Rome just as the objective Parthenon, perched on its Acropolis like a (very distinguished) ornament upon a mantelpiece, stands for Hellas.

Mortimer Wheeler, *Roman Art and Architecture*, London, Thames & Hudson, 1964, p. 13. Copyright © Thames & Hudson 1964.

ART

1　In dealing with ancient art it is particularly important to try to see or envisage objects as they were intended, to remember that both sculpture and architecture were coloured, that the sculpture had a setting quite unlike that of any modern gallery, that even the most precious objects were for use and never displayed as in a museum showcase.

John Boardman, *Greek Art*, London, Thames & Hudson, 4th edn 1996, p. 14. Copyright © 1964, 1973, 1985 and 1996 Thames & Hudson Ltd, London.

2　No one, of course, should claim that there is only one right question to ask about Athenian painted pottery. But it is all too easy to be dazzled by the skills of connoisseurship, by the complex arguments used to assign a pot to one particular artist of one very precise date – and so fail to see that there are more immediate and, for most of us, more central questions to ask: What do the images on Athenian pottery tell us about Athenian culture, society and ideas? How can we understand this quite alien system of visual meaning?

Mary Beard, 'Adopting an approach', in Tom Rasmussen & Nigel Spivey (eds), *Looking at Greek Vases*, Cambridge, CUP, 1991, p. 17.

3　A deep-seated need to discover an order in, or superimpose an order on, the flux of physical and psychological experience is a continuing feature of all Greek artistic and philosophical expression. While it is true that every conscious creature feels this need to some extent, the intensity with which the quest for order was carried on by the Greeks was exceptional. Whether as a result of some mysterious tendency in the national psyche or as a spontaneous reaction to their turbulent historical experience after the break-up of the Mycenaean world, the Greeks felt that to live with changing, undefined, unmeasured, seemingly random impressions – to live, in short, with what was expressed by the Greek word *chaos* – was to live in a state of constant anxiety. An awareness of this anxiety which often haunts Greek thought and expression is of crucial importance in understanding and evaluating Greek art.

J.J. Pollitt, *Art and Experience in Classical Greece*, Cambridge, CUP, 1972, p. 3.

Where scholars had once devotedly catalogued and classified the **4** materials in terms of type and provenance, style and accomplishment, on the assumption that their Greece had been a formative part of the story of 'civilization', a founding chapter in the history of 'Humanity' and its abiding values, a world where 'Geniuses' *must* have sprouted – for our every dig, museum, store, history of 'Art' said no less than that – 'The Greeks' were reconceptualised as 'other' than their investigators, their independence from us as deserving of 'recognition' as any emergent post-colonial culture . . . Why, who knows?, we might even learn something of 'our' own difference, the dynamic, unOlympian, temporal, difference, that arises from our distance and difference from Greek culture.

John Henderson, 'Amazons in Greek art and pottery', in Simon Goldhill & Robin Osborne (eds), *Art and Text in Ancient Greek Culture*, Cambridge, CUP, 1994, p. 135.

Greek art is the source of most Western art, and no branch of it has **5** survived in such quantity as the painted pottery. But there is no need for historical reasons to justify the study of this pottery. It is one of the few subjects of archaeology that can give aesthetic enjoyment.

R.M. Cook, *Greek Painted Pottery*, London and New York, Routledge, 3rd edn 1997, p. 3.

Many keen students of art have called Roman art Greek art in the **6** Roman period – as Greek literature of the Roman empire from the first century B.C. to the fifth century A.D. is Greek and not Roman. Others have compared Roman art to modern art in the nineteenth century, as an art which had so many earlier arts to draw on that it was in danger of succumbing to a purely synthetic method of selective reproduction . . . When the Romans began to feel the urge to create an art expressive of their own concerns, they lived in a world which had just seen the full development of the most revolutionary cycle art has ever witnessed – that of anthropomorphic Greek art. Everything that man could wish to express seemed to be at hand. The Romans sought to appropriate this heritage to their ends; and the dramatic conflict between the adaptation of Greek art and the outbursts of original creativity sways Roman art like a pendulum. Yet to see Roman art only as a foil to the Greek does no justice to the Roman achievement.

George M.A. Hanfmann, *Roman Art: a modern survey of the art of imperial Rome*, London, Cory, Adams & Mackay, 1964, p. 17.

7   In looking at the transformation of Roman art, there are, it seems to me, two attitudes in particular by which one might characterize the nature of scholarly approaches. These may be summarized (and parodied) by the sentences: 'Everything changed' and 'Nothing changed'. In a way, I agree with both these views.

Jas Elsner, *Art and the Roman Viewer: the transformation of art from the pagan world to Christianity*, Cambridge, CUP, 1995, pp. 6–7.

8   Rebirth is meaningless without death: revival presupposes disuse. This, in simple terms, is the major problem to be considered in any study of Roman art after the third century. But it would be pointless to confine a study of late Antique art within such narrow limits. In the first place a renaissance is a metaphor drawn from living bodies; this may be an interesting idea, even a good working model, but its use is bound to lead to trouble, for it presupposes a life-span, finite but renewable, which develops inexorably from birth to maturity. There is no reason at all why art and architecture should share the constraints of biological life. An art style need not die; it changes rather than develops; and it usually co-exists with other styles and intermingles in a way totally foreign to biology. Change, revival, and co-existence seem therefore to be better ideas for examination than the death of classical art or the fifth-century renaissance.

Richard Reece, 'Late Antiquity', in Martin Henig (ed.), *A Handbook of Roman Art*, Oxford, Phaidon, 1983, p. 234.

AUGUSTUS

The rule of Augustus brought manifold blessings to Rome, Italy and   **1**
the provinces. Yet the new dispensation, or 'novus status', was the
work of fraud and bloodshed, based upon the seizure of power and
redistribution of property by a revolutionary leader. The happy
outcome of the Principate might be held to justify, or at least to
palliate, the horrors of the Roman Revolution: hence the danger of
an indulgent estimate of the person and acts of Augustus. It was the
avowed purpose of that statesman to suggest and demonstrate a sharp
line of division in his career between two periods, the first of
deplorable but necessary illegitimacies, the second of constitutional
government. So well did he succeed that in later days, confronted with
the separate persons of Octavianus the Triumvir, author of the
proscriptions, and Augustus the Princeps, the beneficial magistrate,
men have been at a loss to account for the transformation and have
surrendered their reason in extravagant fancies. Julian the Apostate
invoked philosophy to explain it. The problem does not exist: Julian
was closer to the point when he classified Augustus as a chameleon.
Colour changed, but not substance.
Ronald Syme, *The Roman Revolution*, Oxford, OUP, 1939, p. 2.

The present discussion has maintained that for him the Restored   **2**
Republic was more than a fiction; that he sincerely desired to
reestablish, so far as was consistent with the peaceful administration
of a vast empire, the Senate and the Roman People in that primacy
over the civilized world to which their ancestors' energy and ability
had advanced them; and, furthermore, that Tacitus was biased in
his portrayal of Augustus as a diplomatic hypocrite . . . The West
definitely rejected absolutism at Actium. In consequence, Augustus
returned to the ideals of Cicero and Pompey, to a Republic in which
the sovereignty of wisdom and birth should be recognized. As Rome
stood at the head of the civilized world, so the Senate should stand
at the helm of Rome. As the great men of the second century B.C.
had put their talents at the disposal of the state, the prince, *princeps inter
pares*, of the new Republic should serve and guide, not rule and
coerce. Augustus failed because Rome was no longer the Rome
that had marched and fought through the Mediterranean basin, the
Senate no longer that collection of rulers who impressed even the
self-satisfied Greeks. Augustus, like Cromwell, was driven towards
autocracy by the abdication of the republican institutions, not by his
own ambitions.

Mason Hammond, *The Augustan Principate in Theory and Practice during the Julio-Claudian Period*, Cambridge Mass., Harvard University Press, 1933, pp. 195–6. Copyright © 1933 by the President and Fellows of Harvard College.

3   Augustus' restoration of the Republic was not simply the result of his
    – often presumed – conservative attitude or of his genuine desire to
    reform Rome while retaining as much of the republican constitution
    as possible. Whatever his attitude may have been – nobody knows
    for sure – the Republic confronted him not only with opinions,
    beliefs, and traditions, and not only with the expectations raised by
    his own promises, but with concrete interests, which he himself
    considered significant – even and especially within the framework of
    the civil game he had decided to play . . . Because he had set limits to
    his power, within these limits his power was all the more firmly
    established.

C. Meier, 'C. Caesar Divi filius and the formation of the alternative in Rome', in Kurt A. Raaflaub & Mark Toher (eds), *Between Republic and Empire: interpretations of Augustus and his Principate*, Berkeley, Los Angeles and London, University of California Press, 1990, p. 68.

4   In dealing with the reign of Augustus, Tacitus and Dio alike had for
    the most part used the accounts written in the first century AD; in
    these accounts there were no doubt already differing interpretations
    of Augustus. Both historians obviously followed those versions which
    best fitted their overall political vision. For Tacitus, monarchy was the
    only way out of the civil wars; for Dio, it was in absolute terms
    the best possible form of government for a state of his own day and
    the guarantor of true liberty.

Emilio Gabba, 'The historians and Augustus', in Fergus Millar & Erich Segal (eds), *Caesar Augustus: seven aspects*, Oxford, OUP, 1984, p. 75.

5   History was kind to him, and even if sycophantic allusions in the
    Augustan poets are considered worthless adulation, and even if the
    bitter criticism by Tacitus, who never mentions the Res Gestae,
    is fully accepted, one would still have to admit that on the whole
    Augustus enjoyed a 'good press' in subsequent historiography.
    Augustus, and not Julius Caesar, became the accepted model for
    subsequent Roman emperors; his actions were recognised as binding
    precedents, and the name 'Augustus' was supposed to remind people
    of the man upon whom it was first bestowed. Provincial writers would
    recall that Augustus healed the sicknesses common to Greeks and

barbarians and that the title 'averter of evil' would suit him well. To later Roman historians any regime other than monarchy would have appeared unthinkable and undesirable, and the ideal was 'felicior Augusto – melior Traiano'. Christian historians were able to see the *pax Augusta* as a preliminary stage to the *pax Christiana* . . . In modern scholarship, however, Augustus' self-praise in the Res Gestae is, if not despised, at least not taken seriously. Mommsen uttered the warning that no sane man would seek the truth about the imperial government there, and for Syme the Res Gestae is 'no less instructive for what it omits than for what it says'.

Zvi Yavetz, 'The *Res Gestae* and Augustus' public image', in Millar & Segal (eds), *Caesar Augustus*, p. 22.

Rarely has art been pressed into the service of political power so   **6**
directly as in the Age of Augustus. Poetry and art are filled with the imagery of a blessed world, an empire at peace under the sway of a great ruler. The suggestive power of this imagery lives on in our own day, as its frequent use in contemporary advertising attests. This ennobled image of Augustan art became clearly established first in the 1930s . . . In 1937, as the two thousandth year from the birth of Augustus was commemorated, those in power in Italy and their supporters were drawn, consciously or not, to exploit Roman art in general and the Augustan Age in particular as an aesthetic justification for the folly of their mad ambition. The image of the Augustan period created then is, in one form or another, still with us today.

Paul Zanker, *The Power of Images in the Age of Augustus*, trans. A. Shapiro, Ann Arbor, University of Michigan Press, 1988, p. v.

BARBARIANS

No concern, perhaps, was (and is) more basic than that of identity,   **1**
whether collective or individual, ethnic, tribal, political, or whatever. Beginning at the highest level of generality, the Classical Greeks divided all humankind into two mutually exclusive and antithetical categories: Us and Them, or, as they put it, Greeks and barbarians. In fact, the Greek–barbarian antithesis is a strict polar dichotomy, being not just contradictory but jointly exhaustive and mutually exclusive. Greeks + barbarians = all humankind. Not that the Greeks are unique in so distinguishing themselves from others: compare the division and opposition between Jews and *goyim* (gentiles), for example, or Europeans and orientals. But for the Classical Greeks the Greek–barbarian polarity was but one instance of the ideological habit of

polarization that was a hallmark of their mentality and culture. Moreover, they pressed polarization to its (ideo)logical limits. Thus whereas Greeks were ideally seen as not-barbarians, barbarians were equally envisaged as being precisely what Greeks were not.

Paul Cartledge, *The Greeks: a portrait of self and others*, Oxford, OUP, 1993, p. 11.

2   Our fancy may create, or adopt, a pleasing romance, that the Goths and Vandals sallied from Scandinavia, ardent to avenge the flight of Odin, to break the chains and to chastise the oppressor of mankind; that they wished to burn the records of classic literature, and to found their national architecture on the broken members of the Tuscan and Corinthian orders. But in simple truth, the northern conquerors were neither sufficiently savage, nor sufficiently refined, to entertain such aspiring ideas of destruction and revenge. The shepherds of Scythia and Germany had been educated in the armies of the empire, whose discipline they acquired, and whose weakness they invaded; with the familiar use of the Latin tongue, they had learned to reverence the name and titles of Rome; and, though incapable of emulating, they were more inclined to admire, than to abolish, the arts and studies of a brighter period.

Edward Gibbon, *The History of the Decline and Fall of the Roman Empire* [1776–88], D. Womersley (ed.), Harmondsworth, Penguin, 1994; Chapter LXXI, Volume III pp. 1068–9.

3   We have seen that the Emperors of the second half of the third century, Claudius, Aurelian and Probus, had succeeded as if by a miracle in stopping the Germans and even in driving into the steppes of South-Eastern Europe the most formidable amongst them, the Goths, new arrivals who had come from Scandinavia towards the end of the second century. These great men rendered to Italy, Gaul and civilization, the same service as Marius and Caesar. What a deep night would have fallen on the world if barbarism had mastered the West two or three centuries sooner! Thanks to the barrier which they raised between it and *Romania*, ancient civilization was enabled to grow old slowly, change partially, and hand on some fragments of itself to the new generations and even to the barbarians themselves. Nevertheless the danger was not exorcized. The waves of barbarism broke constantly against the frail barrier separating it from the Empire.

Ferdinand Lot, *The End of the Ancient World and the Beginnings of the Middle Ages*, trans. P. & M. Leon, London, Routledge & Kegan Paul, 1931, pp. 187–8. Originally published in French.

According to this traditional schema, the Germanic peoples had been **4**
in motion since the third or first century BC, engaging in periodic
migrations that pressed northern tribes down upon earlier emigrants
to the south with such increasingly disruptive force that the Roman
frontier, which had impeded the migrants' progress for several
centuries, was torn down around AD 400. The moving Germanic
masses then surged forward and halted in imperial territory. Yet
this final step turns out to be remarkably modest: those involved in
it were a mere handful of peoples, each group numbering at the
most in the low tens of thousands, and many of them − not all − were
accommodated within the Roman provinces without dispossessing or
overturning indigenous society. In other words, the barbarians whom
we actually find coming to grips with the Roman Empire in the
fourth to sixth centuries, and leading the earliest successor kingdoms
of the West, are remarkably deficient in numbers, cohesiveness,
assertiveness and skills − altogether a disappointment when juxtaposed
with the long and massive migrations that are thought to characterize
their past.

Walter Goffart, *Barbarians and Romans AD 418–584: techniques of accommodation*, Princeton, Princeton University Press, 1980, pp. 4–5. Copyright © 1980 by Goffart, W. Reprinted by permission of Princeton University Press.

Yet, the moment Germanic villagers and ranchers found themselves **5**
confronted by true nomads, such as the Huns, they had no illusion
as to which world they belonged: they were agrarian peoples, a
northern extension of a peasant economy that stretched, without
significant interruption, from the Mediterranean to the southern
Ukraine. When the Visigoths of Moldavia and the Ukraine began
to be subjected to Hunnish raids, in 374, their first reaction was to
seek permission to enter the Roman empire. What has been grossly
misnamed as a 'barbarian invasion' was, in fact, the controlled immi-
gration of frightened agriculturalists, seeking to mingle with similar
farmers south of the border.

Peter Brown, *The Rise of Western Christendom: triumph and diversity AD 200–1000*, Oxford, Basil Blackwell, 1996, p. 12.

BATHS AND BATHING

Bathing in the ancient world, especially in the world of the Romans, **1**
went far beyond the functional and hygienic necessities of washing. It
was a personal regeneration and a deeply rooted social and cultural
habit − in the full sense of the word, an *institution*.

Fikret Yegül, *Baths and Bathing in Classical Antiquity*, New York, Architectural History Foundation, and Cambridge Mass. and London, MIT Press, 1992, p. 1.

2   There could also be a darker side to the world of beauty and pleasure which the baths create. Excessive beauty, like any other exceptional achievement, risks provoking *phthonos*, the envy which works through the Evil Eye of the envious, with disastrous consequences. Such danger could threaten every sort of human activity, and buildings of every type are found protected by apotropaic inscriptions and symbols; but there is evidence enough to suggest that baths and bathers were especially vulnerable.

Katherine Dunbabin, '*Baiarum grata voluptas*: pleasures and dangers of the Baths', *Papers of the British School at Rome* 57 (1989), p. 33.

3   Hadrian's measure to give the sick the exclusive use of the baths till the eighth hour was perhaps motivated by a wish to protect the healthy from the unhealthy rather than from a desire to spare the sick the embarrassment of exposing their ailments to the gaze of the curious and derisive. Yet it is not clear that the Romans were aware that diseases such as cholera and dysentery could be transmitted by water as well as by direct contact . . .

It seems probable, then, that Roman public baths might not have been as sanitary as is commonly assumed, and that the risks of becoming infected with a wide range of contagious and infectious diseases in such establishments would have been great.

Alex Scobie, 'Slums, sanitation and mortality in the Roman world', *Klio* 68 (1986), pp. 425, 426.

BYZANTIUM

See also LATE ANTIQUITY

1   Historians who use the phrase 'Byzantine Empire' are not very consistent or precise as to the date at which the 'Roman Empire' ends and the 'Byzantine Empire' begins. Sometimes the line is drawn at the foundation of Constantinople by Constantine the Great, sometimes at the death of Theodosius the Great, sometimes at the reign of Justinian, sometimes . . . at the reign of Leo the Isaurian; and the historian who adopts one line of division cannot assert that the historian who adopts a different line is wrong. For all such lines are purely arbitrary. No

'Byzantine Empire' ever began to exist; the Roman Empire did not come to an end until 1453.
J.B. Bury, *A History of the Later Roman Empire*, London, Macmillan, 1899, Vol. I p. v.

If we ask the question can we still, despite Bury's objection, use the **2** term 'Byzantine Empire'? that question may be answered in the affirmative, since thereby we are reminded of the historical significance of the fact that it was precisely at the Greek city of Byzantium and not elsewhere that Constantine chose to create his new imperial capital. Attempts have been made of recent years to minimize the importance of that fact; the capital, it is said, might equally well have been set in Asia Minor, just as the capital of the Turkish Empire has, in our own day, been transferred to Ankara. But Asia Minor of the Byzantines was overrun by hostile armies time and again and its cities captured by the foe. Constantinople, posted on the waterway between the continents and guarded by the girdle of its landward and seaward walls, through all assaults remained impregnable. At moments the Empire might be confined within the circle of the city's fortifications, but the assailants retired discomfited and still the capital preserved the heritage of civilization from the menace of the barbarian.
Norman H. Baynes, 'Introduction', in N.H. Baynes & H.St.L.B. Moss (eds), *Byzantium: an introduction to East Roman civilization*, Oxford, OUP, 1948, pp. xvi–xvii.

No longer simply a 'new' Rome, a replica of Rome offered to the **3** east, Constantinople now stood alone as the sole surviving capital of the 'true' Roman empire. To call this empire 'Byzantium', and its subjects 'Byzantines' (from Byzantium, the former site of Constantinople), is a modern practice that denies the continuity with the Roman empire to which the men of the sixth century were fiercely attached. They thought of themselves as members of 'the fortunate race of the Romans'. Learned folklore, treasured in government departments, insisted that the Praetorian Prefect's court used the plural form, 'we', because it had been used by Romulus and Remus, when they sat together in judgement. It was also believed that the uniforms of the guards of the imperial bedchamber had been designed by Romulus, who had received the pattern from Aeneas!
Peter Brown, *The Rise of Western Christendom: triumph and diversity AD 200–1000*, Oxford, Basil Blackwell, 1996, p. 121.

Of that Byzantine Empire the universal verdict of history is that it **4** constitutes, without a single exception, the most thoroughly base and despicable form that civilisation has yet assumed . . . There has been no other enduring civilisation so absolutely destitute of all the forms and elements of greatness . . . Its vices were the vices of men who had ceased to be brave without learning to be virtuous . . . Slaves, and willing slaves, in both their actions and their thoughts, immersed in sensuality and in the most frivolous pleasures, the people only emerged from their listlessness when some theological subtlety, or some chivalry in the chariot races, stimulated them to frantic riots . . . The history of the Empire is a monotonous story of the intrigues of priests, eunuchs and women, of poisonings, of conspiracies, of uniform ingratitude, of perpetual fratricides.

W.E.H. Lecky, *History of European Morals* [1869], quoted in John Julius Norwich, *Byzantium: the early centuries*, London, Guild, 1988, p. 25.

CHRISTIANITY

See also RELIGION, BROWN

1   For Cicero's spiritual descendants of the early Principate, Roman religion was part of the very stuff of Roman life and Roman greatness; and they were prepared to extend their protection also to the cults of the peoples of their empire, whose devotion to their ancestral religions seemed to their rulers only right and proper. Can we imagine that such men, however intellectually emancipated from the superstitions of the vulgar, would have had any compunction about executing the devotees of a new-fangled sect which threatened almost every element of Roman religion, and indeed of all the traditional cults conducted by the inhabitants of the Roman world? I would be prepared to speak of persecution so motivated as being conducted for religious reasons, though I realize that other people might prefer to use another word – political, perhaps.

G.E.M. de Ste Croix, 'Why were the early Christians persecuted?', *Past & Present*, 26 (1963), pp. 30–1.

2   It was not so much the positive beliefs and practices of the Christians which aroused pagan hostility, but above all the negative element in their religion: their total refusal to worship any god but their own. The monotheistic exclusiveness of the Christians was believed to alienate the goodwill of the gods, to endanger what the Romans called the *pax deorum* (the right harmonious relationship between gods

and men), and to be responsible for disasters which overtook the community.
Ibid., p. 24.

The persecutions, therefore, connect neatly with the features which **3**
we have identified as the living heart of pagan religiousness: honour
and anger, and the appeasing advice of oracles. Persecution would
have occurred at any period, because it attached to the bedrock of this
religiousness . . . The persecutions are good evidence that the essential
continuity of pagan religiousness was still significant. It was not the
preserve of a few antiquarians: it still animated whole cities.
Robin Lane Fox, *Pagans and Christians in the Mediterranean World from the
Second Century AD to the Conversion of Constantine*, Harmondsworth, Penguin,
1986, p. 425. Reproduced with permission of Curtis Brown Ltd, London on
behalf of Robin Lane Fox. Copyright © Robin Lane Fox 1986.

A sort of invisible minefield, ready to produce scowls and pointed **4**
derision aimed in both directions at important parts of a person's
culture, and occasionally exploding in violence (always anti-Christian,
in the period before 312), thus divided church and town. To cross it
required a conscious decision.

From the outside, that decision was occasionally made by people of
leisure, education, and some special interest in cults and philosophies.
They tried Saint Cyprian's work and found it little to their taste. They
tried Scripture with the same result – more often than not, I would
judge from the defensiveness about the style of Scripture on the part
of various church writers, and from the obvious unacceptability of
New Testament Greek, according to the usual literary conventions
of the time. If Christians wanted to have their Apologies widely
circulated, as seems certain, there is no sign they succeeded. In sum,
initiative and movement on the part of the educated observer toward
the church, like the latter's success in reaching out to such an audience,
amounted to very little.

The mass of ordinary people had apparently no greater inclination
to cross the barriers of prejudice and find out more about their
Christian fellow townsmen.
Ramsay MacMullen, *Christianizing the Roman Empire AD 100–400*, New
Haven and London, Yale University Press, 1984, p. 104.

To be a rationalist in that age Constantine would have been an **5**
intellectual prodigy, and he was, in fact, so far as we can discern him,
a simple-minded man. And even if, by some freak of nature, he had

been a sceptical freethinker, he would not on any rational calculation of his interests have chosen to profess Christianity. The Christians were a tiny minority of the population, and they belonged for the most part to the classes of the population who were politically and socially of least importance, the middle and lower classes of the towns. The senatorial aristocracy of Rome were pagan almost to a man; the higher grades of the civil service were mainly pagan; and above all the army, officers and men, were predominantly pagan. The goodwill of the Christians was hardly worth gaining, and for what it was worth it could be gained merely by granting them toleration.

A.H.M. Jones, *Constantine and the Conversion of Europe*, London, Hodder & Stoughton, 1948, p. 79.

6 Constantine's decision to favour the Christians gave a new twist to the social and political developments of the third century. Through his conversion to Christianity the innovations of the later third century produced a Christian empire. It was no inevitable development but the direction of the emperor's sympathies that opened new doors of power and influence to Christians. Christians of the fourth century were men whom success had taken by surprise.

R.A. Markus, *Christianity in the Roman World*, London, Thames & Hudson, 1974, p. 91. Copyright © 1974 by Thames & Hudson Ltd, London.

7 When Christianity came upon the scene, indeed, the polytheism of the State-religion was not yet eradicated, nor was it eradicated for some time to come; but there were plenty of forces already encompassing its ruin. It had survived the critical epoch during which the republic had changed into a dual control and a monarchy; but as for the fresh swarm of religions which were invading and displacing it, polytheism could no more exorcise them with the magic wand of the imperial cultus than it could dissolve them under the rays of a protean cultus of the sun, which sought to bring everything within its sway. Nevertheless polytheism would still have been destined to a long career, had it not been attacked secretly or openly by the forces of general knowledge, philosophy, and ethics; had it not also been saddled with arrears of mythology which excited ridicule and resentment. Statesmen, poets, and philosophers might disregard all this, since each of these groups devised some method of preserving their continuity with the past. But once the common people realized it, or were made to realize it, the conclusion they drew in such cases was ruthless. The onset against deities feathered and scaly, deities adulterous and loaded with vices, and on the other hand against idols of wood and

stone, formed the most impressive and effective factor in Christian preaching for wide circles, circles in which all ranks of society down to the lowest classes (where indeed they were most numerous) had, owing to experience and circumstances, reached a point at which the burning denunciations of the abomination of idolatry could not but arrest them and bring them over to monotheism.

Adolf Harnack, *The Expansion of Christianity in the First Three Centuries*, trans. J. Moffatt, London, Williams & Norgate, 1904, pp. 27–8. First published in German in 1902.

A polytheist society had been made up of innumerable small cells. **8** Though supported by immemorial custom, it was as delicate and as brittle as a honeycomb. The Christian Church, by contrast, brought together activities that had been kept separate under the old system of *religio*, in such a way as to form a compact, even massive, constellation of commitments. Morality, philosophy and ritual were treated as being intimately connected: all were part of 'religion'; all were to be found in their only true form in the Church. In the polytheist world, by contrast, these were separate spheres of activity.

Peter Brown, *The Rise of Western Christendom: triumph and diversity AD 200–1000*, Oxford, Blackwell, 1996, p. 32.

If we are to use notions such as 'religion' and 'culture', or 'sacred' and **9** 'secular' in our own sense, well and good; but we must know what we are doing. It is one thing for Late Antique Christians to debate these matters – as they did with passionate intensity in the decades around 400; it is quite another for modern scholars to make judgements about the extent of conversion, to speak of 'half-Christians' and so forth, without defining some conception of a whole Christian or what a genuine conversion would be . . . We encounter the same problem when we consider what historians used to call 'pagan survivals'. Talk about 'pagan survivals' is the obverse of an uncritical use of the notion of 'christianisation': pagan survivals are seen simply as what resists the efforts of Christian clergy to abolish, to transform or to control. What such talk fails to take into account is the sheer vitality of non-religious, secular institutions and traditions and their power to resist change.

Robert Markus, *The End of Ancient Christianity*, Cambridge, CUP, 1990, pp. 8–9.

If the decline of the Roman empire was hastened by the conversion of **10** Constantine, his victorious religion broke the violence of the fall, and mollified the ferocious temper of the conquerors.

Edward Gibbon, *The History of the Decline and Fall of the Roman Empire* [1776–88], D. Womersley (ed.), Harmondsworth, Penguin, 1994; Chapter XXXVIII, Volume II p. 511.

11 In these respects as in respect of the institution of slavery, where I can really detect no change in attitudes across time, non-Christian moral history runs parallel to Christian. Or the two are one. In both we can discover some variation in moral values up and down the social spectrum. In both we can detect the views of individuals especially interested and sensitive about morals, who rise above everyday norms of actual behaviour. We know them from their words, which inspire. If we look to deeds, however, and try to see patterns of action in the population at large that clearly reflect Christian preaching, we are hard put to find anything very significant.
Ramsay MacMullen, 'What difference did Christianity make?', *Historia*, 35 (1986), pp. 341–2.

CITIZENSHIP

See also POLITICS

1 The abstract word *politeia* reflected the unity of the citizens, not only the sum of the individuals but the living body composed of rulers and ruled, and the political life that was the very life and nature of the citizens. The use of the same word for individual participation in the state and for its general structure shows that the participation was in the main not a purely legal act between individual and state; it reflected the vital adherence of the individual to the citizen body, as also to the other communities inside the state, and therewith was bound to them, bound to religion and soil.
Victor Ehrenberg, *The Greek State*, London, Methuen, 2nd edn 1969, p. 39.

2 During the whole period of the Empire the nature of citizenship was undergoing change. It continued to confer a personal status which was useful especially from the procedural point of view, and it still provided access to the extremely narrow channel through which a tiny minority could aspire to administrative office; but in the heyday of the Empire it lost what had been its essential feature under the Republic, by ceasing to be a guarantee of participation in political life . . . Under the Republic this was all quite different. True, citizenship was not restricted to a close community after the fashion of the Greek *polis*. The process that led to universal citizenship in imperial times began early, and the expansion of Rome made it a power on an imperial scale by the end of the fourth century BC. From its very beginning the City had absorbed alien elements and been free in granting citizenship to foreigners. But in spite of Rome's territorial expansion, and also the existence of what were in effect degrees of citizenship, the latter was not merely a guarantee of juridical status, though this was its fundamental purpose; it also conferred on its holders a political character, that of moral and physical participation in a coherent system of rights and duties, the *munera* of a citizen.

Claude Nicolet, *The World of the Citizen in Republican Rome*, trans. P.S. Falla, London, Batsford, 1980, p. 21. First published in French in 1976.

CITY

See also FINLEY, WEBER

So self-evident did the urban underpinning of civilisation seem to the ancients that they scarcely engaged in a serious analysis of the city. They did not even attempt a formal definition (apart from administrative 'definitions', to which I shall return briefly). Writing a glorified guidebook of Greece late in the second century AD, Pausanias dismissed the claim of a little town in central Greece to city status: 'no government buildings, no theatre, no town square, no water conducted to a fountain, and . . . the people live in hovels like mountain cabins on the edge of a ravine' (104.1). That at least points to a definition: a city must be more than a mere conglomeration of people; there are necessary conditions of architecture and amenity, which in turn express certain social, cultural and political conditions. Many centuries before, Aristotle had pointed in the same direction. The siting and planning of a town, he wrote in the *Politics* (1330a34ff), involves four considerations: health, defence, suitability for political activity, and beauty.

Pausanias, it will have been noticed, did not object to the pretentious little town on the grounds of its small size. And Aristotle saw in smallness a virtue, even a governing condition.

M.I. Finley, 'The ancient city: from Fustel de Coulanges to Max Weber and beyond', in Finley, *Economy and Society in Ancient Greece*, B.D. Shaw & R. Saller (eds), London, Chatto & Windus, 1981, pp. 3–4.

2 The level of urbanization in the Roman Empire was not equalled or surpassed for at least a millennium. That is a plausible claim or even probable; but how does one demonstrate that it is true? There are several indices which can be used: the size of the urban population, the inhabited areas of towns, the area enclosed by walls, the sheer number of towns, the splendour of public monuments, the size of public benefactions, the sophistication of artefacts found by archaeologists, the known division of labour. Each index has its shortcomings, but all the indices seem to point in a similar direction, that is to a high level of urbanization.

Keith Hopkins, 'Economic growth and towns in classical antiquity', in P. Abrams & E.A. Wrigley (eds), *Towns in Societies: essays in economic history and historical sociology*, Cambridge, CUP, 1978, pp. 68–9.

3 Where city life on the Mediterranean pattern did not already exist, everything possible was done to create it, and as much as any single factor it was the slow breakdown of urban prosperity under the twin burden of warfare and taxation that brought about the final downfall of Roman rule. The history of the classical town is in a very real sense the history of classical civilization itself.

J.B. Ward-Perkins, *Cities of Ancient Greece and Italy: planning in classical antiquity*, London, Sidgwick & Jackson, 1974, p. 8.

4 In the end, I believe that the history of *individual* ancient towns is a *cul-de-sac*, given the limits of the available (and potential) documentation, the unalterable condition of the study of ancient history. It is not wholly perverse to see an advantage in the weakness. There is mounting criticism of contemporary urban history for allowing the deluge of data to obscure the questions being asked and their purpose, a danger that the ancient urban historian is happily safe from. But what questions do we wish to ask about the ancient city, whether they can be asked satisfactorily or not? This is the first thing to be clear about, before the evidence is collected, let alone interrogated. If my evaluation of the current situation is a bleak one, that is not because I dislike the questions that are being asked but because I usually fail to discover any questions at all, other than antiquarian ones – how big? how many? what monuments? how much trade? which products?

Finley, 'The ancient city', p. 20.

5 How did an ancient city pay for its necessities, some produced internally, the rest obtained abroad? . . . We cannot draw up a balance-sheet of imports and exports, not even an approximation; we cannot

indeed offer quantities at all; we must therefore resort to models and indicators again.
M.I. Finley, *The Ancient Economy*, London, Hogarth Press, 2nd edn 1985, pp. 131–2.

Present-day overtones of the word 'consumer' should not be allowed **6** to intrude or mislead. No one is suggesting that the urban lower classes were a host of beggars and pensioners, though it has become a favourite scholarly pastime to 'disprove' that contention for the city of Rome; though, too, the extent of begging, unemployment and famine is not to be underestimated. The issue implicit in the notion of the consumer-city is whether and how far the economy and the power relations within the town rested on wealth generated by rents and taxes flowing to, and circulating among, town-dwellers. Even the quintessential consumer-city, Rome, required innumerable crafts-men and shopkeepers for intra-urban production and circulation. In so far as they were engaged on 'petty commodity production', the production by independent craftsmen of goods retailed for local consumption, they do not invalidate the notion of a consumer-city.
Finley, 'The ancient city', pp. 21–2.

I do not remember a passage in any ancient author, where the growth **7** of a city is ascribed to the establishment of a manufacture. The commerce, which is said to flourish, is chiefly the exchange of those commodities, for which different soils and climates were suited.
David Hume, 'On the populousness of antient nations' [1752], in *Essays: moral, political and literary I*, T.H. Green & T.H. Grose (eds), London, Longmans, Green & Co., 1875, p. 411.

It is basic to Finley's view of the Greek city that the economic **8** relationship between town and country turned on the demand of the town for food. The town created a demand for food which the country as a whole, or simply the immediate hinterland of the town, met. In what I have said I have tried to move the emphasis by stressing that the social and political obligations of the wealthy created a need for cash which demanded that they enter the market. The goods which they supplied to the market may have made possible and indeed encouraged the growth of the town as a population centre, but it was occasioned by the existence of the town as a political centre, something which is, conceptually at least, quite a different thing. The public spending of the polis, and particularly of the democratic polis, can be seen to have stimulated both town and country.

Robin Osborne, 'Pride and prejudice, sense and subsistence: exchange and
society in the Greek city', in J. Rich & A. Wallace-Hadrill (eds), *City
and Country in the Ancient World*, London and New York, Routledge, 1991,
p. 140.

9 Among the images which evoke the way cities siphoned off resources
from their territory, we may briefly recall two centripetal movements:
the channelling of water and the stockpiling of grain. Running water
was an element of Mediterranean sociability (the fountain functioning
like the village pump), of urban comfort and of city culture. The
aqueduct was often only a preliminary to the construction of baths,
the function of which was not solely hygienic . . .

On the siphoning off of grain to make up reserves in town, the best
text is that of Galen (6.749ff.), who shows the peasants of the
countryside of Asia Minor starving after the grain harvest – and also
that of beans – had been transported to town.

Mireille Corbier, 'City, territory and taxation', in Rich & Wallace-Hadrill,
City and Country, pp. 222–3.

10 The final question addressed in this work is to explain why the
primitivist, consumer-city paradigm is so widely accepted, regardless
of the rather limited evidence for it. The reasons seem to lie in the
widespread preconceptions Western man has had concerning cities
since the late Roman Empire and early Dark Ages (ca. AD 285–600).
These preconceptions include a view that cities and city people are
evil, and the country and country people are good. Another is the
concept of primitivism – the belief in the superiority of non-industrial
societies to those of more advanced cultures, which has contributed
to the view that the classical world was innocent of the market forces
that later characterized the West. Since classical men and women did
not regard their cities as the focus of evil, where did the notion come
from?

Donald Engels, *Roman Corinth: an alternative model for the classical city*, Chicago,
University of Chicago Press, 1990, p. 134. Copyright © 1990 by The
University of Chicago. All rights reserved.

11 So why then do I think urban economic theories unsatisfactory,
including even Weber's consumer city? The reasons are the same as
those which caused Weber himself to lose interest in the consumer
city when he came to write *Die Stadt*: because of the ambiguity
of spatial distinctions in the ancient city between the *pars urbana* and
the *pars rustica*; because of the indifference of a specifically economic

relationship between urban and rural; but above all because the study of cities is only an imperfect way of studying the operations of power in society.
C.R. Whittaker, 'Do theories of the ancient city matter?', in T.J. Cornell & K. Lomas (eds), *Urban Society in Roman Italy*, London, UCL Press, 1995, p. 22.

With this markedly pragmatic attitude to the problems of planning **12** went a strong concern for the prosaic virtues of material comfort. In most ancient civilizations comfort spelled luxury and was the prerogative of the privileged few. Urban life was the medium by which the Romans contrived to spread an unusually high standard of material well-being surprisingly far down the social scale. Water supply and drainage, public order, the maintenance of streets and public buildings, public entertainment, security for private property – these are only a few of the municipal services available to every citizen. By modern standards there are notable gaps: education and health for example. But the list is a long one, and it has left its mark on many forms of urban planning.
Ward-Perkins, *Cities of Ancient Greece and Italy*, pp. 33–4.

The rectilinear patterns of the Roman towns, which survive in **13** the street patterns and even the country lanes of old imperial lands, from Scotland to Sudan, are often thought to be the by-product of a utilitarian surveying technique. This is not how the Romans themselves saw it: the city was organized according to divine laws.
Joseph Rykwert, *The Idea of a Town: the anthropology of urban form in Rome, Italy and the ancient world*, London, Faber & Faber, 1976, p. 25.

Many sites of ancient cities are occupied by flourishing cities today. **14** Not a few of them have continuous histories since Antiquity. So the Ancient City can be said to have come to an end only in a special sense, the disappearance of those characteristics which distinguished the Graeco-Roman city from others. Of these the most spectacular and influential have been cultural. They involve a particular style of architecture, sculpture and town planning, and a very distinctive literary and intellectual tradition. But the origin of the Ancient City was political and administrative. Its essential feature was the creation of a political, religious and cultural centre ('the city' in the narrow sense) for a rural territory around it. The political centre together with its territory represented the city state, or 'city' in a wider sense.

Wolfgang Liebeschuetz, 'The end of the ancient city', in J. Rich (ed.), *The City in Late Antiquity*, London and New York, Routledge, 1992, p. 1.

15 The inhabitants of cities and towns were, after the fall of the Roman Empire, no more favoured than those of the country. They consisted, indeed, of a very different order of people from the first inhabitants of the ancient republics of Greece and Italy. These last were composed chiefly of the proprietors of land, among whom the public territory was originally divided, and who found it convenient to build their houses in the neighbourhood of one another, and to surround them with a wall, for the sake of common defence. After the fall of the Roman Empire, on the contrary, the proprietors of land seem generally to have lived in fortified castles on their own estates, and in the midst of their own tenants and dependants. The towns were chiefly inhabited by tradesmen and mechanics, who seem to have been of servile or very nearly servile condition.
Adam Smith, *An Inquiry into the Nature and Causes of the Wealth of Nations* [1776], R.H. Campbell & A.S. Skinner (eds), Oxford, OUP, 1976, p. 397.

16 So far as the empire's cities were concerned, the ill effects of this practice [the evasion of curial duties] were concealed, or at least mitigated, through the profits of extortion and venality being generously lavished on building, entertainment, piety, and other socially approved objectives, in the old tradition of civic beneficence. Yet the benefactors were a new nobility. They were the winners in the rush for refuge somewhere, anywhere, within a now enormously expanded bureaucracy. It constituted the chief means of social, political, and of economic advancement. And while officials took advantage of their *cingulum* to grow rich, the older classes and groups of contributors to the state grew poorer.
Ramsay MacMullen, *Corruption and the Decline of Rome*, New Haven and London, Yale University Press, 1988, p. 195.

CLASS AND STATUS

See also WEBER

1 There are really only two ways of thinking theoretically about class: either as a structural *location* or as a social *relation*. The first and more common of these treats class as a form of 'stratification', a layer in a hierarchical structure, differentiated according to 'economic' criteria

. . . In contrast to this geological model, there is a socio-historical conception of class as a relation between appropriators and producers, determined by the specific form in which, to use Marx's phrase, 'surplus labour is pumped out of the direct producers'.
Ellen Meiksins Wood, *Democracy Against Capitalism: renewing historical materialism*, Cambridge, CUP, 1995, p. 76.

Class (essentially a relationship) is the collective social expression of   **2**
the fact of exploitation, the way in which exploitation is embodied in a social structure. By *exploitation* I mean the appropriation of part of the product of the labour of others: in a commodity-producing society this is the appropriation of what Marx called 'surplus value'.

A class (a particular class) is a group of persons in a community identified by their position in the whole system of social production, defined above all according to their relationship (primarily in terms of the degree of ownership or control) to the conditions of production (that is to say, the means and labour of production) and to other classes.
G.E.M. de Ste Croix, *The Class Struggle in the Ancient Greek World from the Archaic Age to the Arab Conquests*, London, Duckworth, and Ithaca, Cornell University Press, 1981, p. 43.

Of course I have no wish to pretend that class is the only category we   **3**
need for the analysis of Greek and Roman society. All I am saying is that it is the fundamental one, which *over all* (at any given moment) and *in the long run* is the most important, and is by far the most useful for us, in helping us to understand Greek society and explain the process of change within it.
Ibid., p.45.

There is little agreement among historians or sociologists about the   **4**
definition of 'class' or the canons by which to assign anyone to a class. Not even the apparently clearcut Marxist concept of class turns out to be without difficulties. Men are classed according to their relation to the means of production, first between those who do and those who do not own the means of production; second, among the latter, between those who work themselves and those who live off the labour of others. Whatever the applicability of that classification in present-day society, for the ancient historian there is an obvious difficulty: the slave and the free wage labourer would then be members of the same class, on a mechanical interpretation, as would the richest senator and

the non-working owner of a small pottery. That does not seem a very sensible way to analyse ancient society.

M.I. Finley, *The Ancient Economy*, London, Hogarth Press, 2nd edn 1985, p. 49.

5   One can, of course, discern other divisions in Roman society and other structural principles than this rigid organisation of juridical status and 'orders': economics, wealth, race, and residence played a role as well. However, nothing was as constant, as constraining, and, above all, as official as this political hierarchization of society.

Claude Nicolet, 'The citizen: the political man', in A. Giardina (ed.), *The Romans*, trans. L.G. Cochrane, Chicago and London, University of Chicago Press, 1993, p. 49. First published in Italian in 1989. Copyright © 1993 by The University of Chicago. All rights reserved.

6   A class struggle in the Marxist sense could not occur for two main reasons. The first is that there was no labour market as such, nor a separate sphere of economic activity, in which men could confront one another as employers and employees. There was certainly a conflict between those with and those without property, but this was not on the whole one between the owners of the means of production and their labour force, nor even necessarily between landlords and tenants . . . but rather between two ranks in society whose relationship had to a great extent been sanctioned by the laws of the community . . . The second obvious explanation for the absence of a class struggle is the schism between free labour and slaves.

Andrew Lintott, *Violence, Civil Strife and Revolution in the Classical City 750–330 BC*, London and Canberra, Croom Helm, 1982, pp. 257–8.

7   The exploits, to say nothing of the aims and organization, of the Bacaudae are passed over almost in silence by writers of the time when they were active. All our authorities belonged to a greater or lesser extent to the propertied classes of the Empire, and therefore to a greater or lesser degree had reason to dread the Bacaudae. When it is dangerously threatened, a propertied class will often conceal (if it can), and even deny, the existence of those who seek to overthrow it.

E.A. Thompson, 'Peasant revolts in late Roman Gaul and Spain', in M.I. Finley (ed.), *Studies in Ancient Society*, London and Boston, Routledge & Kegan Paul, 1974, p. 305. Originally published in *Past & Present*, 2 (1952).

8   We should guard against a blind insistence that there *must* be a middle class and that it must be sought where we are used to finding it today,

in the urban commercial and industrial segments of the population
. . . Statistically, there was indeed a middle class. Between the top and
bottom, taking into account in a single glance the entire empire, a
range of intermediate wealth made up the aristocracy of small cities.
In a given city, however, the aristocracy nevertheless stood upon the
summit of a very steep social pyramid. The feel of society, the living
sense of its proportions, thus did not harmonize with statistics.
Ramsay MacMullen, *Roman Social Relations 50 BC to AD 284*, New Haven
and London, Yale University Press, 1974, pp. 89–90.

Whereas descriptions of ancient society in terms of some category **9**
other than class – status, for instance – are perfectly innocuous, in the
sense that they will have no direct relevance to the modern world
(which will of course need to be described in terms of a completely
different set of statuses), an analysis of Greek and Roman society in
terms of class, in the specifically Marxist sense, is indeed something
threatening, something that speaks directly to every one of us today and
insistently demands to be applied to the contemporary world, of the
second half of the twentieth century.
de Ste Croix, *Class Struggle*, p. 45.

COINAGE AND MONEY

Wherever the attribution of coin types is secure, they are always found **1**
to represent the supreme authority in the state, whatever form that
authority may take in each case. It should therefore follow that
coinage developed and spread in the Greek world because in the first
instance it secured the interests of those authorities everywhere. These
interests could be of several kinds. First of all there is evidence for the
increasing use of standard payments to the state whether in the form
of taxes, fines or harbour dues . . .
Colin M. Kraay, *Archaic and Classical Greek Coins*, Berkeley and Los Angeles,
University of California Press, 1976, p. 321.

It is likely that the advent of state pay at Athens significantly extended **2**
the use of coinage within the economy . . . Pay both presupposed and
encouraged a cash-based market.
Christopher Howgego, *Ancient History from Coins*, London and New York,
Routledge, 1995, pp. 18–19.

Money is itself a commodity, an external object capable of becoming **3**
the private property of any individual. Thus the social power becomes

the private power of private persons. Ancient society therefore
denounced it as tending to destroy the economic and moral order.
Modern society, which already in its infancy had pulled Pluto by the
hair of his head from the bowels of the earth, greets gold as its Holy
Grail, as the glittering incarnation of its innermost principle of life.

Karl Marx, *Capital Vol. I* [1867], trans. B. Fowkes, London, New Left Books,
1976, pp. 229–30.

4   In the period I have been considering the Roman government had no
policy concerning supply of coinage and no monetary policy except
in matters which directly affected its own interest or standing or the
interest or standing of those who could get its ear. It was always to
the government's interest to prevent forgeries because they might be
paid in taxes, and when it was to the Emperor's interest to debase
the coinage, beginning with Nero, he did so without thought for the
economic consequences.

Michael Crawford, 'Money and exchange in the Roman world', *Journal of
Roman Studies*, 60 (1970), p. 48.

5   The normal use of coin as a means of exchange was ubiquitous in
the Roman world. That is to say that coin was used both in towns
and in areas of settled agriculture, and in the 'less developed' as well
as the 'more sophisticated' provinces . . . The overall picture . . . is that
money was the dominant means of exchange for goods, at least in
the cities, but that agricultural produce, particularly corn, played a
substantial role alongside money in taxation, rents, wages, and credit.
The use of money in all these areas shows how money use was
embedded in the structure of the economy, and the use of kind does
not need to be explained by a shortage of coin. Nevertheless, the use
of kind within important areas of the economy restrained the level of
monetization, and money use remained relatively unsophisticated.

Christopher Howgego, 'The supply and use of money in the Roman world
200 BC to AD 200', *Journal of Roman Studies*, 82 (1992), p. 30.

6   The ancients had very little idea of economics. They were aware
that in a shortage of goods prices tended to go up, but they were
unaware that the same thing happened if money was over-abundant.
To them the value of a coin depended entirely on its metal content. So
when Diocletian found prices still rising despite good harvests, and
this though he had recently issued silver washed copper *nummi* of
superior quality, he was filled with indignation against merchants, to
whose insatiable avarice he attributed the rise. It would have seemed

irrelevant to him that his mints were turning out floods of new *nummi*.

Ancient governments ought on their own premises to have realised that debasing the coinage would cause prices to rise, but they seem to have hoped to get by with it. At any rate the emperors, as we have seen, did nothing to adjust public finances to price rises caused by debasement, raising neither taxes nor pay of government employees.

A.H.M. Jones, 'Inflation under the Roman empire', in Jones, *The Roman Economy: studies in ancient economic and administrative history*, P.A. Brunt (ed.), Oxford, Basil Blackwell, 1974, pp. 224–5.

What emerges as the central feature of autocracy is the urge to **7** monopolise all symbols of authority. The spread of the head of Augustus to the obverse is the most dramatic sign of this; but no less significant is the spread of supplementary 'images' of imperial power, celebrations of imperial success, power and glory that become characteristic of the reverse. It is this tendency, an intolerance of rival images of power, even of the gods, unless their power can be identified with that of the emperor, which dictates the pattern of the coinage of Augustus' successors.

Andrew Wallace-Hadrill, 'Image and authority in the coinage of Augustus', *Journal of Roman Studies*, 76 (1986), p. 85.

COLONIZATION

Greek colonisation was due, above all else, to the need for land. **1** But the simplicity of this statement must not rob it of its force. Colonisation, it is true, implies at all times a need for expansion, and under healthy conditions it is a sign that the population of the home-country is fast out-growing its productive capacity: but Greek colonisation was due to a motive that was peculiarly urgent. Greece is, before all things else, a small country – so small, that the traveller on his first visit needs time to grow familiar with the shock of this discovery. Cultivable land, moreover, is precious where bare rocks are so plentiful.

Aubrey Gwynn, 'The character of Greek colonisation', *Journal of Hellenic Studies*, 38 (1918), p. 89.

The assumption that all Greek colonial foundations were made purely **2** to ease population or subsistence problems at home dies hard. These are the only reasons usually offered by ancient writers but archaeology, geography and common sense combine to suggest that trade normally preceded the flag and that in the case of some of the earliest colonies trade rather than land was the dominant factor in choosing a site.

John Boardman, *The Greeks Overseas*, London, Thames & Hudson, 2nd edn 1980, p. 162. Copyright © John Boardman, 1964, 1973. New and enlarged edition copyright © 1980 Thames & Hudson.

3   All this emphasis on land becomes intelligible when we reflect that it was the only significant medium of wealth; that it was itself on occasion the personified object of worship and offerings; that a new political system was being widely introduced in which it was the only qualification for citizenship; and that (if I am right) its full fruitfulness was only now in the process of being rediscovered after centuries of neglect. Competition for land was at its most intense in the newly-arising polis. These is little doubt that, as Thucydides held, of the manifold causes and facets of colonization this one is the most fundamental.

Anthony Snodgrass, *Archaic Greece: the age of experiment*, London, Melbourne and Toronto, J.M. Dent & Sons, 1980, p. 40.

4   The chief purpose of colonies was strategic, 'either to hold the earlier inhabitants in subjection or to repel enemy inroads'. It was not until the second century that economic ends came to the fore. Before then colonies were founded in order to make the Roman state more secure. There may have been the incidental benefit that some paupers were removed from the ranks of the indigent Roman proletariat and made eligible for military service, but the chief consideration was the defence of Roman soil and the establishment of future bases for military operations.

E.T. Salmon, *Roman Colonization under the Republic*, London, Thames & Hudson, 1969, p. 15. Copyright © E.T. Salmon 1969.

CRIME AND PUNISHMENT

See also LAW

1   Just as evidence of slavery can be found in every nook and cranny of Roman social structure and can be seen to affect almost every conceivable type of legal action that the state sanctioned, so too banditry appears as integral to the functioning of imperial society. Of course, one would not presume to claim that banditry is ubiquitous in the same way as the institution of slavery. Yet much the same

resurfacing of the subject in the laws can be noted. Unlike slavery, however, banditry appears to have been perceived as marginal to central Roman society, albeit a phenomenon that impinged on the most mundane aspects of Roman social life.

I do not mean this statement to be understood in some obvious sense, as for example in the existence of many laws directed at the repression of bandits. Rather, I am thinking of a more subtle intrusion of the phenomenon into numerous laws that have no obvious or direct connection with banditry. In these laws brigandage constantly surfaces as a peripheral item, though one of common concern, much in the manner of earthquakes, tempests on the high seas and other 'natural disasters'. That is to say, banditry is mentioned as one of those external occurrences that could affect almost any legal act from the deposition of a will to the signing of building contracts, to sales agreements, marriages and the transfer of dowry. Among the common causes of death recognized by the laws are old age, sickness and attacks by bandits.
Brent D. Shaw, 'Bandits in the Roman Empire', *Past & Present*, 105 (1984), pp. 8–9.

Roman tradition tolerated and even encouraged violence in political   **2** and private disputes, and both the law and constitutional precedent recognized the use of force by private individuals . . . Moreover, it was reinforced by the Roman cult of expediency in matters where the physical coercion of people, whether legal or illegal, was involved.
A.W. Lintott, *Violence in Republican Rome*, Oxford, OUP, 1968, p. 4.

Certain areas naturally favored crime; certain forms of society   **3** resisted civilization. Moorish and Arab nomads, Quinquegentanei, Garamantes, Bessi, Maratocupreni, Brisei, Cietae, or whatever tribe it might be, retained their traditional lawlessness, their inexpugnable haunts, ready at the first sign of weakness on the part of the government to launch their raids against farmhouses and cities. Only in the era of most settled rule could they be fenced off to themselves with reasonable success, while civil or foreign wars gave opportunity to sudden explosions of violence from out of wasteland fastnesses.

But a phenomenon much more interesting and important was the outlaw not born to the trade, so to speak, but drawn to it from among its proper enemies. Without such recruits, brigandage could never have challenged the massed authority of Roman laws and armies. Challenge them it did, in the late Empire, and supplied folk heroes – Bulla Felix, Claudius, Amandus, and Aelian – to its very victims. A widespread sympathy felt, or half-felt, for the lives and deeds of outlaws testifies to a loosening loyalty within civilized society, where to be poor, to be rejected, to scrape a living irregularly in the company of others clinging like oneself to the edge of the respectable world; to envy and then to hate the man of property, and to admire the style of his plunderers, to consort with them, then shield them, and at last join them, were the successive steps leading beyond the boundaries of the law.

Ramsay MacMullen, *Enemies of the Roman Order: treason, unrest and alienation in the empire*, Cambridge Mass., Harvard University Press, 1966, pp. 192–3. Copyright © 1966 by the President and Fellows of Harvard College. All rights reserved.

4   The delegation of almost all (or at least the most important) functions of law-enforcement to public authorities has had such a decisive impact on the modern perception of law and order that pre-modern societies are often characterized as showing a lack of necessary institutions and provisions. Such an approach, however, disregards the simple fact that it is not the absence but the very existence of such forces which is exceptional in universal history. That is why the non-existence of a police force in the modern sense cannot as such provide a satisfactory explanation for the problems of, for example, the Late Republic.

Wilfrid Nippel, 'Policing Rome', *Journal of Roman Studies*, 74 (1984), p. 20.

5   The preconditions for the working of a system which depends to such a high degree on the magistrate's authority being indisputably accepted must be rooted in the basic structure of society and its mechanisms of social control. There must be an interdependence between the military discipline imposed almost permanently on the society as a whole, the sacred aura of the magistracy and the function of state cults, the public representation of the success of the Republic and its élite, manifest in buildings, statues, funerals and triumphs, the disciplining effects of patronage, etc. on the one hand, and the general assumption that the magistrates were capable of dealing successfully with problems of public order on the other hand. It is, however, almost impossible to demonstrate the functioning of such mechanisms of social control in actual situations of conflict.

Ibid., pp. 23–4.

6   On this evidence a more satisfactory case can be made for the Roman upper class being callously indifferent to physical suffering than for their being actively sadistic. Moreover, in so far as they are

distinguished in their attitudes from other nations, it is because they followed policy not passion. This is particularly true of acts of mass brutality, where it is the scale of the action, not the individual act, that is striking. Punishment of the innocent seems to have been a policy of expediency founded on fear and compounded with indifference.
Lintott, *Violence*, p. 44.

In the second and third centuries [AD] there was a definite trend **7** towards harsher penalties. Most of the penalties that came to be regularly applied to criminals originated as irregular sanctions, with no basis in the criminal law. Formerly felt to be suitable almost exclusively for slaves, by the Antonine and Severan periods they are found in general use against *humiliores*. Indeed, by the late third and early fourth centuries, they were overtaking even the provincial aristocracy. In the preceding two centuries it was not their position and the position of *honestiores* in general which improved, but that of the *humiliores* that worsened.
Peter Garnsey, *Social Status and Legal Privilege in the Roman Empire*, Oxford, OUP, 1970, p. 152.

CRISIS

Food crisis was endemic in the Mediterranean in classical antiquity. Its **1** origins lay in nature and in man, often operating together. Harvest failure was an underlying cause of food shortage. However, food crisis was the consequence of a sharp reduction not in the absolute level of supply, but in food availability. The causes of famine are to be sought not only in the physical environment and conditions of production, but also in distribution mechanisms, their limitations, and their disruption through human intervention.
Peter Garnsey, *Famine and Food Supply in the Graeco-Roman world: responses to risk and crisis*, Cambridge, CUP, 1988, p. 271.

The results presented demonstrate the highly precarious position of **2** the ancient Greek peasantry. With alarming regularity they would have found themselves running short of food in the face of climatically induced shortfalls in production . . . In order to ensure their survival, they had to resort to a range of strategies, the operation of which would have enabled them to cope with one and possibly two successive crop failures but no more than that.
Thomas W. Gallant, *Risk and Survival in Ancient Greece: reconstructing the rural domestic economy*, Cambridge, Polity Press, 1991, p. 110.

3 The most desperate need of all was the Peninsular Italian peasantry's. The peasants could not dream of competing with the capitalists in occupying and exploiting the huge areas of new Roman ager publicus . . . The Italian peasantry, Roman and non-Roman alike, would have been content if they could have retained the plots of land that they had inherited from their ancestors; but, in this case, the gods were not on the side of the big battalions; they were on the side of the capitalists with their small slave-gangs.

Arnold J. Toynbee, *Hannibal's Legacy: the Hannibalic War's effects on Roman life, Volume II: Rome and her neighbours after Hannibal's exit*, Oxford, OUP, 1965, p. 177.

4 Throughout the last two centuries BC, there were commonly over 100,000 Italians serving in the army, that is more than ten per cent of the estimated adult male population. Global numbers disguise individual suffering; we have to think what prolonged military service meant to individual peasants, what its implications were for their families and for the farms off which they lived.

Keith Hopkins, *Conquerors and Slaves: sociological studies in Roman history I*, Cambridge, CUP, 1978, p. 4.

5 The period being considered appears to be characterised by a major increase in productivity, obtained by means of the most drastic separation of producers from their means of production and their products that history had known before the modern expropriation of the 'yeomen', which opened the way to [economic] 'take-off' . . . that is to say to capitalism. We are dealing, for the last two centuries of the republic, with the ruin and emigration of the Roman 'yeomen' (if I am not mistaken, between one and two million individuals: between a quarter and a fifth of the population) and the importation of masses of peasants reduced to slavery (around two million).

Andrea Carandini, 'Sviluppo e crisi delle manifatture rurali e urbani', in A. Giardina & A. Schiavone (eds), *Società Romana e Produzione Schiavistica, Vol. II: merci, mercati e scambu nel mediterraneo*, Rome and Bari, Laterza, 1981, p. 250. Trans. N. Morley.

6 Economic evolution was stronger than the efforts of government. The main cause – the emancipation of the provinces – could not be eliminated nor even rendered less dangerous for the economic prosperity of Italy. The gradual economic decline of Italy, due primarily to the decay of its industry and commerce, was aggravated by the crisis which befell the scientific and capitalistic rural economy of the country at the end of the first century.

M.I. Rostovtzeff, *Social and Economic History of the Roman Empire*, rev. P.M. Fraser, Oxford, OUP, 2nd edn 1957, p. 199.

Crisis: what crisis?   7
Title of article by J.R. Patterson, *Papers of the British School at Rome*, 55 (1987), p. 115.

At the beginning, the problems to be solved seemed and were familiar.   8
No one could be blamed for not predicting their consequences or for not understanding as one whole the layers of difficulty that were subsequently to unfold. Hard times there had been before. If some particular affliction aroused the fear that 'the inhabited world' approached the hour of its death, there was little the emperor's jurisconsults or chief accountants could do about it. They had troubles enough of their own. Rumours and visions they left to the masses, something a little more conventional remained for them. They had their national faith and their national history. Neither served pragmatic analysis of the contemporary scene.
Ramsay MacMullen, *Roman Government's Response to Crisis AD 235–337*, New Haven and London, Yale University Press, 1976, p. 198.

DEATH AND BURIAL

Funerals help to create an ideal social structure, which constrains and   1
gives meaning to action without determining it. At least in principle, burial evidence might be questioned about social structure, the way that members of a community were supposed to see themselves.
Ian Morris, *Death-Ritual and Social Structure in Classical Antiquity*, Cambridge, CUP, 1987, p. 43.

The elaborate and lengthy process by which the Greek dead loosened   2
their connections with their kin and became integrated in the society of their own kind is perhaps an analogue for an innate Greek insistence on the preservation of a system of categorisation which, in this instance, was designed to keep the world of the living rigidly apart from that of the dead.
Robert Garland, *The Greek Way of Death*, London, Duckworth, 1985, p. 121.

In burying its dead, then, the Athenian community appropriated them   3
forever, and at the demosion sema all distinctions, individual or family, economic or social, that might divide Athenians even in their graves were abolished.

Nicole Loraux, *The Invention of Athens: the funeral oration in the classical city*, trans. A. Shapiro, Cambridge Mass. and London, Harvard University Press, 1986, p. 23. First published in French in 1981 by Mouton. Copyright © 1986 by the President and Fellows of Harvard College.

4   Death is a protracted social process. Commemorative inscriptions and funerary portraits are only the long-surviving residues of social rituals and personal experience. If we are to understand how the Romans coped with death, we should be careful not to overrate the historical importance of monuments which were made of stone and have survived. We have to try to understand what Romans felt, and that is very difficult.

Keith Hopkins with Melinda Letts, 'Death in Rome', in Hopkins, *Death and Renewal: sociological studies in Roman history II*, Cambridge, CUP, 1983, p. 217.

5   Conditions in death probably mirrored living conditions in the city of Rome . . . It is striking, but I suppose not surprising, that tens of thousands of Roman citizens, living packed together in a culture which set a high value on a proper burial, tolerated the dehumanisation of mass graves.

Ibid., pp. 208–9.

6   High density living in insanitary urban dwellings and surroundings can have only one major consequence in a preindustrial society which lacks effective and cheap medical care: a short, often violent life. That this was the common lot of the millions of people in the Roman world who lived on or below subsistence level, can hardly be doubted, given the conditions discussed above.

Alex Scobie, 'Slums, sanitation and mortality in the Roman world', *Klio*, 68 (1986), p. 433.

7   The aspirations of Romans were increasing steadily, and the simple but decent burials of the past – themselves more difficult to arrange because of the demographic pressure – were sufficient for only a dwindling stratum of the free population. The change was inherent in aristocratic competition: the introduction of the proastion and the luxury of the élite tomb encouraged imitation. It was in this way, through imitation, that the distinctive Roman funerary architecture of *cepotaphia*, *columbaria*, mausolea, catacombs and so on, and the physical layout of cemeteries along roads in suburbs, came to spread from one city to another. This degree of homogeneity throughout the Empire

would not have been possible had the associations of funerary style not been with status, honour, display and benefaction.

Nicholas Purcell, 'Tomb and suburb', in Henner von Hesberg & Paul Zanker (eds), *Römische Gräberstraßen: Selbstdarstellung, Status, Standard. Abhandlung der Philosophisch-historischen Klasse der Bayerischen Akademie der Wissenschaften, Neue Folge, Heft* 96. Munich, Verlag der Bayerischen Akademie der Wissenschaften, 1987, p. 33.

DECLINE AND FALL

See also LATE ANTIQUITY, BARBARIANS, GIBBON

Roman civilisation did not die a natural death; it was assassinated. **1**

André Piganiol, *L'Empire chrétien (325–395)*, Paris, Presses Universitaires de France, 1947, p. 422.

There are, of course, historians who see the Middle Ages making **2** their appearance and the Roman empire sinking into oblivion with the conversion of Constantine in 312 or with the inauguration of Constantinople in 330. And there are historians who would delay the end of the Roman empire to that year 1806 – more precisely to that day 6 August 1806 – in which Napoleon I compelled the Austrian emperor Francis II to underwrite the end of the Holy Roman empire. Between these two extreme dates there are plenty of intermediate choices.

Arnaldo Momigliano, 'Christianity and the decline of the Roman empire', in Momigliano (ed.), *The Conflict between Paganism and Christianity in the Fourth Century*, Oxford, OUP, 1963, p. 1.

The civilization of Antiquity did not decline because the Empire fell, **3** for the Roman Empire as a political structure existed for centuries after ancient civilization had passed its prime. In fact, this civilization had been in eclipse for a long time. By the early third century Roman literature was played out, and Roman jurisprudence deteriorated together with its schools. Greek and Latin poetry were moribund, historiography faded away, and even inscriptions started to fall silent. Latin itself soon gave way to dialects. When, after one and a half centuries, the Western Empire finally disappeared, barbarism had already conquered the Empire from within.

Max Weber, *The Social Causes of the Decline of Ancient Civilization*, in *The Agrarian Sociology of Ancient Civilizations*, trans. R.I. Frank, London, New Left Books, 1976, p. 389. First published in German in 1909.

4   The exclusiveness of the *bourgeoisie* and the system of economic exploitation prevented the lower classes from raising themselves to a higher level and improving their material welfare. On the other hand, the state required more money and labour to maintain internal peace and security. Confining itself, as it did, to the problems of state life and being indifferent to economic progress, the government did nothing to promote and foster the latter. Rather, it helped to accelerate the process of stagnation by protecting the city *bourgeoisie* and taking very little thought for the prosperity of the masses. Thus the burden of supporting the life of the state lay entirely on the working classes and caused a rapid decline of their material welfare. As they were the chief consumers of the industrial goods produced by the cities, their diminished purchasing power reacted adversely on the development of commerce and industry and greatly aggravated the torpor which had come on them. The decay had definitely set in as early as the beginning of the second century. The wars of that century demonstrated the hopeless economic weakness of the Empire and awakened the interest of the emperors in economic problems. But, even when they realized the danger, they were helpless to cure the disease. Their constructive measures were puerile and brought no relief. To save the state they resorted to the old practice of the ancient world – the policy of force and compulsion.

M.I. Rostovtzeff, *Social and Economic History of the Roman Empire*, rev. P.M. Fraser, Oxford, OUP, 2nd edn 1957, pp. xiv–xv.

5   The evolution of the ancient world has a lesson and a warning for us. Our civilization will not last unless it be a civilization not of one class, but of the masses . . . But the ultimate problem remains like a ghost, ever present and unlaid: Is it possible to extend a higher civilization to the lower classes without debasing its standards and diluting its quality to the vanishing point? Is not every civilization bound to decay as soon as it begins to penetrate the masses?

Ibid., p. 541.

6   'Is it *inevitable* for western civilization to suffer the fate of Rome?' This question is urgent, because the answer we give to it will determine the character of our own actions. There is, as we have seen, a clear analogy between the methods adopted by the authoritarian state of the late Empire, and those used by similar regimes in the modern world. In both we see the demands of the State set higher than the happiness and freedom of the individual. In both a fortunate minority, well placed in the mechanism of government, can enjoy luxuries beyond

the scope of the rest, for whom scarcity and hardship are a natural portion. Both foster irrational modes of thought, with new myths, dogmas, and superstitions as a substitute for reason. Moreover, it is a significant and sobering reflection that most of the advanced countries of the world, and not merely those which we call authoritarian, are experiencing a movement away from an age of *laissez-faire* to one of control and state planning.

F.W. Walbank, *The Awful Revolution: the decline of the Roman Empire in the West*, Liverpool, Liverpool University Press, 1969, p. 114.

As the happiness of a *future* life is the great object of religion, we may **7** hear without surprise or scandal, that the introduction, or at least the abuse, of Christianity, had some influence on the decline and fall of the Roman Empire. The clergy successfully preached the doctrines of patience and pusillanimity; the active virtues of society were discouraged; and the last remains of military spirit were buried in the cloyster: a large portion of public and private wealth was consecrated to the specious demands of charity and devotion; and the soldiers' pay was lavished on the useless multitude of both sexes who could only plead the merits of abstinence and chastity. Faith, zeal, curiosity, and the more earthly passions of malice and ambition, kindled the flame of theological discord; the church, and even the state, were distracted by religious factions, whose conflicts were sometimes bloody, and always implacable; the attention of the emperors was diverted from camps to synods; the Roman world was oppressed by a new species of tyranny; and the persecuted sects became the secret enemies of their country.

Edward Gibbon, *The History of the Decline and Fall of the Roman Empire* [1776–88], D. Womersley (ed.), Harmondsworth, Penguin, 1994; Chapter XXXVIII, Vol. II pp. 510–11.

The inevitable accompaniment of the population decline was naturally **8** a corresponding decrease in the manpower available for agriculture, industry, and the public services . . . At the same time there was a corresponding decrease in agricultural and industrial production.

Arthur E.R. Boak, *Manpower Shortage and the Fall of the Roman Empire in the West*, Ann Arbor, University of Michigan Press, 1955, p. 113.

The crisis in the Roman Empire could not be averted because it **9** was provoked by the impulse of young, very prolific peoples to take possession of southern, depopulated lands. It was a kind of physiological compensation which was to a certain extent carried out blindly.

Jacob Burckhardt, *Reflections on History*, London, George Allen & Unwin, 1943, p. 142. First published in German in 1906, from lectures delivered 1868–71.

10   It was in the countryside itself, of course, that the final crisis of Antiquity originated; and while the towns stagnated or dwindled, it was in the rural economy that far-reaching changes now occurred, presaging the transition to another mode of production altogether.
Perry Anderson, *Passages from Antiquity to Feudalism*, London, New Left Books, 1974, p. 93.

11   By contrast with the 'cumulative' character of the advent of capitalism, the genesis of feudalism in Europe derived from a 'catastrophic', convergent collapse of two distinct anterior modes of production, the *recombination* of whose disintegrated elements released the feudal synthesis proper, which therefore always retained a hybrid character. The dual predecessors of the feudal mode of production were, of course, the decomposing slave mode of production on whose foundations the whole enormous edifice of the Roman Empire had once been constructed, and the distended and deformed primitive modes of production of the Germanic invaders which survived in their new homelands, after the barbarian conquests. These two radically distinct worlds had undergone a slow disintegration and slow interpenetration in the last centuries of antiquity.
Ibid., pp. 18–19.

12   As soon as the Germans were established in the country in accordance with the rules of *hospitalitas*, society became once more stabilized. But how was the process of settlement conducted? We may suppose that the Germans took advantage of their position, but their settlement did not involve any absolute upheaval. There was no redistribution of the soil, and no introduction of novel methods of agriculture. The Roman colonists remained tied to the soil to which the impost had attached them. Instead of paying a Roman, they paid a German master. The slaves were divided among the conquerors. As for the peasants, they cannot have noticed any very great changes.
Henri Pirenne, *Mohammed and Charlemagne*, trans. B. Niall, London, George Allen & Unwin, 1939, p. 75. First published in French, 10th edn 1937.

13   In fact the Roman Empire of the West did fall. Not every aspect of the life of Roman subjects was changed by that, but the fall of Rome as a political entity was one of the major events of the history of western

man. It will simply not do to call that fall a myth or to ignore its historical significance merely by focusing on those aspects of Roman life that survived the fall in one form or another. At the opening of the fifth century a massive army, perhaps more than 200,000 strong, stood at the service of the Western emperor and his generals. In 476 it was gone. The destruction of Roman military power in the fifth century AD was the obvious cause of the collapse of Roman government in the West.

Arthur Ferrill, *The Fall of the Roman Empire: the military explanation*, London, Thames & Hudson, 1986, p. 22. Copyright © 1986 Thames & Hudson Ltd, London.

Whatever the frequency of peasant revolts during the third and fourth **14** centuries, they reached such a climax in the first half of the fifth century as to be almost continuous. It would be strange indeed if this fact were considered to be of slight importance in the study of the fall of the Western Empire: Empires only fall because a sufficient number of people are sufficiently determined to make them fall, whether those people live inside or outside the frontier.

E.A. Thompson, 'Peasant revolts in late Roman Gaul and Spain', in M.I. Finley (ed.), *Studies in Ancient Society*, London and Boston, Routledge & Kegan Paul, 1974, p. 318. Originally published in *Past & Present*, 2 (1952).

Suppose we accept what was said in the previous chapter about the **15** patterns of behavior and sense of obligation prevailing among the emperor's servants, military and civilian, in the later empire; how, then, could anyone expect them to mediate effectively, as those in the earlier empire had done, between the directing will at the center and the vast surrounding armature of private power?

Ramsay MacMullen, *Corruption and the Decline of Rome*, New Haven and London, Yale University Press, 1988, p. 172.

In being unable to maintain an acceptable return on investment in **16** complexity the Roman Empire lost both its legitimacy and its survivability. The Germanic kingdoms that succeeded Roman rule in the West were more successful at resisting invasions, and did so at lower levels of size, complexity, permanent military apparatus, and costliness. This indicates a significant difference: with the fall of the Roman Empire, the marginal return on investment in complexity increased significantly in Europe.

Joseph A. Tainter, *The Collapse of Complex Societies*, Cambridge, CUP, 1988, pp. 188–9.

17 The causes of the fall of the western empire in the fifth century have been endlessly debated since Augustine's day, but those who have debated the question have all been westerners, and have tended to forget that the eastern empire did not fall till many centuries later. Many of the causes alleged for the fall of the west were common to the east, and therefore cannot be complete and self-sufficient causes. If, as the pagans said in 410, it was the gods, incensed by the apostasy of the empire, who struck it down, why did they not strike down the equally Christian eastern parts? If, as Salvian argued, it was God who sent the barbarians to chastise the sinful Romans, why did he not send barbarians to chastise the equally sinful Constantinopolitans? If Christianity, as Gibbon thought, sapped the empire's morale and weakened it by internal schisms, why did not the more Christian east, with its much more virulent theological disputes, fall first? We must look then for points in which the two halves of the empire differed.
A.H.M. Jones, *The Decline of the Ancient World*, London, Longmans, 1966, p. 362.

18 The people who were declining should have known it; therefore I turn to them first for their views. Indeed I do find them characterizing the whole world around them in despairing terms; only they do so too often. They think the rot had set in decisively beginning in 154, 146 or 133 B.C., or in the reign of the first emperor, or toward the mid-first century A.D. (all of these judges standing in the capital and taking a survey from that point of view); or it is recognized by Dio Chrysostom a generation afterwards, and in the later second century by Dio Cassius and fifty years after that in Africa and elsewhere; in northern Italy in 386; and (more reasonably, we feel) in 410 and 429 by observers of the sack of Rome and the Vandal invasion of north Africa. At all but the last two of these junctures we also hear people exclaiming about the happiness of the times.
MacMullen, *Corruption and the Decline of Rome*, p. 1.

DEMOCRACY, ATHENIAN

See also POLITICS

1 The Greek word *dêmokratia* can be translated literally as 'the people (*dêmos*) possess the political power (*kratos*) in the state'. In ordinary discourse, 'the people' meant for the Athenians, as for modern democrats, the whole of the citizen body, and citizenship was determined by birthright rather than by property-holding. Much of the appeal of democracy in antiquity, as now, rested upon the attractiveness of two closely related ideas: first, that all citizens, despite differences in their socio-economic standing, should have an equal say in the determination of state policy; second, that the privileges of elite citizens, and the elite collectively, must be limited and restricted when those privileges come into conflict with the collective rights of the citizenry, or the individual rights of non-elite citizens.

Josiah Ober, *Mass and Elite in Democratic Athens: rhetoric, ideology and the power of the people*, Princeton, Princeton University Press, 1989, pp. 3–4. Copyright © 1989 by Ober, J. Reprinted by permission of Princeton University Press.

Ancient historians have always preferred to focus on the age of **2** Perikles, seeing it as the period of the real greatness of Athens in art and literature as well as politics; that philosophy and rhetoric reached their apogee in the fourth century counts for less. That has given especially to English and American accounts of the Athenian democracy a particular shape, namely a historical (diachronic) description of developments down to Ephialtes in 462, crowned by a systematic (synchronic) description of the democracy in the Periklean age . . . In the systematic part, on the institutions of the Periklean age, fourth-century sources are constantly called on, for want of better, and extrapolated back to the Athens of the fifth century. The method rests on two presuppositions that are seldom discussed: that in 403 the Periklean democracy was reintroduced with very few and un-important adjustments, and that the restored democracy maintained itself without further change until 322.

Mogens Herman Hansen, *The Athenian Democracy in the Age of Demosthenes*, Oxford and Cambridge Mass., Basil Blackwell, 1991, pp. 21–2.

What was the reality about the extent of political activity, understand- **3** ing and interest? That there were a substantial number of apathetic citizens may be taken for granted, but we cannot put a figure to them. One common approach is to pretend to statistical 'objectivity' by making disparaging remarks about the numbers who actually attended meetings of the Assembly and to back them by purely hypothetical statements (disguised as facts) about the behaviour of the peasant majority of the population, their lack of culture and education, their unconcern with anything other than the hard struggle for existence, their inability to take the time for a journey to the city on meeting-days. Further support is claimed from passages in the poets and Plato that glorify the man who 'minds his own business', who does not meddle in public affairs. Pericles in the Funeral Oration dismissed such men as 'useless', but that, we are assured, was mere wartime rhetoric. None of this will do.

M.I. Finley, *Politics in the Ancient World*, Cambridge, CUP, 1983, pp. 72–3.

4 The central importance of a study of apragmosynè [quietism] lies in correcting our overall vision of the democracy. It comes as a shock to be reminded, for instance, that a full meeting of the assembly numbered about 6,000 men, but that the citizen population at the outbreak of the war was around 30,000. The Athenians had *never seen* a full meeting of the citizen body, though the very idea of democracy was predicated on it. From the very start they must have accepted that any meeting of the assembly was bound to be a sample of the citizenship – and not even a random sample: the assembly was invariably going to reflect the views of the town-dwellers against those living in the outlying villages and hamlets. This is the first tension inherent in the democracy.

L.B. Carter, *The Quiet Athenian*, Oxford, OUP, 1986, p. 193.

5 We must never forget that as recently as a century ago a lot of people were used to walking sometimes even 10 miles twice a day, six days a week, to get to their place of work in the morning and back home in the evening. The Greeks, and particularly the Athenians, appreciated political participation as a value which made life worth living. Moreover, the assembly pay was probably a sufficient compensation for working hours lost.

Mogens Herman Hansen, *The Athenian Assembly in the Age of Demosthenes*, Oxford, Basil Blackwell, 1987, pp. 9–10.

6 Athens was not going to allow any such powers to her executive officers. None of them presided over or prepared business for her *ekklesia*, nor had any special function in it, except that the most important, the *stratêgoi*, could demand a special meeting of the *ekklesia* to deal with some urgent matter. Naturally, the executive often had matters to report to the *ekklesia*, and therefore were given first hearing; naturally also, if they had been elected to office because they were well known and popular, they would at any time be listened to and applauded; they would sway the meeting; but as citizens like any other, not by right as magistrates. And it is highly characteristic of Athens that many of her most influential politicians for long years held no office at all, and fought shy of it; they were content with their influence as talkers, and wanted no further responsibility.

A.W. Gomme, 'The workings of the Athenian democracy', in Gomme, *More Essays in Greek History and Literature*, D.A. Campbell (ed.), Oxford, Basil Blackwell, 1962, pp. 180–1.

'Mildness' (*praotes*) was indeed supposed to be one of the democratic **7** virtues, but it belonged to the sphere of private conduct, certainly not when it came to magistrates and political leaders. That is the background for the innumerable kinds of public prosecution and the astonishing frequency of their use. Athenian leaders were called to account more than any other such group in history: to be a *rhetor* or a general was to choose a perilous career that could easily lead to condemnation and execution – if you failed to flee into exile in time.
Hansen, *The Athenian Democracy*, p. 310.

In a society where no political parties exist, smaller groups, even less **8** consciously political groups, can have a great importance in political life. They take on many of the functions which we would ascribe to parties. Thus he who would understand Athenian politics must understand Athenian friendship. He must inform himself not only about the meetings of the assembly and the council, but about the gatherings of families and friends as well. If he will understand what happens in the bouleuterion or on the Pnyx, let him study the clubs and the symposia and the genealogical charts of families.
W. Robert Connor, *The New Politicians of Fifth-Century Athens*, Princeton, Princeton University Press, 1971, p. 32.

Of modern societies something of the sort is certainly true, but **9** for Athens it is anachronistic . . . Policy was made by debate in the Assembly and not by the back-room negotiations of political leaders on behalf of political parties, because there were no political parties and no organized interest groups.
Hansen, *Athenian Democracy*, p. 287.

My concern with political institutions has sometimes been taken to **10** imply a denial or at least a minimization of the elitist aspect of Athenian democracy . . . My point is that the elite exercised its power *through* political institutions, not independently of or in opposition to the institutions. If power and political influence had been based primarily on extra-institutional factors, such as family ties, friendship, local influence and wealth, then rhetoric would have played a much smaller role than it obviously did.
Mogens Herman Hansen, 'On the importance of institutions in an analysis of Athenian democracy', *Classica et Mediaevalia*, 40 (1989), p. 111.

11   In matters of legislation the Assembly relinquished its final say to *nomothetai*. Thus the democracy achieved stability, consistency, and continuity when the higher sovereignty of *nomos* limited the sovereignty of the people.

Martin Ostwald, *From Popular Sovereignty to the Sovereignty of Law: law, society, and politics in fifth-century Athens*, Berkeley, Los Angeles and London, University of California Press, 1986, p. 524.

12   Nomothesia has sometimes been regarded as a serious diminution of the sovereignty of the assembly, but it should rather be seen as a brake on the making of decisions which might affect the fundamental laws and institutions of the polis. Nomothesia did not prevent constitutional or legal changes but it did slow down the process and sought to prevent change through snap votes or a single stacked meeting.

R.K. Sinclair, *Democracy and Participation in Athens*, Cambridge, CUP, 1988, p. 84.

13   It would be easy to preach about the irrationality of crowd behaviour at an open air mass meeting, swayed by demagogic orators, chauvinistic patriotism and so on. But it would be a mistake to overlook that the vote in the Assembly to invade Sicily had been preceded by a period of intense discussion, in the shops and taverns, in the town square, at the dinner table – a discussion among the same men who came together on the Pnyx for the formal debate and vote . . . Moreover, as Thucydides said explicitly, many were voting that day to take themselves off on campaign, in the army or the navy. Listening to a political debate with that end in view would have focused the minds of the participants clearly and sharply. It would have given the debate a reality and spontaneity that modern parliaments may once have had but now notoriously lack.

M.I. Finley, *Democracy Ancient and Modern*, London, Chatto & Windus, 1973, p. 22.

14   The contrariness of the expectations placed on the political orator clearly benefited the demos. Politicians competed for public favor in public contests which were played according to certain conventions, but the details of the rules remained vague: when was *charis* good and when was it bad? when would an elitist claim be suitable and when would it be considered evidence of secret demos-hating tendencies? when should one praise the citizens and when should one castigate them? None of the answers were spelt out, and so politicians always operated from a position of uncertainty. When the rules of a contest are ill defined, its judge is given a wide interpretative scope. The masses set the rules and always acted as combined referee and scorekeeper; the vague and internally contradictory rules they devised for those who would play the game of political influence allowed the demos to reserve for itself the right to cast its own judgements according to its own lights – and hence to keep control of the state. As a result, the orators were never able to define a sphere of influence, authority, or power for themselves that was independent of the continued goodwill of the people.

Ober, *Mass and Elite*, pp. 335–6.

Kleisthenes' reforms politicised the Attic countryside and rooted **15** political identity there. Those local political roots continue to be the basis for political activity throughout the classical period . . . For all who would be Athenians the deme group had to be the primary group, a group which both catered for the non-political expression of local identity and which was strong enough in itself to accommodate the interests of members in other, extra-local, groups, whether the product of kinship ties, associates in wealth and in service to the polis, or religious activity. The abiding importance of the deme tie prevents any of those other groups becoming exclusive, and always provides the unavoidable channel for political activity.

Robin Osborne, *Demos: the discovery of classical Attika*, Cambridge, CUP, 1985, p. 189.

We may now treat the funeral oration as a form of democratic **16** discourse, despite its contradictions and perhaps even because of them. In the absence of any theory of democracy, the epitaphioi present a eulogy of the political system; an aristocratic eulogy, in the absence of a democratic theory . . . Old words to describe new institutions: no doubt, in the classical period, there was no other way of speaking of the Athenian system.

Nicole Loraux, *The Invention of Athens: the funeral oration in the classical city*, trans. A. Shapiro, Cambridge Mass. and London, Harvard University Press, 1986, p. 218. First published in French in 1981 by Mouton. Copyright © 1986 by the President and Fellows of Harvard College.

DEMOGRAPHY

The facts, delivered by ancient authors, are either so uncertain or so **1** imperfect as to afford us nothing positive in this matter. How indeed could it be otherwise? The very facts, which we must oppose to them, in computing the populousness of modern states, are far from being either certain or complete. Many grounds of calculation proceeded on by celebrated writers, are little better than those of the Emperor Heliogabalus, who formed an estimate of the immense greatness of Rome, from ten thousand pound weight of cobwebs which had been found in that city.

It is to be remarked, that all kinds of numbers are uncertain in ancient manuscripts, and have been subject to much greater corruptions than any other part of the text; and that for an obvious reason. Any alteration, in other places, commonly affects the sense or grammar, and is more readily perceived by the reader and transcriber. David Hume, 'Of the populousness of ancient nations' [1752], in *Essays: moral, political, and literary I*, T.H. Green & T.H. Grose (eds), London, Longmans, Green & Co., 1875, pp. 413–14.

2   It should be obvious that if we have no conception of the numbers of peoples about whom we write and read we cannot envisage them in their concrete reality. What does a statement about the Romans *mean*, if we do not know roughly how many Romans there were? Without such knowledge even politics and war cannot be understood. For instance, a description of Roman political institutions in the third century B.C. could only be misleading if we did not know that the citizen body was so numerous and so scattered that in the absence of the representative principle the democratic features which they seem to manifest were bound to be illusory in practice, and that Rome could consequently not enjoy a genuinely popular government. Success in war, even more evidently, depended largely on the balance between the forces that Rome and her enemies could mobilize. For a study of social and economic questions an assessment of population is indispensable. P.A. Brunt, *Italian Manpower 225 BC–AD 14*, Oxford, OUP, 1971, p. 3.

3   It seems to me that the burden of proof is firmly on those who wish to assert that the Roman population in general had a lower mortality than other pre-industrial populations with similar technical achievements or towns; they must show that there were present in the Roman Empire factors which could have led to a general diminution of mortality.

In the absence of any such significant factors, it seems reasonable to hypothesize on these general grounds that the Roman population probably had an expectation of life at birth of 20 to 30 years. But by the same token that we rejected the evidence of the inscriptions, we cannot use them now as corroboration. For if we rejected evidence which does not conform to the hypothesis on the ground that it does not conform (e.g. the underrepresentation of infant mortality), we cannot usefully accept evidence which confirms the hypothesis merely because it confirms it. For example, we cannot accept the evidence of Africa on the sole ground that it yields levels of mortality at particular ages similar to those we have hypothesized, but reject the evidence of the city of Rome because it is different. We have to show instead some other grounds for its validity; for example, that in Africa all people who died were commemorated, hence the reasonable demographic levels of mortality at certain ages. But clearly we do not have enough evidence for such an assertion.

Keith Hopkins, 'On the probable age structure of the Roman population', *Population Studies*, 20 (1966–7), p. 264.

DISEASE

Disease and parasitism play a pervasive role in all life. A successful **1** search for food on the part of one organism becomes for its host a nasty infection or disease. All animals depend on other living things for food, and human beings are no exception. Problems of finding food and the changing ways human communities have done so are familiar enough in economic histories. The problems of avoiding becoming food for some other organism are less familiar, largely because from very early times human beings ceased to have much to fear from large-bodied animal predators like lions or wolves. Nevertheless, one can properly think of most human lives as caught in a precarious equilibrium between the microparasitism of disease organisms and the macroparasitism of large-bodied predators, chief among which have been other human beings.

W.H. McNeill, *Plagues and Peoples*, Oxford, Basil Blackwell, 1977, pp. 5–6.

It is perfectly legitimate and interesting to study causes of death, but in **2** view of the understanding of modern evolutionary theory employed here, which puts the accent on differential reproduction rather than mortality, less importance is attached here to diseases as a driving force in human history than McNeill attributed to them . . . It is doubtful that diseases, like other predators, are capable of regulating prey populations, so long as the predator's effects on the prey are purely negative, even though some of them are well capable of causing massive short-term decreases.

Robert Sallares, *The Ecology of the Ancient Greek World*, London, Duckworth, and Ithaca, Cornell University Press, 1991, p. 224.

DRAMA

See also FESTIVALS

1   The more we learn about the original production of tragedies and
    comedies in Athens, the more it seems wrong even to call them plays
    in the modern sense of the word.
    John J. Winkler & Froma I. Zeitlin (eds), *Nothing to do with Dionysos?*
    Athenian drama in its social context, Princeton, Princeton University Press,
    1990, p. 4. Copyright © 1990 by Winkler, J.J. & Zeitlin, F.I. Reprinted by
    permission of Princeton University Press.

2   The festival was truly a civic occasion, then. This could not be more
    strongly emphasized than by the ceremonies that during the period of
    Athenian supremacy took place after the opening sacrifice and before
    the performances . . . Before the drama, the great festival of the city
    puts on stage an assertion and display of the strength of the democracy
    and its civic ideology.
        It may seem somewhat surprising after that introduction to consider
    the nature of the plays that follow. Even in the *Orestaia*, a play often
    taken to support wholeheartedly a civic ideology, we have already seen
    the undercutting of the security of communication (here in the city of
    words) and the questioning of the ideal of Justice (here in the city so
    proud of its legal innovations as well as its overall democratic justices).
    We will go on to see throughout this book how a whole series of
    notions which are important to the city and the development of civic
    ideology are put through a profound questioning in the dramatic texts.
    After the opening ceremony with its display of civic power, tragedy
    explores the problems inherent in the civic ideology. It depicts a crisis
    of belief not only in people who hold power but also in the very
    system and relations by which the hierarchies of power obtain.
    Simon Goldhill, *Reading Greek Tragedy*, Cambridge, CUP, 1986, pp. 76–7.

3   Once the Athenians had known the fear of the 'envy of the gods', now
    they governed a mighty empire. Once they had continually invoked
    justice and the 'customs of the Greeks'; now they offended these
    not just here and there but as an inherent consequence of what
    was becoming a system of power politics. Question upon question was
    bound to arise, questions which could hardly be aired before the
    Assembly without arousing suspicions of vested political interests and
    which required a constant concern for practicability and for the
    constraints of rational argument.

ECONOMY

Could tragedy step into this breach, not maybe in its original form, but in the form which it was to assume? Perhaps it contributed far more than this to the mental infrastructure of this so successful and in a way so adventurous society, this most powerful but also most insecure part of the world which had yet to test its potential and its frontiers, a world suspended in the first instance between the old and the new.
Christian Meier, *The Political Art of Greek Tragedy*, trans. A. Webber, Cambridge, Polity Press, 1993, p. 3. First published in German in 1988.

It can only be learnt from the Greeks what such a sudden and **4** miraculous awakening of tragedy must signify for the essential basis of a people's life. It is the people of the tragic mysteries who fight the battles with the Persians: and again, the people who waged such wars required tragedy as a necessary healing potion.
Friedrich Nietzsche, *The Birth of Tragedy* [1872], trans. W.A. Haussman, London, George Allen & Unwin, 1909, p. 157.

ECONOMY

See also AGRICULTURE, INDUSTRY, TRADE

The ancient economy is an academic battleground. **1**
Keith Hopkins, 'Introduction', in P. Garnsey, K. Hopkins & C.R. Whittaker (eds), *Trade in the Ancient Economy*, London, Chatto & Windus/Hogarth Press, 1983, p. ix.

'Economics' is a late nineteenth century innovation that did not **2** capture the field until the publication of the first volume of Alfred Marshall's *Principles of Economics* in 1890. Marshall's title cannot be translated into Greek or Latin. Neither can the basic terms, such as labour, production, capital, investment, income, circulation, demand, entrepreneur, utility, at least not in the abstract form required for economic analysis. In stressing this I am not suggesting that the ancients were like Molière's M. Jourdain, who spoke prose without knowing it, but that they in fact lacked the concept of an 'economy', and, *a fortiori*, that they lacked the conceptual elements which together constitute what we call 'the economy'. Of course they farmed, traded, manufactured, mined, taxed, coined, deposited and loaned money, made profits or failed in their enterprises. And they discussed these activities in their talk and their writing. What they did not do,

57

however, was to combine these particular activities conceptually into a unit . . . It then becomes essential to ask whether this is merely accidental, an intellectual failing, a problem in the history of ideas in the narrow sense, or whether it is the consequences of the structure of ancient society.

M.I. Finley, *The Ancient Economy*, London, Hogarth Press, 2nd edn 1985, p. 21.

3   If the problem in the beginning was the 'naive anthropology' of Economics, today it is the 'naive economics' of Anthropology. 'Formalism versus substantivism' amounts to the following theoretical option: between the ready-made models of orthodox Economics, especially the 'microeconomics', taken as universally valid and applicable *grosso modo* to the primitive societies; and the necessity − supposing this formalist position unfounded − of developing a new analysis more appropriate to the historical societies in question . . . Broadly speaking, it is a choice between the perspective of Business, for the formalist method must consider the primitive economies as underdeveloped versions of our own, and a culturalist study that as a matter of principle does honor to different societies for what they are.

Marshall Sahlins, *Stone Age Economics*, London and New York, Tavistock, 1974, pp. xi–xii.

4   However, this essential distance from the past can come to resemble a clumsy lurch to save oneself from overbalancing on one side, which ends up in a fall on the other. Distancing ourselves is thus a necessary but not a sufficient condition for a balanced judgement. Stopping obstinately here, one can certainly avoid 'modernism', but cannot avoid falling head long into the more common but hardly less harmful defect of 'primitivism'. Instead of claiming that the dead are like us (Columella is a capitalist) we end up claiming that they are inferior to us (Columella can't keep his books). 'Modernism' and 'primitivism' are two sides to the same coin, the self-deification of the present and the annihilation of the past.

Andrea Carandini, 'Columella's vineyard and the rationality of the Roman economy', *Opus*, 2 (1983), p. 202.

5   The Roman economy was underdeveloped. This means essentially that the mass of the population lived at or near subsistence level. In a typical underdeveloped, pre-industrial economy, a large proportion of the labour force is employed in agriculture, which is the main avenue for investment and source of wealth. The level of investment in

manufacturing industry is low. Resources that might in theory be devoted to growth-inducing investment are directed into consumption or into unproductive speculation and usury. Demand for manufactured goods is relatively low, and most needs are met locally with goods made by small craftsmen or at home. Backward technology is a further barrier to increased productivity. Finally, there is no class of entrepreneurs who are both capable of perceiving opportunities for profit in large-scale organisation of manufacture and prepared to undergo the risks entailed in making the necessary investment.

Peter Garnsey & Richard Saller, *The Roman Empire: economy, society, culture*, London, Duckworth, and Berkeley and Los Angeles, University of California Press, 1987, p. 43. Copyright © 1987 Peter Garnsey and Richard Saller.

Marxist development theory will not help us to understand whether   **6** the ancient economy was primitive or advanced. If we want the answer, we must ask again: primitive compared to whom? Numerous comparative studies are needed on all aspects of classical society, economy and political institutions . . . It is my view that the classical economy will compare favourably to that of fifteenth to sixteenth century Italy or mid-nineteenth century Japan.

Donald Engels, *Roman Corinth: an alternative model for the classical city*, Chicago, University of Chicago Press, 1990, p. 133. Copyright © 1990 by The University of Chicago.

EDUCATION

See also HELLENISM

Early Greek education was essentially aristocratic and its content was   **1** directed towards fitting the pupil for a life of leisure interspersed with warlike pursuits. This accounts for the early emphasis on physical education. This aristocratic tradition continues right down to the end of our period, but the competition of democratic aims becomes stronger and stronger. The final victory was won by Hesiod with his concept of an absolute and ultimate criterion of Justice working retribution on rich and poor alike. The democratic pressures for equal civic rights became exerted towards the usurpation of aristocratic educational privileges, however unsuitable the aristocratic educational forms might be for the new order.

Frederick A.G. Beck, *Greek Education 450–350 B.C.*, London, Methuen, 1964, pp. 305–6.

2   Hellenic education alike at Sparta and at Athens, in theory and in practice, aimed at producing the best possible citizen, not the best possible money-maker; it sought the good of the community, not the good of the individual. The methods and materials of education naturally differed with the conception of good citizenship held in each locality, but the ideal object was always the same.

Kenneth J. Freeman, *Schools of Hellas: an essay on the practice and theory of ancient Greek education from 600 to 300 B.C.*, London, Macmillan, 1907, p. 275.

3   Early Roman education was thus little concerned with the development of intellectual attainments. Its main object was to form that spirit of self-restraint and filial submission which Roman feeling demanded of the young; its chief merit was that it fostered a reverence for childhood which made every boy and girl an object of almost religious veneration. But it would be a mistake to remain blind to the faults of the system. Judged by intellectual standards, Roman education was essentially utilitarian.

Aubrey Gwynn, *Roman Education from Cicero to Quintilian*, New York, Russell & Russell, 1964, pp. 17–18.

4   Under the Republic, as a general rule, parents exercised a rather firm control over their children, and required them to conform to good standards of behavior and to be diligent in their studies; but at the same time they usually took a keen interest in their progress. Under the Empire, there were still such well-regulated families, but there were also many more parents who delegated their responsibilities to nurses and 'pedagogues', who might, or might not, keep a proper check on their conduct. Other parents went to the opposite extreme, and spoilt their children by over-indulgence. Thus in the classroom the schoolmaster's task was made more difficult, for some of his pupils were idle and ill-behaved, and others were self-willed and conceited. To rectify matters, he acted according to his temperament, and either sought to correct them by meting out hard punishment, or took the line of least resistance and gave them what they liked, or found easiest, to do. Neither method succeeded, and the result was deterioration. But we hardly need the Romans to remind us that education cannot remain immune from the influences of contemporary society.

Stanley F. Bonner, *Education in Ancient Rome: from the elder Cato to the younger Pliny*, London, Methuen, 1977, pp. 332–3.

EGYPT

It will be an added bonus if [this study] also helps to shake a conviction common among historians of the Roman empire that Egypt was exceptional, and that its socio-economic history has no bearing on that of the rest of the empire. It was in some ways different, but every province must have had local peculiarities, and some of the apparent exceptions which emerge from the rich Egyptian documentation may justifiably provoke reappraisal of the rules constructed on the more slender basis of the evidence from elsewhere.

Dominic Rathbone, *Economic Rationalism and Rural Society in Third-Century A.D. Egypt: the Heroninos archive and the Appianus estate*, Cambridge, CUP, 1991, pp. 408–9.

EMPEROR AND PRINCIPATE

The emperor was what the emperor did . . . The emperor's role in **1** relation to his subjects was essentially that of listening to requests, and of hearing disputes . . . It is the essential passivity of the role expected of the emperor both by himself and by others which explains the very limited and simple 'governmental' apparatus which he needed.

Fergus Millar, *The Emperor in the Roman World (31 BC–AD 337)*, London, Duckworth, and Ithaca, Cornell University Press, 1977, p. 6.

If it was only the emperor himself who read the petitions addressed to **2** him, then not many petitions can have been read and petitions cannot have been a fundamental aspect of Roman political life; Roman subjects must have devised some other ways of solving problems and redressing grievances. Of course, the belief that the emperor read petitions and redressed grievances may have been important; and dramatic individual cases may have been important in keeping that belief alive – just as Abraham Lincoln's rise from log cabin to the Presidency of the USA has been an important myth in American political culture. But myth and practice should be analysed on separate levels.

Keith Hopkins, 'Rules of evidence', *Journal of Roman Studies*, 68 (1978), p. 184.

The imperial regime simply cannot be adequately characterised **3** in constitutional terms, for while the institutions of the *res publica* persisted, and while the emperor performed his functions partly within them (speaking, and occasionally even voting, in the senate, or having his nominees to office formally elected by the *comitia*), he also assumed from the beginning a direct relationship to cities, institutions and individuals in which his pronouncements and decisions were treated as being of automatic legal validity.

Millar, *Emperor*, pp. 6–7.

4   Both in the theory and in the practice of the constitution the emperor's powers were absolute. He controlled foreign policy, making peace and war at will: he could raise what taxes he willed and spend the money at his pleasure: he personally appointed to all offices, civil and military: he had the power of life and death over all his subjects. He was moreover the sole fount of law and could make new rules or abrogate old at pleasure . . . These constitutional powers were reinforced by a religious sanction. From the conversion of Constantine the emperor was, it is true, no longer worshipped as a god, but he hardly lost by the change. He became instead the divinely appointed viceregent of the one God . . . In official and popular phraseology the emperor and everything connected with him continued to be sacred or divine, and emperors did not hesitate to qualify disobedience to their will as sacrilege.

A.H.M. Jones, *The Later Roman Empire 284–602*, Oxford, Basil Blackwell, 1964, p. 321.

5   [The Principate] was a regime of secrecy in which decisions, wise though they might be, were taken by the emperor in his own council and prepared by administrators who, however able, were answerable to no one. The only outlet for public opinion consisted either in the closely supervised debates of a Senate virtually recruited by the emperor, or in urban riots and military pronunciamentos. There were still citizens, but civic life was extinct.

Claude Nicolet, *The World of the Citizen in Republican Rome*, trans. P.S. Falla, London, Batsford, 1980, p. 21. First published in French in 1976.

6   Hostility to the *nobiles* was engrained in the Principate from its military and revolutionary origins. In the first decade of his consti-tutional rule, Augustus employed not a single *nobilis* among the legates who commanded the armies in his *provincia* . . . A rational distrust persists, confirmed under his successors by certain disquieting incidents, and leads to the complete exclusion of the *nobiles*, the delayed but logical end of Revolution and Empire.

Ronald Syme, *The Roman Revolution*, Oxford, OUP, 1939, p. 502.

Although the formal status of senators remained high, their collective **7** political power was undermined. The functions of the senate within Roman politics had changed completely, partly because the senate was subordinate to the emperors, and partly because the emperors created alternative channels of power which were more directly under their own control . . . Senators acquiesced in their own political demise, we imagine, partly because they were internally divided, in competition with each other for honours and positions bestowed only by the emperor, and partly because their wealth and their social status especially outside the capital did not depend upon their political power in the central government.

Keith Hopkins & Graham Burton, 'Ambition and withdrawal', in Hopkins, *Death and Renewal: sociological studies in Roman history II*, Cambridge, CUP, 1983, pp. 196–7.

While the political influence of the individual Roman citizen was **8** not great, when crowds gathered together in the circuses or at the theatres they expressed their feelings as a collective body; and to such manifestations no ruler dared to remain indifferent . . . Moreover, the efforts made by the emperors to reduce tension among the wider public indicate that the masses were not an entirely negligible factor. For the emperors it was important that the common people should be well-disposed towards them, and to this end they directed a considerable part of their propaganda.

Zvi Yavetz, *Plebs and Princeps*, Oxford, OUP, 1969, p. 132.

The outcome was that those emperors who (either through natural **9** deficiencies or lack of experience) did not acquire sufficient prestige to be able to restrain both the soldiers and the people always failed. And most of the emperors (especially those who came to the throne as new men), when they realised how difficult it was to satisfy these two conflicting tendencies, tried to satisfy the soldiers and worried little about the people being harmed.

Machiavelli, *The Prince* [1513], Q. Skinner & R. Price (eds), Cambridge, CUP, 1988, p. 67.

Political power and legitimacy rest not only in taxes and armies, but **10** also in the perceptions and beliefs of men. The stories told about emperors were part of the mystification which elevated emperors and the political sphere above everyday life. Stories circulated. They were the currency of the political system, just as coins were the currency of the fiscal system. Their truth or untruth is only a secondary problem.

Power is a two-way process; the motive force for the attachment between the king and the gods does not come from the ruler alone. His aides and his lowest subjects, since they cannot usually change the social order, wish to justify, indeed they often wish to glorify, the *status quo* and their own place within it.

Keith Hopkins, 'Divine emperors or the symbolic unity of the Roman empire', in Hopkins, *Conquerors and Slaves: sociological studies in Roman history I*, Cambridge, CUP, 1978, p. 198.

11 The emperor was honoured at ancestral religious festivals; he was placed within the gods' sanctuaries and temples; sacrifices to the gods invoked their protection for the emperor. There were also festivals, temples and sacrifices in honour of the emperor alone which were calqued on the traditional honours of the gods. In other words, the Greek subjects of the Roman empire attempted to relate their ruler to their own dominant symbolic system.

S.R.F. Price, *Rituals and Power: the Roman imperial cult in Asia Minor*, Cambridge, CUP, 1984, p. 235.

12 The imperial cult stabilized the religious order of the world. The system of ritual was carefully structured; the symbolism evoked a picture of the relationship between the emperor and the gods. The ritual was also structuring; it imposed a definition of the world. The imperial cult, along with politics and diplomacy, constructed the reality of the Roman empire.

Ibid., p. 248.

13 As regarded the idealisation of the emperor, on the other hand, the chief obstacle always remained the emperor himself; the obstacle was an ever present reality. For this reason, it was both safer and more practical to leave the ideal emperor ultimately undefined, and to let him be as an image which might be glimpsed as in a mirror or beheld 'as in the innermost sanctuary'.

Sabrine G. McCormack, *Art and Ceremony in Late Antiquity*, Berkeley, Los Angeles and London, University of California Press, 1981, pp. 268–9.

ENVIRONMENT

1 The concerns of ecology are in fact fundamental to understanding the course of history in general (and so the present) and ancient history in particular . . . Indeed I could go so far as to assert that any ancient historian who has not immersed himself or herself fully in the

problems of ecology can have, at best, only an extremely limited comprehension of the course of history in classical antiquity.
Robert Sallares, *The Ecology of the Ancient Greek World*, London, Duckworth, and Ithaca, Cornell University Press, 1991, p. 4.

The Mediterranean Sea with its bordering lands has been a melting-   **2**
pot for the peoples and civilizations which have seeped into it from its continental hinterlands. It has been a catchment basin, and it has also been a distributing center for its composite cultural achievements. This double role in history is an outgrowth of its geographical location and its relation to the neighbouring continents.
Ellen Churchill Semple, *The Geography of the Mediterranean Region: its relation to ancient history*, London, Constable & Co., 1932, p. 4.

The first part [of this book] is devoted to a history whose passage is   **3**
almost imperceptible, that of man in his relationship to the environ-ment, a history in which all change is slow, a history of constant repetition, ever-recurring cycles.
Fernand Braudel, *The Mediterranean and the Mediterranean World in the Age of Philip II*, trans. S. Reynolds, London, Collins, 1972, Volume I, p. 20. First published in French in 1949, 2nd edn 1966, by Armand Colin.

Throughout the Mediterranean basin and the adjoining Near East, the   **4**
ruins of ancient civilizations stand amid the evidences of depleted environments. The conclusion seems inescapable that the natural environment and the course of civilizations were linked.
J. Donald Hughes, *Ecology in Ancient Civilizations*, Albuquerque, University of New Mexico Press, 1975, p. 2.

The modern ecological crisis grew out of roots which lie deep in the   **5**
ancient worlds, particularly in Greece and Rome. The problems of human communities with the natural environment did not begin suddenly with the ecological awareness of the 1960s, nor indeed with the onset of the Industrial Revolution or the Christian Middle Ages. Mankind has been challenged to find a way of living with nature from the earliest times, and many of our habitual answers to that challenge received their first conscious formulation within ancient societies, especially the classical civilizations.
Ibid., p. 154.

There is in this description a note of awestruck admiration as well   **6**
as repugnance that exactly reflected Rome's mixed feelings about the

forest. On the one hand, it was a place which, by definition, was 'outside' (*foris*) the writ of their law and the governance of their state. On the other hand, their own founding myths were sylvan. Classical Greece had venerated groves sacred to Artemis and Apollo and their cults of fertility, the hunt, and the tree-oracle had been transferred to Rome. Arcadia was imagined in both cultures as a wooded, rocky place, the haunt of satyrs, the realm of Pan. According to Virgil, the city itself had sprung from the motherwood Rhea Silvia, where wild-men and giants issued from the trunks of oaks. The fig tree beneath which Romulus and Remus were said to have been suckled by the she-wolf had been removed to the forum, where it too was an active devotional site. And by the time of Tacitus and Pliny it had become commonplace to contrast the mythic simplicity of an archaic 'timbered' Rome, when the first Senate was no more than a rustic hut, with what moralists complained was the gilded decadence of the empire.

Tacitus' wooded Germania, then, was in some ways desirably, as well as deplorably, primitive.

Simon Schama, *Landscape and Memory*, London, HarperCollins, 1995, p. 83. Reprinted by permission of HarperCollins and the Peters Fraser & Dunlop Group.

ETHNICITY

1   There is one surprise that the historian usually experiences upon his first visit to Rome. It may be at the Galleria Lapidaria of the Vatican or at the Lateran Museum, but, if not elsewhere, it can hardly escape him upon his first walk up the Appian Way. As he stops to decipher the names upon the old tombs that line the road, hoping to chance upon one familiar to him from his Cicero or Livy, he finds praenoman and nomen promising enough, but the cognomina all seem awry. L. Lucretius *Pamphilus*, A. Aemilius *Alexa*, M. Coldius *Philostorgus* do not smack of freshman Latin. And he will not readily find in the Roman writers now extant an answer to the questions that these inscriptions inevitably raise. Do these names imply that the Roman stock was completely changed after Cicero's day, and was the satirist recording a fact when he wailed that the Tiber had captured the waters of the Syrian Orontes? If so, are these foreigners ordinary immigrants, or did Rome become a nation of ex-slaves and their offspring? Or does the abundance of Greek cognomina mean that, to a certain extent, a foreign nomenclature has gained respect, so that a Roman dignitary might, so to speak, sign a name like C. Julius Abascantus on the hotel register without any misgivings about the accommodation?

Tenney Frank, 'Race mixture in the Roman empire', in D. Kagan (ed.), *Decline and Fall of the Roman Empire: why did it collapse?*, Boston, D.C. Heath & Co., 1962, p. 44. Originally published in *American Historical Review*, 21 (1916).

The ancient Greeks believed themselves to have Greek nationality   **2** because they were of one blood, one language, one religion, and one culture and outlook on life; and appealed to their own folk-memory in proof of this unity. All these criteria fail, however, when applied to the data now accessible. The Greeks of classical times were of mixed descent, spoke different dialects of a hybrid language, combined Olympian with chthonic cults and rituals, contrasted Doric and Ionic manners and ideas, with growing insistence, throughout the 'great age' of Greece; and their traditions intermixed indigenous stocks, which were not Greek, with immigrant culture-heroes, pervasive Hellenes, migratory Dorians and Aeolians transposed and superposed on other kinds of Greeks. Wherein then does Hellenic unity consist? Who were the Greeks?

Their Aegean cradle-land, with its peculiar physique, and its intimate relations with other Mediterranean coastlands, neighboring sections of the Mountain-zone, and neighboring annexes of the Eurasian steppe, has been for long the recipient of inhabitants from all the three primary breeds of the White Race of mankind. But it also lies sufficiently aloof and self-contained to impose its peculiar geographical controls and each and all, selecting the strains best fitted for acclimatization. As a physical variety of man, a Greek type is always emerging in Greek lands, and during a long interval of quiescence from the eleventh to the seventh centuries B.C., did actually establish itself by elimination of unconformable, uncongenial traits. From mongrel ancestry, the Greek people of classical times had come to consist of closely related types, approximately thoroughbred. Renewed facilities for intercourse, however, intercrossed these secluded types, in the centuries from the sixth to the fourth, and Alexander's conquests disseminated these already cross-bred Greeks over large continental regions; and here heterogeneous interbreeding with foreign stocks once more replaced the 'classical' types by numerous mongrel descendants.

John Linton Myres, *Who Were the Greeks?*, Berkeley, University of California Press, 1930, pp. 531–2.

The problem with the nineteenth-century treatment of Greek ethnic   **3** groups was that its racial model entailed a view of biologically determined, static and monolithic categories whose boundaries were impermeable – indeed, elements of this doctrine still prevail in some current works on Greek history which apply the term 'race' to the Dorians or Ionians . . . The ethnic group is a *social construction* rather than an objective and inherently determined category. Genetic, linguistic, religious or common cultural factors cannot act as an objective and universal definition of an ethnic group. They are instead *indicia*, or the operational sets of distinguishing attributes which tend to be associated with ethnic groups once the socially determined *criteria* have been created and set in place.

Jonathan M. Hall, 'Approaches to ethnicity in the Early Iron Age of Greece', in Nigel Spencer (ed.), *Time, Tradition and Society in Greek Archaeology*, London and New York, Routledge, 1995, pp. 8–9.

4 'The Greeks', however, is an abstraction, and, at times, an inconvenient one. Herodotus may have thought that he could usefully define *to Hellenikon*, literally 'the Greek thing' or 'Greekness', in terms of common blood, language, religion, and mores. But not only did he have to omit political institutions or structures from his definition in order to do so, when there were well over a thousand separate Greek political communities which could never form more than local, shortlived, and usually imposed interstate ties. He also had to create the fiction of genetic homogeneity and gloss over important differences of dialect, religion and mores within the broadly 'Hellenic' world. In other words, *to Hellenikon* was no less of an ideological construct than, say, Christendom was in the Middle Ages or 'the Arab world' is today.

On the other hand, it was no more of an artificial construct than those, either. 'Greekness', that is to say, had at least enough purchase on reality to allow of a definition that was not purely wishful thinking.

Paul Cartledge, *The Greeks: a portrait of self and others*, Oxford, OUP, 1993, p. 3.

5 Many Ancient Greeks shared a feeling very like what would now be called nationalism: they despised other peoples and some, like Aristotle, even put this on a theoretical plane by claiming a Hellenic superiority based on the geographical situation of Greece. It was a feeling qualified by the very real respect many Greek writers had for foreign culture, particularly those of Egypt, Phoenicia and Mesopotamia. But, in any event, this Ancient Greek 'nationalism' was negligible compared to the tidal wave of ethnicity and racialism, linked to cults of Christian Europe and the North, that engulfed

Northern Europe with the Romantic movement at the end of the 18th century. The paradigm of 'races' that were intrinsically unequal in physical and mental endowment was applied to all human studies, but especially to history. It was now considered undesirable, if not disastrous, for races to mix. To be creative, a civilization needed to be 'racially pure'. Thus it became increasingly intolerable that Greece – which was seen by the Romantics not merely as the epitome of Europe but also as its pure childhood – could be the result of the mixture of native Europeans and colonizing Africans and Semites.

Martin Bernal, *Black Athena: the Afroasiatic roots of classical civilization, Volume I: the fabrication of ancient Greece, 1785–1985*, pp. 28–9. First published in the UK by Free Association Books, 57 Warren Street, London W1P 5PA, England; Copyright © Martin Bernal 1987.

EUERGETISM

Let us return to our notables and their cities. Like the kings, they gave *largesse* sometimes for the sake of gratuitous display (voluntary euergetism or patronage) and sometimes symbolically (this was the case . . . of their *euergesiai ob honorem*). But their magnificence had a very special character, which is a good reason for coining the word 'euergetism' with its ending in 'ism'. It was both spontaneous and forced, voluntary and constrained. Every euergesia is to be explained both by the generosity of the *euergetês*, who has his own motives, and by the constraint imposed upon him by the expectations of others, public opinion, the 'role' in which the *euergetês* is caught. This dual character makes euergetism something almost unique: if there were only constraint, *euergesiai* would be in the nature of taxes or liturgies, while if there were only spontaneity, there would be no difference between a *euergetês* of antiquity and an American patron of the arts today, who gives if he chooses to, without such patronage constituting a moral obligation.

Paul Veyne, *Bread and Circuses: historical sociology and political pluralism*, trans. B. Pearce, Harmondsworth, Penguin/Allen Lane, 1990, pp. 103–4. First published in French in 1976 by Editions de Seuil.

FESTIVALS

See also DRAMA

1   In the ancient Greek city there were no purely secular festivals. All holidays were really holy days dedicated to particular gods or goddesses. But also the ancient Greeks had no rigid distinctions between activities of a religious or of a worldly character. Not only was feasting an appropriate act of worship, but even athletics and play-acting were proper institutions for holy days. The pious psalmist, sure in his knowledge of the nature of Jehovah, might assert: 'He hath no pleasure in the strength of an horse: neither delighteth he in any man's legs'. But the Athenian when he took part in chariot-racing or running at the Panathenaic games believed that Athena was honoured by these exertions. Similarly when he laughed at the comedies or wept at the tragedies, he was seated in a theatre consecrated to Dionysus, and the happenings on the stage, however pathetic or ludicrous, were governed by the rules of a religious ceremony.
H.W. Parke, *Festivals of the Athenians*, London, Thames & Hudson, 1977, p. 13. Copyright © 1977 Thames & Hudson Ltd, London.

2   We may go to a secular play or concert which is part of a church festival, is given in a church and is even preceded by some prayers from the priest, but does that make the performance a ritual or attendance a religious experience? You have only to contrast it with the lessons, litany and liturgy of a church service. But surely, it may still be claimed, tragedy was, none the less, a religious experience for the audience, seeing that they were participating in a sacred festival. Is going to the panto a religious experience since it is part of the annual festival commemorating Christ's birth (or marking the winter solstice, if you prefer)? For the Athenians the great Dionysia was an occasion to stop work, drink a lot of wine, eat some meat, and witness or participate in the various ceremonials, processions and priestly doings which are part of such holidays the world over. It was also the occasion for tragedy and comedy; but I do not see any way in which the Dionysiac occasion invades or affects the entertainment.
O. Taplin, *Greek Tragedy in Action*, London, Methuen, 1978, p. 162.

3   The special circumstances of the City Dionysia festival, then, bring the special license of comedy, with its obscenity and lampoons, and the special license of tragedy, with its images of society collapsing. The two faces of Dionysos form the one festival. The tensions and ambiguities that tragedy and comedy differently set in motion, the tensions and ambiguities that arise from the transition from tragedy to comedy, all fall under the aegis of the one god, the divinity associated with illusion and change, paradox and ambiguity, release and transgression.

Simon Goldhill, 'The Great Dionysia and civic ideology', in J.J. Winkler &
F.I. Zeitlin (eds), *Nothing to do with Dionysos? Athenian drama in its social
context*, Princeton, Princeton University Press, 1990, p. 128. Copyright ©
1990 by Goldhill, S. Reprinted by permission of Princeton University Press.

They clearly occupied a very significant place in Roman society, **4**
though what they precisely meant to the individual Roman in
religious or social terms, or how many Romans attended or took part
in such rites, is unfortunately often far from clear. Thus, for instance,
who can say what was in the mind of Ovid when, like a primitive
shepherd, he leapt through the flames of the purificatory rite of the
Parilia festival?
H.H. Scullard, *Festivals and Ceremonies of the Roman Republic*, London,
Thames & Hudson, 1981, p. 12. Copyright ©1981 Thames & Hudson Ltd,
London.

FOOD AND DRINK

Forms of eating and drinking therefore reflect and reinforce the social **1**
system in a variety of complex ways; they also create and maintain a
variety of cultural values. But in modern societies the relationships are
more hidden than in ancient ones.
Oswyn Murray, 'Introduction', in Murray (ed.), *Sympotica: a symposium on the
Symposium*, Oxford, OUP, 1990, p. 5.

Wherever it began, agriculture had from the start been obliged to opt **2**
for one of the major food-plants; and had been built up around this
initial choice of priority on which everything or almost everything
would thereafter depend. Three of these plants were brilliantly
successful: wheat, rice and maize. They continue to share world arable
land between them today. The 'plants of civilization', they have
profoundly organized man's material and sometimes his spiritual life,
to the point where they have become almost ineradicable structures.
Fernand Braudel, *The Structures of Everyday Life: the limits of the possible*, trans.
M. Kochan, rev. S. Reynolds, Berkeley and Los Angeles, University of
California Press, 1981, p. 107. First published in French in 1979 by Armand
Colin.

The olive tree and the vine are such an integral part of Mediterranean **3**
farming that it is easy to fall into the trap of thinking that this has been
the case throughout history, but then no one would guess from its role
in the modern Italian diet that the tomato only arrived in the early

modern period . . . The triad of crops which characterises modern Mediterranean agriculture, namely the olive, vine and the modern types of wheat, was not inherited by the Greeks and Romans from their Bronze Age predecessors living in the same areas but was in the main a product, an innovation, of the first millennium BC.

Robert Sallares, *The Ecology of the Ancient Greek World*, London, Duckworth, and Ithaca, Cornell University Press, 1991, pp. 32–3.

4   The fermented grape was by far the commonest source of alcohol in the ancient world, and alcohol by far the commonest intoxicant available. This created for wine a wholly distinctive pattern of demand and consumption and, associated with it, a rich variety of cultural behaviour.

N. Purcell, 'Wine and wealth in ancient Italy', *Journal of Roman Studies*, 75 (1985), p. 2.

5   Among historians there is indeed an increasing tendency to emphasize the socializing aspects of alcohol. For them the truth in wine is a social truth . . . And yet there remains the fact of the potential for anomie, the power of Dionysus to disrupt society, to send his devotees mad – that is to offer not an alternative order, but the alternative of disorder.

Oswyn Murray, 'Histories of pleasure', in O. Murray & M. Tecusan (eds), *In Vino Veritas*, London, British School at Rome, 1995, pp. 4–5.

6   We have reached the conclusion that hunger endured over long periods and a constant dearth of proteins and calories would have produced a noticeable reduction of motivation and social activity. A vicious circle would be established in which malnutrition led to anorexia and apathy, and this in turn aggravated malnutrition. As a result there would have been a sense of isolation, the loss of effective control over one's own life, a state of profound depression, a sense of isolation from surrounding reality. The plebs would have lived with a kind of 'prisoner syndrome', seeing the world immediately outside the city as a hostile environment, which offered neither land nor work.

Giuseppe Pucci, 'I consumi alimentari', in E. Gabba & A. Schiavone (eds), *Storia di Roma IV: caratteri e morfologie*, Turin, Giulio Einaudi, 1989, p. 385. Copyright © 1989, Giulio Einaudi Editore. Trans. N. Morley.

FREEDMEN

1   This conjectural estimate [of the number of freedmen in the city of Rome] fits the impression to be derived from the thousands of urban

epitaphs, which show an enormous preponderance of freedmen both in general and among the skilled craftsmen. Statistics taken from these epitaphs undoubtedly under-estimate the number of slaves living at any given time; a very high proportion of slaves will have died as freedmen, having spent most of their working lives in servitude. Do they also underrate the proportion of men of free birth? Perhaps: it can be argued that freedmen were more disposed to leave some memorial of themselves, for they may have taken a pride in the exercise of their crafts or merely in having earned their liberation, whereas the ingenuous poor had nothing to commemorate save that they had lived. Moreover a tombstone cost money, and when crafts were mainly in the hands of the freedmen, and the men of free birth were restricted to casual, unskilled labour, they may not have had the means to pay for a memorial. But it remains difficult to dismiss the epigraphic ratio between freedmen and freeborn as wholly misleading . . . It seems to me safe to conclude that slaves and freedmen accounted for well over two-thirds of the urban population in 70 [BC], perhaps three-quarters.

P.A. Brunt, *Italian Manpower 225 BC–AD 14*, Oxford, OUP, 1971, p. 387.

We need to recall that the social being of the freedman was **2** complicated and fragile. A freedman did not have the coherence of the aristocrat, who was sure of his superiority and armed with fortifying values, even if he did not always apply them in his daily life. The freedman had neither the rustic simplicity of the indigenous countryman nor the finely tuned irreverence of the domestic slave. The freedman stood where several divergent and even opposing forces intersected. On the one hand, he had been a slave, and neither he nor others could forget it. On the other, he had the status of freedman, which was in itself partly contradictory, since manumission conferred on him the same citizenship as his patron but also subjected him to a number of regulations and customs that set him apart from the freeborn *ingenuus*.

Jean Andreau, 'The freedman', in A. Giardina (ed.), *The Romans*, trans. L.G. Cochrane, Chicago and London, University of Chicago Press, 1993, pp. 178–9. First published in Italian in 1989. Copyright © 1993 by The University of Chicago.

The position of the freedman depended by and large on the patron's **3** attitude. It was the patron who decided the scale of the *operae* or services to be imposed on the manumitted slave, if indeed he chose to stipulate for *operae* at all. It was his interpretation of the freedman's duty of *obsequium*, respectful conduct, that prevailed.

Peter Garnsey, 'Independent freedmen and the economy of Roman Italy under the Principate', *Klio*, 63 (1981), p. 366.

4   Freedmen had claims that slaves lacked, namely, family and citizenship. Nonetheless, they occupied a marginal position in society, and the stain of a servile past left them continually vulnerable to denigration and to insiders' disdain for any accomplishment in the present. The loss of origin was permanent and, with it, full physical integrity, at least in relation to the former master. For some, the claim to one's own labor continued to be a resistance to that loss. By altering the standard of assessment from birth to economic activity, the claim gives the freedman a central rather than marginal position.

Sandra R. Joshel, *Work, Identity and Legal Status at Rome: a study of the occupational inscriptions*, Norman and London, University of Oklahoma Press, 1992, p. 166.

5   Neither a parvenu, nor a capitalist, nor a bourgeois: these anachronistic categories tend to blur what is original in the reality of the epoch. The life of Trimalchio is characteristic of this reality . . . Trimalchio epitomises or reflects his times, if one replaces him in the system of possibilities and impossibilities across which he must clear a way for himself.

Paul Veyne, 'Vie de Trimalcion', *Annales ESC*, 16 (1961), p. 214. Trans. N. Morley.

FRONTIERS

1   There is, therefore, a consistent pattern in Roman frontier policy, and a hierarchy of priorities: first, the frontier must facilitate strategic transit between the continental regions of the empire; second, it should *not* include areas inherently difficult to settle, urbanize, and Romanize (such as Scotland); third, it *should* include lands suited for settlement – lands that would enhance the strength of the empire in men and resources. Finally, as a distinctly secondary priority, the frontier should be as short as possible, in order to reduce the manpower required for outposts and patrols.

Edward N. Luttwak, *The Grand Strategy of the Roman Empire: from the first century AD to the third*, Baltimore and London, Johns Hopkins University Press, 1976, p. 96.

Rome had no institutes of strategic studies. In military matters as in **2** government, within a broad framework of the simplest form, Rome tended less to *act* than to wait for things to happen and then *react*. Frontier development shows this admirably. Each developed merely as the local response to local circumstances. It is impossible to force them into rigid strait-jackets.

J.C. Mann, 'Force and the frontiers of the empire', *Journal of Roman Studies*, 69 (1979), p. 180.

The Romans faced a dilemma. The very existence of stability created **3** by a frontier, and the prosperity that frontiers brought in terms of goods and markets changed and developed the social and ecological conditions that, as I have argued in this chapter, halted the progress of the imperial armies. Either frontiers expanded to incorporate these new regions, or the frontiers themselves came under attack and pressure.

C.R. Whittaker, *Frontiers of the Roman Empire: a social and economic study*, Baltimore and London, Johns Hopkins University Press, 1994, p. 97. Copyright © 1994 by The Johns Hopkins University Press. All rights reserved.

GAMES

No one can fail to be repelled by this aspect of callous, deep-seated **1** sadism which pervaded Romans of all classes.

J.P.V.D. Balsdon, *Life and Leisure in Ancient Rome*, London, Sydney and Toronto, Bodley Head, 1969, p. 308.

Can we expect a Roman, even a cultured Roman, not to reason as a **2** Roman? If we are astonished at the attitude of the Roman elite in this matter, it means only that we are putting the question wrongly. We start from the idea that they should have taken a stand against the cruelties of which we disapprove. We must, on the contrary, start from the idea that such disapproval was out of the question . . . The Roman attitude cannot be explained without admitting from the start that it is conditioned by the existence of slavery, that is to say, by the idea that a human being can be simply an instrument.

Roland Auguet, *Cruelty and Civilization: the Roman games*, London, Allen & Unwin, 1972, p. 197. First published in French in 1970.

The popularity of gladiatorial shows was a by-product of war, disci- **3** pline and death. Rome was a militaristic society. For centuries, it had been devoted to war and to the mass participation of citizens in battle. They won their huge empire by discipline and control . . . When long-term peace came to the heartlands of the empire, particularly after 31 BC, these militaristic traditions were preserved at Rome in the domesticated battlefield of the amphitheatre. War had been converted into a game, a drama repeatedly replayed, of cruelty, violence, blood and death. But order still needed to be preserved, and the fear of death still had to be controlled or assuaged by ritual. In a city as large as Rome, without an adequate police force, disorder always threatened. And without effective medicine, death-rates must have been very high. No one was safe. Sickness spread occasionally like wild-fire through crowded apartment blocks. Gladiatorial shows and their accompanying executions provided opportunities for the reaffirmation of the moral order through the sacrifice of criminal victims, of slave gladiators, of Christian outcasts and wild animals. The enthusiastic participation of spectators, rich and poor, raised and then released collective tensions, in a society which traditionally idealised impassivity (*gravitas*). The gladiatorial shows provided a psychic and a political safety valve for the population of the capital.

Keith Hopkins, 'Murderous games', in Hopkins, *Death and Renewal: sociological studies in Roman history II*, Cambridge, CUP, 1983, pp. 29–30.

4   This constant struggle between emperor and people as to how power was to be distributed and (more formally) where sovereignty lay, was particularly liable to surface in the amphitheatre, since the three categories of activities that went on there were particularly symbolic of the exercise of power: power over the natural world, the enforcement of law, and the power to decide whether a particular gladiator was or was not to be classified as a virtuous Roman.

Thomas Wiedemann, *Emperors and Gladiators*, London and New York, Routledge, 1992, p. 169.

5   The gladiator was at first a defeated warrior: but he was also, even at this early stage, a man given a special privilege, like Hannibal's captives: he was allowed another opportunity to redeem his honor and display his valor before the eyes of his enemy (as an alternative to enslavement or execution). Centuries later it still served this purpose for the prisoner of war, but now it was voluntarily resorted to by free Roman citizens. It offered the would-be soldier a sphere of competition in which victory with honor was at least possible, and both victory and defeat could be accompanied by honor depending on the gladiator himself, on his self-control, his *firma frons*.

The gladiator was thus, in one aspect, a metaphor of empowerment; the *munus*, a ritual of empowerment. It gave both individual and community a redress against arbitrary and unpredictable fortune and the Powers That Be: the audience could give a man (or woman) honor where fortune had withheld it.

Carlin A. Barton, *The Sorrows of the Ancient Romans: the gladiator and the monster*, Princeton, Princeton University Press, 1993, pp. 34–5. Copyright © 1993 by Barton, C.A. Reprinted by permission of Princeton University Press.

GENDER AND SEXUALITY

This book was conceived when I asked myself what women were 1 doing while men were active in all the areas traditionally emphasized by classical scholars. The overwhelming ancient and modern preference for political and military history, in additional to the current fascination with intellectual history, has obscured the record of those people who were excluded by sex or class from participation in the political and intellectual life of their societies.

The 'glory of classical Athens' is a commonplace of the traditional approach to Greek history. The intellectual and artistic products of Athens were, admittedly, dazzling. But rarely has there been a wider discrepancy between the cultural rewards a society had to offer and women's participation in that culture.

Sarah B. Pomeroy, *Goddesses, Whores, Wives, and Slaves: women in classical antiquity*, New York, Schocken Books, 1975, pp. ix–x. Copyright © 1975 by Sarah B. Pomeroy. Reprinted by permission of Pantheon Books.

There are three possible ways of defining women's history, which in 2 the early stages of the use of the term tended to overlap, but which now need separating: history by women, history about women, history written from a feminist point of view. In its early stages 'women's history', like 'women's studies', was closely linked to the consciousness-raising polemics of the women's movement. But there are now signs of increasing awareness that history written exclusively about, by and for women can never achieve more than ghetto significance . . . Women's history has to define its subject-matter as the history of conceptions of gender (i.e. of 'men' and 'women' as social, not natural, beings) and of the social relationships and experiences to which gender ideologies are tied.

Sally Humphreys, 'What is women's history?', *History Today*, 35 (June 1985), p. 42.

3   Gender is the social organization of sexual difference. But this does not mean that gender reflects or implements fixed and natural physical differences between women and men; rather gender is the knowledge that establishes meaning for bodily differences.
Joan Wallach Scott, *Gender and the Politics of History*, New York, Columbia University Press, 1988, p. 2.

4   In the case of a society dominated by men who sequester their wives and daughters, denigrate the female role in reproduction, erect monuments to the male genitalia, have sex with the sons of their peers, sponsor public whorehouses, create a mythology of rape, and engage in rampant saber-rattling, it is not inappropriate to refer to a reign of the phallus. Classical Athens was such a society. The story of phallic rule at the root of Western civilization has been suppressed, as a result of the near-monopoly that men have held in the field of Classics, by neglect of rich pictorial evidence, by prudery and censorship, and by a misguided desire to protect an idealized image of Athens.
Eva C. Keuls, *The Reign of the Phallus: sexual politics in ancient Athens*, New York, Harper & Row, 1985, p. 1.

5   There is no first Athenian woman; there is not, and never has been, a real female Athenian. The political process does not recognize a 'citizenness', the language has no word for a woman from Athens, and there is even a myth to make the exclusion of women a corollary of the invention of the *name of Athens* – indeed, this name was invented by women only for the city of men to deprive them of it for ever.
Nicole Loraux, *The Children of Athena: Athenian ideas about citizenship and the division between the sexes*, trans. C. Levine, Princeton, Princeton University Press, 1993, p. 10. First published in French in 1984. Copyright © 1993 by Loraux, Nicole. Reprinted by permission of Princeton University Press.

6   Chapter 3 sketched the patterns of values, norms, and social practices which define prestige and reputation in many modern Mediterranean communities. Within that context the values and beliefs associated with honour and shame occupy a prominent place, and one may begin investigating the politics of gender by recalling those central features of honor and shame that connect to sexuality. The crucial point here is that the honor of men is, in large part, defined through the chastity of the women to whom they are related. Female honor largely involves sexual purity and the behavior which social norms deem necessary to maintain it in the eyes of the watchful community. Male honor receives the active role of defending that purity. A man's honor is therefore involved with the sexual purity of his mother, sisters, wife and daughters — of him chastity is not required.

David Cohen, *Law, Sexuality, and Society: the enforcement of morals in classical Athens*, Cambridge, CUP, 1991, pp. 139–40.

Alongside the heroines of the imperial aristocracy, the irreproachable   **7** wives and excellent mothers who were still found within its ranks, it is easy to cite 'emancipated', or rather 'unbridled', wives, who were the products of the new conditions of Roman marriage. Some evaded the duties of maternity for fear of losing their good looks; some took a pride in being behind their husbands in no sphere of activity, and vied with them in tests of strength which their sex would have seemed to forbid; some were not content to live their lives by their husband's side, but carried on another life without him at the price of betrayals and surrenders for which they did not even trouble to blush.

Jerome Carcopino, *Daily Life in Ancient Rome*, trans. E.O. Lorimer, Harmondsworth, Penguin, 1941, p. 104. First published in French in 1939. Reprinted by permission of Routledge and Yale University Press.

Merely a superficial inquiry into the position of women among   **8** the Roman upper classes reveals what scholars appear to regard as a paradoxical fact: that many well-born women are remembered as possessing forceful personalities and exerting a substantial impact on men's public affairs, despite their society's extolling of domesticity as women's only proper concern, and despite their own legal disabilities and formal exclusion from political participation.

Judith P. Hallett, *Fathers and Daughters in Roman Society*, Princeton, Princeton University Press, 1984, p. 6. Copyright © 1984 by Hallett, J.P. Reprinted by permission of Princeton University Press.

Actually, I'm going to propose that Satire isn't 'about' women at all.   **9** Nor is it about 'Woman', that is to say about 'Images of women' — or Reflections, Representations or what have you — . Rather, I'll treat Satire as one area within the Roman discourse on *gender*. It participates in and contributes to the way Roman culture constructed norms, ideals and fantasies for its people (both) as individuals (and) within its social structures.

John Henderson, ' . . . when Satire writes "Woman"', in S.H. Braund (ed.), *Satire and Society in Ancient Rome*, Exeter, University of Exeter Press, 1989, p. 94.

10   If sex were simply a natural fact, we could never write its history . . .
But sex is not, except in a trivial and uninteresting sense, a natural fact.
Anthropologists, historians, and other students of culture (rather than
of nature) are sharply aware that almost any imaginable configuration
of pleasure can be institutionalized as conventional and perceived by
its participants as natural. Indeed, what 'natural' means in many such
contexts is precisely 'conventional' and 'proper'.

John J. Winkler, 'Laying down the law', in D.M. Halperin, J.J. Winkler &
F.I. Zeitlin (eds), *Before Sexuality: the construction of erotic experience in the ancient
Greek world*, Princeton, Princeton University Press, 1990, p. 171. Copyright
© 1990 by Winkler, J.J. Reprinted by permission of Princeton University
Press.

11   Even the relevant features of a sexual object in classical Athens were
not so much determined by a physical typology of sexes as by the
social articulation of power. Sexual partners came in two significantly
different kinds – not male and female but 'active' and 'passive', dominant and submissive. That is why the currently fashionable distinction
between homosexuality and heterosexuality (and, similarly, between
'homosexuals' and 'heterosexuals' as individual types) had no meaning
for the classical Athenians: there were not, so far as they knew, two
different modes of 'sexuality', two differently structured psychosexual
states or modes of affective orientation, corresponding to the sameness
or difference of the anatomical sexes of the persons engaged in a sexual
act; there was, rather, but a single form of sexual experience in which
all free adult males shared – making due allowance for variations in
individual taste, as one might for individual palates.

David M. Halperin, *One Hundred Years of Homosexuality and other essays on
Greek love*, New York and London, Routledge, 1990, p. 33.

HELLENISM

See also EDUCATION

1   What now does Hellenism mean? To one, it means a new culture
compounded of Greek and Oriental elements; to another, the
extension of Greek culture to Orientals; to another, the continuation
of the pure line of the older Greek civilisation; to yet another, that
same civilisation modified by new conditions.

W.W. Tarn, *Hellenistic Civilisation*, London, Edward Arnold, 2nd edn 1930,
pp. 1–2.

We can now define the specific character of Hellenism in contrast 2
to the Orient. By discovering man, the Greeks did not discover
the subjective self, but realized the universal laws of human nature.
The intellectual principle of the Greeks is not individualism but
humanism, to use the word in its original and classical sense . . . It
meant the process of educating man into his true form, the real and
genuine human nature. That is the true Greek paideia, adopted by the
Roman statesmen as a model. It starts from the ideal, not from the
individual. Above man as a member of the horde, and man as a
supposedly independent personality, stands man as an ideal; and that
ideal was the pattern towards which Greek educators as well as Greek
poets, artists, and philosophers always looked.
Werner Jaeger, *Paideia: the ideals of Greek culture, Volume I: Archaic Greece:
the Mind of Athens*, trans. G. Highet, Oxford, Basil Blackwell, 1946,
pp. xxiii–xxiv. First published in German; 2nd edn 1935.

A civilization must achieve its true form before it can create the 3
education in which it is reflected. That is why classical education did
not attain its own distinctive form until after the great creative epoch
of Greek civilization. We have to wait until the Hellenistic era before
we find it in full possession of its own specific forms, its own curricula
and methods. Once it reached maturity, however, the inertia that is
characteristic of all the achievements of civilization – and particularly
of any phenomenon connected with educational routine – enabled it
to preserve its structure and method for many centuries without
any important change. The extension of classical education beyond
the boundaries of the Greek world to Rome, Italy, and the Latinized
West, was to involve changes and adaptations of merely secondary
importance – even though it was originally as completely unexpected
and as staggering a phenomenon as the conversion of the Mediterranean world to Christianity.
H.I. Marrou, *A History of Education in Antiquity*, trans. G. Lamb, London,
Sheed & Ward, 1956, p. xiii. First published in French in 1948.

The contrast is extreme between the older tradition of Roman 4
education and the new Graeco-Roman culture which was soon to
take its place. On the one side a tradition of family life and national
custom, with no higher form of literary education than the elementary instruction necessary for life's work. On the other, an ideal of
culture which included Greek literature, rhetoric, and philosophy, and
was necessarily dependent on school instruction for the acquisition of
this knowledge. The change was inevitable once Rome, hitherto the

centre of a small group of Italian towns, became the metropolis of a world empire.

Aubrey Gwynn, *Roman Education from Cicero to Quintilian*, New York, Russell & Russell, 1964, p. 34.

5   The lure of Hellenism stirred the consciousness of Rome's leaders in this era, driving them to a new plane of self-awareness. The reaction was complex, enigmatic, and dissonant. Roman *nobiles* projected themselves as custodians of the nation's principles, champions of its characteristic virtues, and guardians of the *mos maiorum*. Yet these very same *nobiles* were the persons most drawn to Greek literary achievements, religion and visual arts. Hellenic culture challenged and intimidated them – even when it proved irresistible.

Erich S. Gruen, *Culture and National Identity in Republican Rome*, Ithaca, Cornell University Press, and London, Duckworth, 1992, p. 1.

6   Our return to Greece, our spontaneous renewal of this influence, does not mean that by acknowledging the timeless and ever-present intellectual greatness of the Greeks, we have given them an authority over us which, because it is independent of our own destiny, is fixed and unchallengeable. On the contrary: we always return to Greece because it fulfils some need of our own life, although that need may be very different at different epochs. Of course each of the Helleno-centric nations feels that even Hellas and Rome are in some respects fundamentally alien to herself . . . But there is a gigantic difference between that feeling and the sense of complete estrangement we have when we confront the Oriental nations, who are both racially and intellectually different from us.

Jaeger, *Paideia*, p. xv.

7   Nearly every age and stage of culture has at some time or other sought with deep displeasure to free itself from the Greeks, because in their presence everything self-achieved, sincerely admired and apparently quite original, seemed all of a sudden to lose life and colour and shrink to an abortive copy, even to caricature.

Friedrich Nietzsche, *The Birth of Tragedy* [1872], trans. W.A. Haussman, London, George Allen & Unwin, 1909, p. 113.

8   Greek antiquity began to absorb the interest of Europeans in the second half of the eighteenth century when the values, ideas, and institutions inherited from the Roman and Christian past became problematized. The search for new cultural roots and alternative

cultural patterns developed out of the need to understand and articulate the disruptive political, social, and intellectual experience that Europeans confronted in the wake of the Enlightenment and of revolution. In some cases the appeal to Greece served to foster further change, in others to combat the forces of disruption. In both cases the turn to Greece on the part of scholars, critics, and literary figures constituted an attempt to discern prescriptive signposts for the present age in the European past that predated Rome and Christianity. These writers were, of course, actually erecting new landmarks.

Frank M. Turner, *The Greek Heritage in Victorian Britain*, New Haven and London, Yale University Press, 1981, p. 2.

HELLENISTIC AGE

After the generation of Alexander, the political action of Greece becomes cramped and degraded – no longer interesting to the reader, or operative on the destinies of the future world.   **1**

George Grote, *A History of Greece*, London, John Murray, new edn 1869, Vol. I p. x.

Greek achievement was still to a remarkable extent identified with   **2**
the Greek *polis*, so that Philip of Macedon's victory over a handful of leading Greek states at Chaeronea in 338 came to be seen as a watershed in Greek history, after which nothing, in a sense, mattered; Hellenistic culture was bourgeois, decadent, and materialist; Periclean idealism was dead; the *idiotai* and *apragmones* had triumphed, *ataraxia* was the goal. When this society fell victim, finally, to the Roman military machine, with its crass and philistine efficiency, the feeling was that these degenerate Greeklings had got no more than they deserved.

Peter Green, 'Introduction: new approaches to the Hellenistic world', in Green (ed.), *Hellenistic History and Culture*, Berkeley, Los Angeles and London, University of California Press, 1993, p. 7.

It is hardly necessary to insist upon the importance of the so-called   **3**
'Hellenistic' age in the history of mankind. As every student of ancient history knows, the old-fashioned conception of this age as a time of decay of Greek civilization and of a pitiful collapse of Greek political life is unfounded or at least one-sided and misleading. Without doubt the Greeks of the Hellenistic period developed great creative activity in all departments of their life and were responsible for many, sometimes fundamental, novelties in the political, social, economic,

and cultural development of the ancient world. Under their bene-
ficent influence other nations remodelled their own institutions and in
consequence achieved brilliant results in many directions.
M.I. Rostovtzeff, *The Social and Economic History of the Hellenistic World*,
Oxford, OUP, 1941, p. v.

4   By their political rivalry and jealousy the Greeks gave the Romans a
    pretext for active interference in their political affairs, and the same
    rivalry and jealousy prevented them from uniting to check the rapid
    progress of the intruders. These failings were fatal to Greece. Roman
    destruction was radical. But the Romans alone cannot be blamed for
    it: they accelerated the process of disintegration and destruction, but
    they did not initiate it.
    Ibid., pp. 1311–12.

5   The Hellenistic age has one great advantage for us: it is easily
    definable.
    Peter Green, *Alexander to Actium: the Hellenistic age*, Berkeley and Los Angeles,
    University of California Press, 1993, p. xv.

6   One result both of an over-ready assumption of 'cultural fusion' and
    of a lop-sided 'Hellenocentric' focus has been the perception of
    the Hellenistic world as a relatively unitary phenomenon: sharing a
    common tongue, imbibing Greek culture, trading and exchanging
    at an unprecedented rate, displaying the 'unity and homogeneity of
    the Hellenistic world from the point of view of civilisation and mode
    of life'. Such an approach to the study of the Hellenistic period can
    be traced to the scholarly stress laid on the dominant persuasive power
    of Greek influence in these foreign lands. Yet it is also due in part
    to the nature of the sources most frequently consulted . . . In short,
    much Hellenistic history is fundamentally colonialist history . . .
    Nowhere does 'Hellenism' meet 'Orientalism' more forcefully than
    in Hellenistic scholarship.
    Susan E. Alcock, 'Breaking up the Hellenistic world: survey and society', in
    I. Morris (ed.), *Classical Greece: ancient histories and modern archaeologies*,
    Cambridge, CUP, 1994, pp. 171–3.

7   Even when given every possible benefit of the doubt, for most
    scholars and teachers the Hellenistic era remains an untidy, unwieldy
    and confusing interregnum between 'Greek' and 'Roman' history.
    Ibid., 173.

HISTORY

I should like to point out how remarkable a thing is this creation of **1**
scientific history by Herodotus, for he was an ancient Greek, and
ancient Greek thought as a whole has a very definite prevailing
tendency not only uncongenial to the growth of historical thought
but actually based, one might say, on a rigorously anti-historical
metaphysics.

R.G. Collingwood, *The Idea of History*, J. van der Dussen (ed.), Oxford,
OUP, rev. edn 1993, p. 20.

So if the atmosphere in which Herodotus set to work was saturated **2**
with myth of that sort, the prognosis for the birth of 'History' in
something like a modern professional sense – critical, disinterested,
objective, accurate, and explanatory – was not exactly favourable, even
if we stress (as I would) the open-boundedness as opposed to the
supposed scientificity of all history-writing. Nevertheless, something
that some of us anyway would want to call at least 'proto-history' did
emerge.

Paul Cartledge, *The Greeks: a portrait of self and others*, Oxford, OUP, 1993,
pp. 26–7.

'History' is an abstract word to moderns (except when applied to a **3**
particular work); to ancients, the notion was concrete even before
the word *historia* came to describe it. When we write history, we
conceive of our work as a partial and incomplete selection from a
theoretical totality of past events, developments, occurrences and so
on. By definition, written history can never attain the 'whole truth'
after which it searches. But the ancients did not begin or end by
considering history as a sum total. History was for them a specific and
sharply delineated slice of the present or the past. The definition they
started with was that of Herodotus, who defined his subject as the
memorable deeds of men, and this definition, with some expansions
relating to the treatment of notable individuals, remained standard
thereafter. History, therefore, was *res gestae*, accomplishments, of a
particular kind.

Charles William Fornara, *The Nature of History in Ancient Greece and Rome*,
Berkeley, Los Angeles and London, University of California Press, 1983,
p. 92.

History then and history now are alike in name only. Not that history **4**
then was imperfect and had only to progress to fully become the

science it would then forever be. In its own genre, ancient history was as complete a means of creating belief as our journalism of today, which it resembles a great deal.

Paul Veyne, *Did the Greeks Believe in their Myths? an essay on the constitutive imagination*, trans. P. Wissing, Chicago and London, University of Chicago Press, 1988, p. 5. First published in French in 1983. Copyright © 1988 by The University of Chicago. All rights reserved.

HOMERIC SOCIETY

1   It can no longer be doubted, when one surveys the state of our knowledge today, that there really was an actual historical Trojan War, in which a coalition of Achaeans, or Mycenaeans, under a king whose over-lordship was recognised, fought against the people of Troy and their allies.

Carl Blegen, *Troy and the Trojans*, London, Thames & Hudson, 1963, p. 20. Copyright © Carl W. Blegen 1963.

2   Homer says that Troy was sacked. The world smiled, when it did not sneer. Now Hissarlik has been fully excavated, and nobody doubts that Troy VIIa was destroyed within the Mycenaean period. Homer says that the centre of Achaean power was at Mycenae, rich in gold. This too was surely a fable; few believed it. After nearly a hundred years of excavation at Mycenae and other palaces on the mainland, there is (I suppose) not a sceptic left. Homer says that Troy was besieged by Achaeans. Archaeology has brought the Mycenaeans into very close contact with Troy . . . Now come the Hittite documents, and (if we accept the equation of Ahhijawa with Achaia) we can add many touches of colour to the picture of Achaeans and others on the west coast of Anatolia.

D.G. Page, 'Homer and the Trojan War', *Journal of Hellenic Studies*, 84 (1964), p. 18.

3   But again Homer and archaeology part company quickly. On the whole, he knew where the Mycenaean civilization flourished, and his heroes lived in great palaces unknown in Homer's own day (but unlike the Mycenaean, or any other, palaces). And that is virtually all he knew about Mycenaean times, for the catalogue of his errors is very long. His arms bear a resemblance to the armour of his time, quite un-like the Mycenaean, although he persistently casts them in antiquated bronze, not iron. His gods had temples, and the Mycenaeans built none, whereas the latter constructed great vaulted tombs in which to

bury their chieftains and the poet cremates his. A neat little touch is provided by the battle chariots. Homer had heard of them, but he did not really visualize what one did with chariots in a war. So his heroes normally drove from their tents a mile or less away, carefully dismounted, and then proceeded to battle on foot.

M.I. Finley, *The World of Odysseus*, London, Chatto & Windus, rev. edn 1964, pp. 44–5.

If it is to be placed in time, as everything we know about heroic poetry **4** says it must, the most likely centuries seem to be the tenth and the ninth.

Ibid., p. 51.

What we have in Homer is surely not just archaism in material culture, **5** but artificial conflation of historical practices.

A.M. Snodgrass, 'An historical Homeric society?', *Journal of Hellenic Studies*, 94 (1974), p. 124.

Homer was describing the Heroic Age, and this was supposed to be **6** different from the everyday world. So while we speak of Homer drawing on his own culture, which must have been his main model, it is in no way implied that Homer was in any way consciously attempting to describe the world of the eighth century. But on the other hand, in trying to describe the world of the heroes, Homer had to build upon the shared assumptions of his own culture, embellishing them in collectively acceptable ways, to create an alternative reality.

Ian Morris, 'The use and abuse of Homer', *Classical Antiquity*, 5 (1986), p. 120. Copyright © 1986 by the Regents of the University of California.

Although there is no doubt that the *written* version of the epics **7** originated in Greece, the thesis is here advanced that the *oral* version originated in western Europe at a much earlier date. This, of course, in no way detracts from the prestige of classical Greek culture as it developed after Homer, and which is rightly admired by all.

Someone reading the *Iliad* for the first time, with no preconceived ideas, would not, on the evidence of the text, locate the theatre of war in the eastern Mediterranean (if it were not for a number of familiar place-names) as there is mention of tides, a salty, dark or misty sea and a climate of rain, fog and snow, while the trees are generally more typical of regions with a temperate climate rather than of subtropical southern Europe. Also the tall, long-haired warriors, travelling overseas in 'symmetrical' ships, 'eager to kill their enemies' are more reminiscent of the dreaded Norsemen of the Dark Ages than the more peaceful Greeks of the classical era. Several commanders even had the honorific but little reassuring title of 'sacker of cities'. As the ancient Greeks themselves could hardly imagine that these people were their ancestors, they relegated them to an imaginary 'heroic age'.

Iman Wilkens, *Where Troy Once Stood: the mystery of Homer's Iliad and Odyssey revealed*, London, Sydney, Auckland and Johannesburg, Rider, 1990, p. 15.

HOUSEHOLD

1   *Oikos* and *polis* – household and city – are two of the Greek words which ancient historians are most prone to avoid translating. It is a charitable, and I think also a reasonable, inference that the concepts have a central and problematical position in the Greek scheme of values.

S.C. Humphreys, *The Family, Women and Death: comparative studies*, London, Boston, Melbourne and Henley, Routledge & Kegan Paul, 1983, p. 1.

2   This was the origin of monogamy, as far as we can trace it among the most civilised and highly-developed people of antiquity. It was not in any way the fruit of individual sex love, with which it had absolutely nothing in common, for the marriages remained marriages of convenience, as before. It was the first form of the family based not on natural but on economic conditions, namely, on the victory of private property over original, naturally developed, common ownership. The rule of the man in the family, the procreation of children who could only be his, destined to be the heirs of his wealth – these alone were frankly avowed by the Greeks as the exclusive aims of monogamy . . .

This monogamy does not by any means make its appearance in history as the reconciliation of man and woman, still less as the highest form of such a reconciliation. On the contrary, it appears as the subjection of one sex by the other, as the proclamation of a conflict between the sexes entirely unknown in prehistoric times . . . The first class antagonism which appears in history coincides with the development of the antagonism between man and woman in monogamian marriage, and the first class oppression with that of the female sex by the male.

Frederick Engels, *The Origin of the Family, Private Property and the State* [1884], in Marx and Engels, *Selected Works in One Volume*, London, Lawrence & Wishart, 1968, pp. 502–3.

The household embodies the unification of the male/female **3**
opposition. This is analogous to the idea, prevalent in Greek medicine
and philosophy, that the bodily health of an individual resulted from
the presence in equal balance of a collection of complementary
opposites: wet and dry, hot and cold elements had to be present in
equal amounts. The balance of the opposites in a household, manifest
in the genders, ages and statuses of its individual members, is similarly
expressive of its health and well-being as a properly constituted social
body. The household is the context in which male and female
individuals operate as a single social entity.
Lin Foxhall, 'Household, gender and property in classical Athens', *Classical
Quarterly*, 39 (1989), p. 23. Reprinted by permission of Oxford University
Press and the Classical Association.

The house is seen as sheltering the private sphere, including the **4**
sexual purity and reputation of the women on whom the honour of a
family in significant part depends. Community opinion sanctions this
protection, for reputation and shame require vengeance for injuries
done to a sister, her children, or one's wife. The law provides further
reinforcement by allowing the adulterer or thief to be killed with
impunity if caught within the house, and by making offences against
personal autonomy and honour a major public offence.
David Cohen, *Law, Sexuality, and Society: the enforcement of morals in classical
Athens*, Cambridge, CUP, 1991, p. 83.

In its determination to maintain the numbers of the *oikoi* the Athenian **5**
state interfered extensively in men's private property: there was
complex legislation designed to protect the persons and property of
epikleroi, orphans, and *oikoi* without an heir.
W.K. Lacey, *The Family in Classical Greece*, London, Thames & Hudson,
1968, p. 125. Copyright © 1968 W.K. Lacey.

Greek discussions of economics which present 'the *oikos*' as the natural **6**
economic base of the city-state have an obvious bias. Since there was
no concept of economic policy to provide a framework within which
the economic interests of citizens as individuals could be recognised as
having a legitimate claim to consideration in discussions of public
affairs, it was open to each class to accuse the other of pursuing private
advantage at the expense of the city. Hence it was in the economic
sphere that the citizen's duty to subordinate private interests and
responsibilities to the claims of the city was most insistently proclaimed.
Humphreys, *Family, Women and Death*, p. 13.

7   In the early fifth century, the basic building-block of Athenian society, the *oikos*, had been perceived as self-sufficient, producing for its own private consumption. But by the fourth century, agricultural products were increasingly being raised for cash sale; consumer items were now often produced by commercial workshops; aristocratic marriages for dynastic continuity had disappeared.

Edward E. Cohen, *Athenian Economy and Society: a banking perspective*, Princeton, Princeton University Press, 1992, p. 6. Copyright © 1992 by Cohen, E.E. Reprinted by permission of Princeton University Press.

8   The individual as a separate entity has entirely disappeared; the State and the law recognise only family communities, groups of persons, and thus regulate the relations of family to family, not of individual to individual. As to what happens within the household they do not trouble themselves. In the economic autonomy of the slave-owning family lies the explanation of all the social and a great part of the political history of Rome. There are no separate classes of producers, as such, no farmers, no artisans. There are only large and small proprietors, rich and poor.

Karl Bücher, *Industrial Evolution*, trans. S.M. Wickett, New York, 1901. First published in German as *Entstehung des Volkswirtschaft* in 1893.

9   Consider for a moment the fact that one of the cardinal characteristics of a good Roman marriage was *concordia*, a state of harmony between husband and wife that was hoped for when marriage began and that was celebrated, once attained, by outsiders or commemorated at the time of spousal death by a surviving partner . . . Think how odd it would seem if you were to describe a successful marriage today by saying that it was full of concord or harmony between husband and wife. The virtue is rather passive in its associations, implying a state of tranquil and stable unanimity but suggesting little of the romance or intimacy typical of modern marriage . . .

What can be inferred is that because marriage at Rome was generally a matter of outside arrangement, not of personal choice on the part of the marrying couple (among the prosperous, at least), there could never at the outset be any assurance of harmony between husband and wife, and in the likely absence of any strong affective tie characteristic of modern marriage, the potential for discord was always as great as that for concord.

Keith R. Bradley, *Discovering the Roman Family: studies in Roman social history*, New York and Oxford, OUP, 1991, pp. 6–8. Copyright © 1991 by Oxford University Press, Inc. Used by permission of Oxford University Press, Inc.

The Roman family was unquestionably patriarchal, in the sense that   **10**
it was defined with reference to the father, who was endowed with a
special authority in the household. But, I have argued, the characterization of an 'excess of domination' has been the result of both a
misinterpretation of the legends and, above all, an overly legalistic
approach to the family. The law endowed the *pater* with a striking
potestas encompassing extensive coercive and proprietary rights, yet a
purely legal understanding of the Roman family is as incomplete and
misleading as would be a solely legal understanding of the twentieth-
century family.
Richard P. Saller, *Patriarchy, Property and Death in the Roman Family*,
Cambridge, CUP, 1994, p. 225.

The seventeenth-century house, like the Roman house, was one   **11**
where distinctions of rank and etiquette were dominant. The house
did not merely reflect, but generated status. Social success depended
partly on playing a game of contact with others of widely varying
social rank with skill and understanding; on treating the distinguished
with distinction and the obscure with sufficient distance. In a world
oiled by patronage, social success could be heavily dependent on this
domestic game. Consequently the formal house of the period, like the
grand Roman house, was arranged in terms of suites and apartments,
with a succession of rooms differing more in hierarchic value than
function. Here 'privacy' takes on a different meaning; it involves
separation from the vulgar crowd, but not from the battles of the social
world outside.
Andrew Wallace-Hadrill, 'The social structure of the Roman house', *Papers
of the British School at Rome*, 56 (1988), pp. 95–6.

HOUSING

The abundance of public meeting places, shops, baths, fora,   **1**
colonnades and loggias, together with the fact that most of the actual
living units of the town were small, cramped, and in some cases
inadequately lighted, suggests that the entire city was intended
to function as a single unit. In the modern world each house or
apartment ideally supplies, insofar as possible, the needs of its
inhabitants. In ancient Ostia almost all the requirements of the vast
majority of citizens were taken care of outside the home. Thus, in
some sense, the whole city constituted a single complex habitation of
which the individual residence was perhaps the least important part.
Ancient Ostia represents communal living on a massive scale, which

by its very intensity and public nature is entirely foreign to the modern Western conception of privacy.

James E. Packer, *The Insulae of Roman Ostia*, Rome, American Academy at Rome, 1970, p. 74.

2 Life for the poor in Rome's high rise tenements was dangerous not merely because of the constant risks of fire, collapse, and the rapid spread of communicable diseases in overcrowded badly ventilated rooms, but also because such conditions frequently produce a high level of violence and crime.

Alex Scobie, 'Slums, sanitation and mortality in the Roman world', *Klio*, 68 (1986), p. 432.

3 Postindustrial society has become accustomed to a divorce between home and place of work. Status is generated at work not home, so the home becomes endowed with a 'privacy' alien to the Roman. It is significant that comparable patterns can be found in other societies where public and private life similarly interpenetrate. The nobility of the French ancien régime offers a particularly striking parallel. Private houses were, according to the prescriptions of the *Encyclopédie*, hierarchically classified and labeled: Only a prince of royal blood inhabited a *palais*; the nobility had their *hôtels*; the third estate lived in *maisons*. Each of these had its proper architectural form . . .

So dominant are the axes of public and private, grand and humble, that without them there can be no form. For the *Encyclopédie*, it is only the palais and the hôtels that have perceptible architectural form; the maison is, so to speak, formless, though in fact the upper echelons of the third estate went far in imitating the forms of the nobility. This is equally true in the Roman house, both that of Vitruvius's description and that of the archaeological remains. The noble house is where Vitruvius starts in attempting to give an account of form; the houses of the humble he can only describe in negative terms, citing their lack of public space and their absence of need for elegance of decor; and the houses of the financiers and lawyers he describes in relative terms, as more endowed with the characteristics of the noble house. This chimes with the archaeological evidence, where the humbler housing is characterized by the relative lack of predictable and analyzable form, and the intermediate levels by their imitation of the forms of the upper class.

Andrew Wallace-Hadrill, *Houses and Society in Pompeii and Herculaneum*, Princeton, Princeton University Press, 1994, pp. 12, 13–14. Copyright ©1994 by Wallace-Hadrill, A. Reprinted by permission of Princeton University Press.

IMPERIALISM

The concept of 'imperialism' arose in political circumstances and was **1** appropriated for scholarly debate. Its manipulation has not necessarily brought us closer to the truth. The negative ring of the term can prejudice rather than facilitate understanding.

Erich S. Gruen, *The Hellenistic World and the Coming of Rome*, Berkeley, Los Angeles and London, University of California Press, 1984, p. 7.

To suggest, for example, that we should abandon 'empire' as a **2** category in Greek history and speak only of 'hegemony' does not seem to me helpful or useful. It would have been small consolation to the Melians, as the Athenian soldiers and sailors fell upon them, to be informed that they were about to become the victims of a hegemonial, not an imperial, measure.

M.I. Finley, 'The fifth-century Athenian empire: a balance sheet', in P.D.A. Garnsey & C.R. Whittaker (eds), *Imperialism in the Ancient World*, Cambridge, CUP, 1978, p. 124.

There never was a people which made the principle that all its **3** citizens were equal a more live reality than the Athenians made it; and no state to my knowledge was more cunningly contrived to insure the government of the people than was theirs. Yet they became imperialists with ardor and conviction, and with this much of logical consequence, that, while they believed in democracy for everybody, they did not doubt that the Athenians had earned the right to rule both Greeks and barbarians by the acquisition of superior culture. Equality among its citizens Athens carefully distinguished from equality among all men.

William Scott Ferguson, *Greek Imperialism*, New York, Houghton Mifflin, 1941, pp. 38–9.

The charges levelled against the Athenians, the so-called 'abuses', **4** when assembled to form a single bill of particulars, create a misleading impression. This assembling of complaints is modern; no-one put them together in the fifth century. The truth is that no single imperial practice could be judged gravely oppressive, irritating in individual cases though it might be.

Malcolm F. McGregor, *The Athenians and their Empire*, Vancouver, University of British Columbia Press, 1987, p. 174. Reprinted with permission of the publisher. Copyright © University of British Columbia Press 1987. All rights reserved by the publisher.

5   The Aegean world gained considerably from the use made by Athens of the wealth that she drew from the cities and, as the Athenians claimed at Sparta in 432, they made considerably less use of force than imperial powers were expected to use; but they could have made more concessions to the general Greek passion for autonomy without undermining their position.
Russell Meiggs, *The Athenian Empire*, Oxford, OUP, 1972, p. 412.

6   That Athens profited financially from her empire is of course true. But these profits were not necessary to keep the democracy working. They enabled Athens to be a great power and to support a much larger citizen population at higher standards of living.
A.H.M. Jones, *Athenian Democracy*, Oxford, Basil Blackwell, 1957, p. 6.

7   Imperialism, as we have already seen, is deeply rooted in instinct, in *the need for fuller being* in men and peoples. This need is satisfied through the egoistic appetite for domination, but it is equally satisfied through solidarity and mutual aid. And often imperialism derives part of its strength from the benefits conferred by the increased solidarity. No empire has been better able to assimilate its conquests than the Roman.
Henri Berr, 'Foreword', in Léon Homo, *Primitive Italy and the Beginnings of Roman Imperialism*, trans. V. Gordon Childe, London, Kegan Paul, Trench, Trübner & Co., and New York, Alfred A. Knopf, 1926, p. x. Originally published in French.

8   Early forms of imperial expansion were directed less to any permanent occupation and government of foreign countries than to the capture of large supplies of slave labour to be transmitted to the conquering country. The early Imperialism of the Greek states and of Rome was largely governed by this same motive.
J.A. Hobson, *Imperialism: a study*, London, George Allen & Unwin, 3rd edn 1938, p. 247.

9   If, therefore, we hope to understand the groping, stumbling, accidental expansion of Rome, we must rid ourselves of anachronistic generalizations and 'remote causes' and look instead for the specific accidents that led the nation unwittingly from one contest to another until, to her own surprise, Rome was mistress of the Mediterranean.
Tenney Frank, *Roman Imperialism*, New York, Macmillan, 1914, pp. 120–1.

10   The modern student, accustomed to seeing history – at least at second or at tenth hand – through the blood-red spectacles of Marx, may by now have become impatient with my approach, observing that a discussion of Roman imperialism in terms of politics, strategy, social *ethos* and even psychology, surely misses the point: what (he will say) about revenues, markets, exports? These (we are constantly taught) are the real stuff of imperialism . . . Though I would not deny the importance of economic motives for political actions, it seems to me clear that this importance can vary considerably in different conditions and even in different cases, and that failure to recognise this, and over-emphasis on economic factors, has led, not only to many mistaken historical interpretations, but also to many wrong political decisions. However, our main point at present is that no such motives can be seen, on the whole, in Roman policy, during the period that we are now considering.

E. Badian, *Roman Imperialism in the Late Republic*, Oxford, Basil Blackwell, 2nd edn 1968, pp. 16–17.

Huge tracts of land came into Roman hands, as did enormous **11** quantities of gold and silver and plunder of every kind; millions of people were enslaved; tribute in different forms flooded in; the ingenuity of Roman officials and businessmen exacted its profits in large areas of the Mediterranean world. There is therefore something paradoxical in denying that economic motives were important in Roman imperialism.

William V. Harris, *War and Imperialism in Republican Rome 327–70 BC*, Oxford, OUP, 1979, pp. 54.

Economic gain was to the Romans (and generally in the ancient **12** world) an integral part of successful warfare and of the expansion of power. Land, plunder, slaves, revenues were regular and natural results of success; they were the assumed results of victory and power . . . No Roman senator had to convince other senators that victory was, in general, wealth-producing.

Ibid., p. 56.

It seems certain that the Romans' capacity to conquer did for a time **13** outrun their will or capacity to devise means of regularly extracting a surplus from the conquered peoples. This in turn defines the extent to which we can attribute economic imperialism to the decision-takers. It does not mean that their war-decisions were not aggressive, nor does it mean that they had no economic motive; but it does mean that their economic objectives were either short-term or unconsidered

– either they wanted slaves and quick profits, or they had simply not considered the problems in advance.

J.A. North, 'The development of Roman imperialism', *Journal of Roman Studies*, 71 (1981), pp. 2–3.

14 Two factors are of particular significance. Firstly, the pattern of Roman office-holding itself encouraged military expansion, since Roman magistrates, in their role as generals, traditionally had only one year to win the glory of a successful military campaign. A general could gain nothing for himself by deferring military action; for if it was put off to the next year, the prize of victory might fall to his successor. The competitive aspirations of the Roman elite thus encouraged year after year (consul after consul) the undertaking of wars that would give victory to the Roman people and prestige to their leaders. Secondly, Rome's system of dominance over her Italian allies also led to a high level of military activity and, with it, imperial expansion. For Rome demanded of the allies no yearly taxes in money or kind, but simply required that they provide troops for the Roman armies. Thus she had just one way to express her leadership in Italy: that is to make use of these troops . . . by undertaking further wars. Without military activity Rome's position as leader of Italy would not have been manifest.

Mary Beard & Michael Crawford, *Rome in the Late Republic*, London, Duckworth, 1985, pp. 74–5. Reprinted by permission of Gerald Duckworth & Co. Ltd.

15 Thus a double standard of behaviour developed. In the East, a hegemonial policy was pursued in a cautious and, on the whole, fairly civilised way, at least without violence and open treachery and certainly (as long as it proved possible) without direct control and major wars. But against the barbarians, where publicity need not be feared and where, incidentally, the gradual advancing of the frontier did not, on the whole, lead to any major new commitment at any one time, so that the whole process would not easily become obvious – there policy was openly brutal and aggressive, and triumph-hunting an accepted technique.

Badian, *Roman Imperialism*, p. 11.

INDUSTRY

See also TRADE

Essentially the ability of ancient cities to pay for their food, metals, **1**
slaves and other necessities rested on four variables: the amount of
local agricultural production, that is, of the produce of the city's own
rural area; the presence or absence of special resources, silver, above all,
but also other metals or particularly desirable wines or oil-bearing
plants; the invisible exports of trade or tourism; and fourth, the
income from land ownership and empire, rents, taxes, tribute, gifts
from clients and subjects. The contribution of manufactures was
negligible; it is only a false model that drives historians in search of
them where they are unattested, and did not exist.
M.I. Finley, *The Ancient Economy*, London, Hogarth Press, 2nd edn 1985,
p. 139.

Industrial production [in Athens] remained fragmented and indi- **2**
vidual. For the slave owner, his income was often no more than a rent,
not very different from land rents. For the small artisan, production
was a means of insuring his livelihood by working for the community.
Claude Mossé, *The Ancient World at Work*, trans. J. Lloyd, London, Chatto &
Windus, 1969, p. 95. First published in French in 1966.

The slight sketch which I have given of the development of the three **3**
basic industries, pottery, metal-working and textiles, in the Hellenistic
period, will enable the reader of this short summary to grasp the
leading features of Hellenistic industry in general: its slow technical
progress and its restricted range of output, never reaching the stage of
mass production concentrated in a few industrial centers. The causes
of these limitations are chiefly to be found, on the one hand in local
production of manufactured goods and the arrest of development of
large industrial centers, and on the other in the low buying capacity
and the restricted number of customers.
M.I. Rostovtzeff, *The Social and Economic History of the Hellenistic World*,
Oxford, OUP, 1941, p. 1230.

It is true that ancient aristocrats, as absentee land-lords, did not **4**
hesitate to spend much of their agriculturally generated wealth on
their cities. But that does not mean that all cities were, so to speak,
parasites of the adjacent countryside. The city of Pompeii, that is the
urban component of the Pompeian *polis*, was so far as the wool trade
was concerned economically viable. And the above investigation of
the wool processing plants should lay to rest the view that ancient
workshops were uniformly small and that the ancients were incapable
of rationalizing their production by dividing labor and regulating the

flow of materials through a system. In Pompeii some of the plants were true factories and the formula of one craftsman = one production unit did not apply to the production of woollen cloth.
Walter O. Moeller, *The Wool Trade of Ancient Pompeii*, Leiden, Brill, 1976, pp. 108–9.

5   The Pompeian textile industry was quite unlike its counterparts in such later centres of growth as the communes of northern Italy or Flanders. Its scale was incomparably smaller, and there are no signs that it did any more than cater for a fairly local market.
Willem Jongman, *The Economy and Society of Pompeii*, Amsterdam, Gieben, 1991, p. 184.

6   We know of only a handful of large or middling privately owned manufacturies engaged in making cloth. All their owners seem to have been primarily interested in other activities, as landowners or officials. So far as I know, no fortunes in the ancient world were based on cloth-making, even if textiles contributed to some fortunes.
Too much is often made of the small scale of manufacturing units. Of course, most manufacturing units in a pre-industrial economy are small; so they were still in Germany and France at the beginning of the twentieth century. What matters are the number and size of the exceptions and whether there was any system by which a host of small producers, each engaged in one stage of production, was integrated by the activities of capitalistic entrepreneurs, who took a share of the profits in return for their effort and capital risk. There is only slight evidence that such integration did take place in the Roman world, and it seems probable that in textiles, as in other handicrafts, the roles and institutions of integrating fragmented piece workers were never highly developed.
Keith Hopkins, 'Economic growth and towns in classical antiquity', in P. Abrams & E.A. Wrigley (eds), *Towns in Societies: essays in economic history and historical sociology*, Cambridge, CUP, 1978, p. 53.

JEWS AND JUDAISM

See also CHRISTIANITY

1   The world-historical importance of Jewish religious development rests above all in the creation of the *Old Testament*, for one of the most significant intellectual achievements of the Pauline mission was that it

preserved and transferred this sacred book of the Jews to Christianity as one of its own sacred books . . . Jewry has, moreover, been the instigator and partly the model for Mohammed's prophecy. Thus, in considering the conditions of Jewry's evolution, we stand at a turning point of the whole cultural development of the West and the Middle East.

Max Weber, *Ancient Judaism*, trans. H.H. Gerth & D. Martindale, Glencoe, The Free Press, 1952, pp. 4–5. Copyright © 1952, renewed 1980 by The Free Press. First published in German, 1917–19.

How were the Jews to react to this [Greek] cultural invasion, which **2** was opportunity, temptation and threat all in one? The answer is that they reacted in different ways . . . At one extreme, the coming of the Greeks pushed more fundamentalists into the desert, to join the absolutist groups who kept up the Rechabite and Nazarite traditions, and who regarded Jerusalem as already irredeemably corrupt. The earliest texts found in the Qumran community date from about 250 BC, when the noose of Greek cities around Judah first began to tighten. The idea was to retreat into the wilderness, recapture the pristine Mosaic enthusiasm, then launch back into the cities. Some, like the Essenes, thought this could be done peacefully, by the word, and they preached in villages on the edge of the desert: John the Baptist was later in this tradition. Others, like the Qumran community, put their trust in the sword . . . At the other extreme, there were many Jews, including pious ones, who hated isolationism and the fanatics it bred.

Paul Johnson, *A History of the Jews*, London, Weidenfeld & Nicolson, 1987, pp. 98–9.

To the Romans, embroiled in a turbulent ideological atmosphere the **3** likes of which they had never encountered in any other administered territory, it could not have been easy to distinguish between those who passively awaited God's miraculous intervention, those who would render unto Caesar the things that were Caesar's provided their religious integrity was respected, and those who wished to hasten the end of days by fire and sword. From this heady and dangerously confusing brew would result not only the Jewish revolt against Rome but also the Christian schism within Judaism.

David J. Goldberg & John D. Rayner, *The Jewish People: their history and their religion*, London, Viking, 1987, p. 75.

One of the most striking characteristics of the Jew has always been his **4** ability to preserve his national identity even after generations of residence among gentiles and to resist assimilation except in the superficial matter of language assimilation for everyday contacts . . . The Jews of the Diaspora remained aloof, and their refusal to compromise one jot or tittle of their religion either by abandoning or modifying their own practices or by making courteous concessions to paganism bred the unpopularity out of which anti-semitism was born. The Jew was a figure of amusement, contempt or hatred to the gentiles among whom he lived . . .

In dealing with a religious minority which would countenance neither compromise nor assimilation and which was liable to be at loggerheads with its gentile host, Rome was faced with the alternatives of suppression on the one hand and on the other toleration with the corollary of active measures to protect the sect from gentile molestation. The normal Roman attitude towards foreign religions was one of toleration, provided that they appeared to be both morally unobjectionable and politically innocuous. Judaism with its high moral code and non-subversive character fulfilled the criteria for permitted survival, and received toleration on an *ad hoc* basis in the late republic.

E. Mary Smallwood, *The Jews under Roman Rule from Pompey to Diocletian*, Leiden, Brill, 1976, pp. 123–4.

5 Time and again, confrontation tends to be seen as the dominant mode of relations between Jews and others, acted out in different ways between the different parties and sometimes erupting in physical conflict. Such conflict was, of course, by no means absent from the scene; nor, however, was it omnipresent . . . The market-place model preferred by us gives primacy to the overall pattern of coexistence, within which both interaction and breakdown can find their place. This model acknowledges, as we have said, what was in effect a society developing towards pluralism: varied options, each carrying its own attractions, its own advantages and liabilities, became available.

Judith Lieu, John North & Tessa Rajak (eds), *The Jews among Pagans and Christians in the Roman Empire*, London and New York, Routledge, 1992, p. 6.

LABOUR

See also SLAVERY

[Cicero] calls a whole range of employments mean and illiberal, but he **1**
restricts the slave metaphor to those who work for wages, to hired
labour. Free men were found in all occupations, but usually as self-
employed workers, either as smallholders or tenants on the land, or as
independent craftsmen, traders and moneylenders in the towns . . .
Free hired labour was casual and seasonal, its place determined by
the limits beyond which it would have been absurd to purchase and
maintain a slave force.
M.I. Finley, *The Ancient Economy*, London, Hogarth Press, 2nd edn 1985,
p. 73.

If freedom as most Athenians conceived it implied, among other **2**
things, the freedom of labour, in contrast to the freedom *from* labour,
and if the contempt for servility must be distinguished from a disdain
for labour as such, then clearly something more needs to be said about
the very common proposition that one of the principle characteristics
of Athenian culture was a general contempt for labour.
Ellen Meiksins Wood, *Peasant-Citizen and Slave: the foundations of Athenian
democracy*, London and New York, Verso, 1988, p. 137.

The distinctive character of Athenian democracy was not the degree **3**
to which it was based on dependent labour, the labour of slaves, but
on the contrary, the extent to which it *excluded* dependence from the
sphere of production, that is, the extent to which production rested on
free, independent labour to the exclusion of labour in varying forms
and degrees of juridical dependence or political subjection. Athenian
slavery, then, must be explained in relation to other forms of labour
which were *ruled out* by the democracy.
Ibid., p. 82.

There was certainly a considerable but fluctuating demand for **4**
unskilled labour in building operations and other trades at Rome, and
this demand could not have been met economically by exclusive
reliance on slaves. Free labour must have been cheaper, and it was
available; the free poor needed employment. The inference seems to
me *certain* that free labour was extensively employed on public works
at Rome. This makes it *probable* that the policy of promoting public
works was *in part* designed to provide such employment.
P.A. Brunt, 'Free labour and public works at Rome', *Journal of Roman Studies*,
70 (1980), p. 84.

Anyone who wants to make out that the hiring of free labour in **5** construction works played a major part in the economic life of ancient cities should ask himself how, in that case, the men concerned were able to live at all when – as often happened – there was little or no public building going on.

G.E.M. de Ste Croix, *The Class Struggle in the Ancient Greek World*, London, Duckworth, and Ithaca, Cornell University Press, 1981, p. 190.

LATE ANTIQUITY

See also DECLINE AND FALL, BYZANTIUM, BROWN

1   Classical archaeologists and art historians have taught us to recognize the distinctive character of the art of these later centuries . . . We now realize how fallacious it is to think only in terms of the debasement of classical art. The men of these centuries – whether pagan or Christian – experienced a new vision of the human and the divine, which made them capable of new forms of expression. In Germany the period we are concerned with here is known as the age of *Spätantike*, in recognition of its individual quality.

Joseph Vogt, *The Decline of Rome: the metamorphosis of ancient civilization*, trans. G. Weidenfeld, London, Weidenfeld and Nicolson, 1967, p. 6. First published in German in 1965.

2   To study such a period one must be constantly aware of the tension between change and continuity in the exceptionally ancient and well-rooted world round the Mediterranean. On the one hand, this is notoriously the time when certain ancient institutions, whose absence would have seemed quite unimaginable to a man of about AD 250, irrevocably disappeared. By 476, the Roman empire had vanished from western Europe; by 655, the Persian empire had vanished from the Near East. It is only too easy to write about the Late Antique world as if it were merely a melancholy tale of 'Decline and Fall': of the end of the Roman empire as viewed from the West; of the Persian, Sassanian empire, as viewed from Iran. On the other hand, we are increasingly aware of the astounding new beginnings associated with this period: we go to it to discover why Europe became Christian and why the Near East became Muslim; we have become extremely sensitive to the 'contemporary' quality of the new, abstract art of this age; the writings of men like Plotinus and Augustine surprise us, as we catch strains – as in some unaccustomed overture – of so much that a sensitive European has come to regard as most 'modern' and valuable

LAW

in his own culture. Looking at the Late Antique world, we are caught between the regretful contemplation of ancient ruins and the excited acclamation of new growth.
Peter Brown, *The World of Late Antiquity*, London, Thames & Hudson, 1971, p. 7. Copyright © 1971 by Thames & Hudson Ltd, London.

'Late antiquity' is in danger of having become an exotic territory,   **3**
populated by wild monks and excitable virgins and dominated by the clash of religions, mentalities and lifestyles . . . This very different perspective is, however, largely based on the evidence of religious and cultural developments; whether it can be extended to economic and administrative history remains to be seen.
Averil Cameron, *The Mediterranean World in Late Antiquity, AD 395–600*, London and New York, Routledge, 1993, p. 6.

The newly formed governing class that had emerged throughout the   **4**
empire by 350 thought of itself as living in a world restored to order: *Reparatio Saeculi*, 'The Age of Restoration', was their favorite motto on coins and inscriptions. The fourth century is the most prosperous period of Roman rule in Britain. As soon as the emperors had pacified the Rhineland, a new aristocracy sprang up in Gaul like mushrooms after rain; men like Ausonius, who could remember how his grandfather had died as a refugee from barbarian invasion in 270, founded landed fortunes that would last for the next two centuries. In Africa and Sicily, a series of splendid mosaics illustrate the *dolce vita* of great landowners, without any significant interruption, from the third to the fifth centuries.

It is important to stress this fourth-century revival. The headlong religious and cultural changes of Late Antiquity did not take place in a world living under the shadow of a catastrophe. Far from it: they should be seen against the background of a rich and surprisingly resilient society, that had reached a balance and attained a structure significantly different from the classical Roman period.
Brown, *World of Late Antiquity*, p. 34.

LAW

See also CRIME AND PUNISHMENT

Νομος, in all its senses, signifies an 'order' and implies that this order   **1**
is, or ought to be, generally regarded as valid and binding by the

members of the group in which it prevails. This usually means that
the members of a given group accept νομος without question,
and general if not universal acceptance is especially in evidence in
the most general senses of the term, when it refers to a way of life, to
the normal order of things, to normal procedures, and to normal
behavior, or when it describes the authority on the basis of which or
by which norms are issued, or the condition of law-and-order, in
which the νομοι are obeyed.
Martin Ostwald, *Nomos and the Beginnings of the Athenian Democracy*, Oxford,
OUP, 1969, p. 54.

2   The problem of Greek or, to be more precise, Athenian law is that it
is not simply a stepchild, but a stepchild overawed by several over-
bearing (not to say ugly) sisters.
Stephen Todd & Paul Millett, 'Law, society and Athens', in P. Cartledge,
P. Millet & S. Todd (eds), *Nomos: essays in Athenian law, politics and society*,
Cambridge, CUP, 1990, p. 1.

3   The population of Athens was growing, and ordinary Athenians were
becoming readier to stand up and speak up for what they believed to
be their rights. Yet the amount of the time which the assembly
of citizens could spend hearing cases was not unlimited; they had to
make a living too. How could the right of appeal to the people be
preserved without bringing the work and other activities of the people
to a standstill?
    The solution found to this problem was brilliant, one of the greatest
contributions ever made to democracy and the administration of
justice. It was to regard a limited number of ordinary citizens as
representing all the citizens: a part of the community stood for the
whole, and the decisions of the part counted as decisions of the whole.
The right to trial by a jury of ordinary citizens is commonly regarded
in modern states as a fundamental part of democracy. It was in Athens
that it was invented.
Douglas M. MacDowell, *The Law in Classical Athens*, London, Thames &
Hudson, 1978, pp. 33–4. Copyright © 1978 Thames & Hudson Ltd,
London.

4   Athenian law . . . was not only intended to solve conflicts between
individual citizens by resorting to a formal legal standard, but also, and
perhaps more importantly, legal action ensured ongoing communication between Athenians in a context that made explicit the power
of the masses to judge the actions and behavior of elite individuals.

What scholars of Greek law often forget is that reconstructing what   **5**
penalties the statutes provided is, in itself, not particularly interesting.
The bare statutes tell us relatively little about the law as applied,
interpreted, violated, and avoided in the social system of which the
law is but one part. In other words, one must move from the legal
positivist interpretation of the criminal law as a set of prohibitory rules
that impose order upon society to an understanding of legal norms as
but a part of the complex structure of social practices through which
a social order is maintained and reproduced.
David Cohen, 'The social context of adultery at Athens', in Cartledge,
Millett & Todd (eds), *Nomos*, p. 148.

Demosthenes regards the variety of legal actions as a positive feature of   **6**
Athenian law, but the open texture of law on which it relies was not
seen as unambiguously welcome. The issue is well discussed in the
Aristotelian writings. In *Ath. Pol.* 9.2 it is noted that because Solon's
laws were not written simply or clearly there were many ambiguities
leaving a major rôle for the courts, and that some thought that this was
a deliberate move on Solon's part 'in order that the people might
control judicial decisions'. This suggestion is criticised here, and in the
Rhetoric (1354a 31ff) Aristotle stresses that it is important that the
lawgiver define as much as possible himself and leave as small a part as
possible to the *dikastai*. Thus Aristotle is concerned both to deny that
Solon can in fact have desired a law of open texture and to prescribe
that such a feature is undesirable in any circumstances. In doing so he
sets himself up against a whole school of thought on what law courts
should do. Modern critics have often assumed that Athenian courts
performed badly the formalist exercise which Aristotle prescribed
for them, but just as various other legal systems have exploited 'open
texture' as a (limited) virtue to be controlled by such means as
precedent, so it is at least worth exploring the possibility that Athenian
courts were able to use the open texture of the law in a positive way,
and to control it by the openness and variety of legal process.
Robin Osborne, 'Law in action in classical Athens', *Journal of Hellenic Studies*,
105 (1985), pp. 43–4.

In complex societies everyone is enmeshed in a vast network of legal   **7**
rules, although people may go through their lives unconscious of most

of them . . . Roman society was quite complex enough for this to be true of it, but it is likely that more Romans knew more about their legal institutions than Englishmen do about theirs. For reasons connected with the amateurism (until quite late in its history) of Roman public life – whereby the standard education included forensic rhetoric, and the law was run by members of a financially independent upper class in the interstices of pursuing political careers or just managing their estates, so that the talkers of law were also the readers and quite often the writers of literature – for such reasons, legal talk and terminology seem rather more frequent and more at home in Roman literature than in ours. Legal terms of art could be used for literary metaphor, could be the foundation of stage jokes or furnish analogy in philosophical discussion. And a corollary of this is that many a passage of Latin *belles lettres* needs a knowledge of the law for its comprehension.

J.A. Crook, *Law and Life of Rome*, London, Thames & Hudson, 1967, pp. 7–8. Copyright © 1976 J.A. Crook.

8 Actual legislation remained throughout the Principate at least nominally in the hands of the republican organs and was only indirectly controlled by the princeps. But there existed also from the beginning a number of other forms in which the princeps was active, inconspicuously but none the less effectively, as an independent creator of new legal rules. All these forms were connected to a greater or lesser degree with the model of magistral creation of law but the standards were at all times quite different; for the power of the princeps, in practice almost unlimited in scope and lifelong in duration, lent his ordinances a degree of authority which was never possessed by the measures of the annual republican magistrates . . .

The free and independent advisory activity of the jurists lost more and more ground through the competition of the highest power in the State, and, probably as early as the first half of the third century, the jurists found themselves able to take part in the development of law only as officials of the emperor . . . The Principate, to which the legal profession had once owed such extraordinary advancement, now crushed it with its overwhelming power and extended its unlimited dominance to the field of the creation of law.

Wolfgang Kunkel, *An Introduction to Roman Legal and Constitutional History*, trans. J.M. Kelly, Oxford, OUP, 2nd edn 1973, pp. 127, 129. First published in German, 6th edn 1971.

LITERACY AND ORALITY

Against our modern ways of thinking about written documents, there **1**
are puzzling or inexplicable features in the classical use of documents.
These can only be understood against the background of oral
communication and with the recognition that the uses of writing
are not obvious and predictable but influenced both by attitudes to it
and by non-written features. The relation between inscriptions and
archive documents, for instance, is curious. There are occasions when
an Athenian orator relies on oral tradition and his audience's memory
when we might expect a reference to written record. It is not clear
that Athenians actually read inscriptions much.
Rosalind Thomas, *Oral Tradition and Written Record in Classical Athens*,
Cambridge, CUP, 1989, p. 35.

In non-literate society, it was suggested, the cultural tradition functions **2**
as a series of interlocking face-to-face conversations in which the very
conditions of transmission operate to favour consistency between past
and present, and to make criticism – the articulation of inconsistency
– less likely to occur; and if it does, the inconsistency makes a less
permanent impact, and is more easily adjusted or forgotten . . .

In literate society, these interlocking conversations go on; but they
are no longer man's only dialogue; and in so far as writing provides
an alternative source for the transmission of cultural orientations it
favours awareness of inconsistency. One aspect of this is a sense of
change and of cultural lag; another is the notion that the cultural
inheritance as a whole is composed of two very different kinds of
material; fiction, error and superstition on the one hand; and, on the
other, elements of truth which can provide the basis for some more
reliable and coherent explanation of the gods, the human past and the
physical world.
Jack Goody & Ian Watt, 'The consequences of literacy', in J. Goody (ed.),
Literacy in Traditional Societies, Cambridge, CUP, 1968, pp. 48–9.

Fifth-century Athens was not a 'literate society', but nor was it quite **3**
an 'oral society' either. Clearly oral communication and writing
are far from incompatible here (nor are they now, of course, in the
modern world, though people often speak as if they were). We can
see that the presence of writing does not necessarily destroy all
oral elements of a society, and orality does not preclude complex
intellectual activity . . . The written word was more often used in the
service of the spoken.

Rosalind Thomas, *Literacy and Orality in Ancient Greece*, Cambridge, CUP, 1992, p. 4.

4   Three crucial factors, however, prevent us from thinking that more than, say, 10% of the population as a whole was literate: we have reasons to think that the mid-Republican Romans possessed no more than a rudimentary network of schools; no economic or other incentive led the rulers of Rome to attach importance to the education of the ordinary citizen; and no set of beliefs, such as existed in classical Athens and probably in a number of Hellenistic cities, told the citizens at large or a large section of them that they had any duty to acquire enough elementary education to be able to read and write.

William V. Harris, *Ancient Literacy*, Cambridge Mass. and London, Harvard University Press, 1989, p. 173. Copyright © 1989 by the President and Fellows of Harvard College.

5   If adult male literacy was about 10% across the Roman empire, then there were roughly 2 million adult males who *could* read and write to some extent in the empire as a whole . . . The sheer mass of people who could read and write, living in towns (and, as I shall show, in some villages), made a political, economic, social, and cultural difference in the experience of living in Roman society. Over time, these literates increased the stored reserves of recorded knowledge, and thereby allowed both state and religion unprecedented control over the lives of the illiterate.

Keith Hopkins, 'Conquest by book', in M. Beard et al., *Literacy in the Roman World*, Ann Arbor, Journal of Roman Archaeology Supplementary Series, 1991, pp. 134–5.

LUXURY

1   People have declaimed against luxury for two thousand years, in verse and in prose, and people have always delighted in it.

What has not been said of the early Romans when these brigands ravaged and pillaged the harvests; when, to enlarge their poor village, they destroyed the poor villages of the Volscians and the Samnites? They were disinterested, virtuous men; they had not yet been able to steal either gold, silver or precious stones, because there were not any in the little towns they plundered. Their woods and their marshes produced neither pheasants nor partridges, and people praise their temperance.

When gradually they had pillaged everything, stolen everything from the far end of the Adriatic Gulf to the Euphrates, and when they had enough intelligence to enjoy the fruit of their plundering; when they cultivated the arts, when they tasted of all pleasures, and when they even made the vanquished taste of them, they ceased then, people say, to be wise and honest men.
Voltaire, *Philosophical Dictionary* [1764], trans. H.I. Woolf, London, George Allen & Unwin, 1923, p. 200.

Had the Roman empire been governed with order and tranquillity, **2** this taste of luxury, by precipitating money into the hands of the numerous classes, would, in time, have wrought the effects of multiplying the number of the industrious; consequently, of increasing the demand for vendible subsistence; consequently, of raising the price of it . . . But while either despotism or slavery were the patrimonial inheritance of every one on coming into the world, we are not to expect to see the same principles operate, as in ages where the monarch and the peasant are born equally free to enjoy the possessions made for them by their forefathers.
James Steuart, *An Inquiry into the Principles of Political Economy* [1770], in *The Collected Works of James Steuart*, London, Routledge, 1995, Vol. II pp. 139–40.

A further source of error is the habit of assenting unreservedly to the **3** condemnation by Roman writers of certain forms of luxury, whereas an unprejudiced examination would have shown them innocent and sensible, even welcome symptoms of advance in civilization and prosperity. For the idea of luxury is relative.
Ludwig Friedländer, *Roman Life and Manners under the Early Empire*, trans. J.H. Freese & L.A. Magnus, London, Routledge & Kegan Paul, 1908, Volume II, p. 141. First published in German in 1862–4; translated from 7th edition.

Leading Romans habitually accused one another of luxury and sexual **4** immorality and were in turn accused of hypocrisy. Accusations of immorality were a fundamental part of the political vocabulary of the elite in ancient Rome. We cannot separate the substance, the 'real' issues, of the disputes from the language in which they were articulated.
Catharine Edwards, *The Politics of Immorality in Ancient Rome*, Cambridge, CUP, 1993, p. 26.

In each of these forms [self-indulgence, *avaritia* and *ambitio*], luxury **5** perverts the good and politic order. What these three forms have in common is that they are species of desire. These desires, when they have been stimulated, are capable of perverting good order because they all place a premium upon self-gratification. The more such 'selfish' pleasures are indulged, the less responsibility and commitment to the public good will be exhibited.

Christopher J. Berry, *The Idea of Luxury: a conceptual and historical investigation*, Cambridge, CUP, 1994, pp. 85–6.

MAGIC AND DIVINATION

1   But if in the most backward state of human society now known to us we find magic thus conspicuously present and religion conspicuously absent, may we not reasonably conjecture that the civilised races of the world have also at some period of their history passed through a similar intellectual phase, that they attempted to force the great powers of nature to do their pleasure before they thought of courting their favour by offerings and prayers – in short that, just as on the material side of human culture there had everywhere been an Age of Stone, so on the intellectual side there had everywhere been an Age of Magic?

J.G. Frazer, *The Golden Bough: a study in magic and religion*, London, Macmillan, abridged edition 1922, p. 55. Reprinted by permission of A.P. Watt Ltd on behalf of Trinity College, Cambridge.

2   In antiquity, magic was itself a religious ritual which worked on pagan divinities. It was not a separate technology, opposed to religious practice. To the ancients, magic was distinguished from respectable rites and prayers by the malevolence of its intentions and the murkiness of the materials which it used. It was not a new force, different in kind from conventional cults: cults, too, compelled their gods with symbols and aimed to work on them for beneficial ends.

Robin Lane Fox, *Pagans and Christians in the Mediterranean World from the Second Century AD to the Conversion of Constantine*, Harmondsworth, Penguin, 1986, p. 36. Reproduced with permission of Curtis Brown Ltd, London on behalf of Robin Lane Fox. Copyright © Robin Lane Fox 1986.

3   Papyri, amulets and curse tablets remain; incantations, gestures, incense and sacrifices cannot reach us, though they are often enough described in written sources; the total of the evidence affirms the belief of people of the time that the strength of their spirit could be increased by the right practices or that another spirit could be engaged

to reach out against their enemies. The ancient world was as tangled in a crisscross of invisible contacts, so it might be thought, as our modern world is entangled in radio beams.

Aggressive magic was only one of many kinds, and by no means the most common. Among amulets, it was pain and sickness that were most often aimed at; among curse tablets, the wrong horse or chariot in the hippodrome. Nothing so very horrible here. And the picture of star spells and of demons with whips or hooks in their hands, ready to strike where they were told, should be further corrected by mention of magical powers used for good purposes.

Ramsay MacMullen, *Enemies of the Roman Order: treason, unrest and alienation in the empire*, Cambridge Mass., Harvard University Press, 1966, pp. 103–4. Copyright © 1966 by the President and Fellows of Harvard College. All rights reserved.

Astrology emerged as the Roman Republican system began to **4** collapse, a coincidence which, in my view, was no accident. Astrology belonged with the sole ruler, as the state diviners belonged with the Republic.

Tamsyn Barton, *Ancient Astrology*, London and New York, Routledge, 1994, p. 38.

To sum up the history of the Delphic oracle is not easy, because it **5** diffused itself into every branch of Greek life and thought, and everywhere presented itself under the curious and ambiguous forms which are to be expected of such an obscure activity as prophecy. But even if one could form a judgement on the perplexing problem of each particular response and be prepared to assert which are genuine and which not, the influence of the oracle itself is not defined by those limits.

H.W. Parke & D.E.W. Wormell, *The Delphic Oracle*, Oxford, Basil Blackwell, 1961, Vol. I p. 416.

METICS

Aristotle weighs into the slavery issue, and ponders long upon the **1** *polites*. But the metic? A mere footnote to the definition of the citizen, observing that the metic is the converse, the mirror-image. Here, in paradigm, the *durability* of the ideology – *its general acceptability to metics as well as citizens*.

David Whitehead, *The Ideology of the Athenian Metic*, Cambridge, Cambridge Philological Society, 1977, p. 174.

111

2   So if the metic had no overmastering desire, or no means of expressing a desire, for a substantial improvement in his status (even short of citizenship and full assimilation), what citizen body this side of Utopia would have given him one? Revolution, even simple protest, did not arise; the conventions were known and accepted by all concerned.
Ibid., pp. 174–5.

MYTH

1   The specific character of myth seems to lie neither in the structure nor in the content of a tale, but in the use to which it is put; and this would be my final thesis: *myth is a traditional tale with secondary, partial reference to something of collective importance.* Myth is traditional tale applied; and its relevance and seriousness stem largely from this application.
Walter Burkert, *Structure and History in Greek Mythology and Ritual*, Berkeley, Los Angeles and London, University of California Press, 1979, p. 23.

2   There are seven main types of theory of myth: that which treat myth as a form of explanation and, in particular, a form which occurs at a certain stage in the development of human society and culture; that which treats myth as a form of symbolic statement which has the function, not of explanation, but of expression as an end in itself, and which reflects a particular type of thought, the mythopoeic; that which treats it as an expression of the unconscious; that which accounts for it in terms of its function in creating and maintaining social solidarity, cohesion, etc.; that which stresses its function in legitimating social institutions and social practices; that which treats it as a form of symbolic statement about social structure, possibly linked with ritual; and, finally, there is the structuralist theory.
Percy S. Cohen, 'Theories of myth', *Man* n.s., 4 (1969), p. 338.

3   In a non-literate and highly traditional culture tales are a primary form not only of entertainment but also of communication and instruction – communication between coevals and also between older and younger, and therefore between generations . . . Development in that kind of society over several generations gave myths their characteristic density and complexity, their imaginative depth and their universal appeal. At the same time they tend to have a limited range of themes, which are made to perform multiple functions and reflect different interests. That is why global theories of myth are so peculiarly disastrous.
G.S. Kirk, *The Nature of Greek Myths*, Harmondsworth, Penguin, 1974, p. 29.

One of the basic truths about myths, which cannot be repeated too **4** often, is that they are traditional tales. Such tales develop manifold implications and meanings according to the character, wishes and circumstances of their tellers and audiences. Therefore they are likely to vary in their qualities and functions. The main fault in the modern study of myths is that it has consisted so largely of a series of supposedly universal and mutually exclusive theories, each of which can be easily disproved by marshalling scores of agreed instances that do not accord with it. Yet most of these theories have seemed to illuminate *some* myths at least; for example those of a particular form, or those associated with a particular kind of community or culture. After all, a theory could never begin to establish itself if there were not certain phenomena to which it seemed more or less relevant. My own conviction, nevertheless, is that there can be no single and comprehensive theory of myths – except, perhaps, the theory that all such theories are necessarily wrong. The only exception would be a theory so simple as hardly to deserve the name (like that implied by the 'traditional tale' definition); or so complicated, and containing so many qualifications and alternatives, as not to be a single theory at all.
Ibid., p. 38.

The atmosphere in which the Fathers of history set to work was **5** saturated with myth. Without myth, indeed, they could never have begun their work. The past is an intractable, incomprehensible mass of uncounted and uncountable data. It can be rendered intelligible only if some selection is made, around some focus or foci . . . What 'things' merit or require consideration in order to establish how they 'really were'? Long before anyone dreamed of history, myth gave an answer. That was its function, or rather one of its functions; to make the past intelligible and meaningful by selection, by focusing on a few bits of the past which thereby acquired permanence, relevance, universal significance.
M.I. Finley, 'Myth, memory and history', in *The Use and Abuse of History*, London, Chatto & Windus, 1975, p. 13.

Myth, in its original form, provided answers without ever explicitly **6** formulating the problems. When tragedy takes over the mythical traditions, it uses them to pose problems to which there are no solutions.
Jean-Pierre Vernant, *Myth and Society in Ancient Greece*, trans. J. Lloyd, Sussex, Harvester, 1980, p. 214. First published in French in 1974.

NERO

1 Did the rôle that Nero initially played so well embody conflicts that he ultimately found it impossible to resolve? Did the system offer particular temptations to a man of his temperament? Was the more successful Vespasian simply an *empereur de bon sens* or was he less exposed than Nero to certain features of the Principate and more aware, because of recent history, of the need to change others?
Miriam T. Griffin, *Nero: the end of a dynasty*, London, Batsford, 1984, p. 17.

2 The essentially positive picture we have of Augustus is – even in our sources – sufficiently *ambivalent* for us to find it plausible in a world where nothing is ever black and white. The traditional picture we have of Nero is, by contrast, impossibly crude. The historical sources constantly revile him: he is depicted as a monster of lust, a tyrant, an egomaniac, a murderer, an incompetent, indeed, in every way the antithesis of the ideal Roman statesman; and he is granted only so many virtues as will throw his vices into sharper relief. However attractive this may be as a story – and it does, undeniably, have its appeal – it is hard in the end to believe that any historical figure could have been so uniformly depraved, or any era so hopelessly steeped in crime and sycophancy.
Jás Elsner & Jamie Masters (eds), *Reflections of Nero: culture, history and representation*, London, Duckworth, and Chapel Hill, University of North Carolina, 1994, pp. 1–2.

PATRONAGE

1 First, it involves the *reciprocal* exchange of goods and services. Secondly, to distinguish it from a commercial transaction, the relationship must be a personal one of some duration. Thirdly, it must be asymmetrical, in the sense that the two parties are of unequal status and offer different kinds of goods and services in the exchange – a quality which sets patronage off from friendship between equals.
Richard P. Saller, *Personal Patronage under the Early Empire*, Cambridge, CUP, 1982, p. 1.

2 In a recent study it was thought significant that both Roman poets and their aristocratic supporters were called *amici*, adhering to the 'familiar code of *amicitia*'. But . . . the fact that men of varying social statuses could be called *amici* does not indicate that all *amicitiae* fit into a single category of social relationships with a single code of conduct.

Conversely, we should not jump to the conclusion that patronage existed only where the words *patronus* and *cliens* were used.
Ibid., p. 7.

It is an easy step to connect the strength and longevity of the Athenian **3** democracy with the apparent absence of information about patronage. It seems a plausible hypothesis that the democratic ideology, with its emphasis on political equality, was hostile to the idea of personal patronage, which depended on the exploitation of inequalities in wealth and status.
Paul Millett, 'Patronage and its avoidance in classical Athens', in A. Wallace-Hadrill (ed.), *Patronage in Ancient Society*, London and New York, Routledge, 1989, p. 17.

To stand at the door of an upper-class Roman house of the late republic **4** or early empire is already to glimpse something of the centrality of patronage in Roman society . . . The way the Roman house invites the viewer from the front door, unparalleled in the Greek world, flows from the patronal rituals so often described in the Roman sources.
Andrew Wallace-Hadrill, 'Patronage in Roman society: from republic to empire', in Wallace-Hadrill (ed.), *Patronage in Ancient Society*, p. 63.

PEASANTS

See also AGRICULTURE, CRISIS

Although Athens almost certainly remained an area of many small **1** land-holders it is only misleading to treat these as peasants in any strong sense of that word. Certainly Athenian farmers shared a low level of technological development, the linking of farm with family . . . the economic dependence upon agriculture, and probably the use of the immediate family for labour, with the classic peasant; but it is far less clear that they were dominated by outsiders or exploited in any direct way by outsiders, and there is no evidence at all for their possessing a distinct cultural tradition.

The two crucial factors which mark Athenian farmers out from peasants are the lack of a clear distinction between town and country . . . and the absence of a recognisable division separating small and large landowners.
Robin Osborne, *Demos: the discovery of classical Attika*, Cambridge, CUP, 1985, p. 142.

2   One way of defining the significance of the peasant-citizen (and increasingly also the artisan-citizen) might be to consider this phenomenon against the background of other peasant societies . . . In all these cases, agriculture and production were dominated by people who were politically subject to or juridically dependent upon privileged classes or a central authority to whom they were obliged to render tribute and/or labour services in one form or another. In fact, this is a characteristic which these states had in common with most known advanced civilizations of the ancient world. The generality of such social arrangements is what makes it useful to characterize the contrasting situation of Athenian democracy in terms of its exclusion of dependence from the sphere of production, instead of emphasizing, as is more commonly done, the predominance of dependent labour in the form of chattel slavery. In comparison to the conditions of other advanced civilizations of the ancient world – and indeed many later societies – the absence of a dependent peasantry and the establishment of a regime of free smallholders stands out in sharp relief.

Ellen Meiksins Wood, *Peasant-Citizen and Slave: the foundations of Athenian democracy*, London and New York, Verso, 1988, p. 83.

3   It is, of course, impossible to say that the culture of democratic Athens, the climax of these cultural developments, was the product of the smallholders' regime in the sense that Athenian poets and philosophers were peasants, or even craftsmen . . . The small producers of Athens were its cultural mainspring in a different sense – not least, of course, in their own craft-productions, to which we have already referred, or in their demands as audiences for Athenian drama and comedy, but above all in the challenge which they represented to aristocratic dominance.

Ibid., p. 169.

4   The more fundamental point concerns the relationship of the slave and peasant systems of production. The growth of the former at the expense of the latter is one of the best known facts of Roman history. But the extent of their inter-dependence has not been noted, nor has recognition been given to the dilemma this posed for the slave system. Large landowners needed a stable labour force near their estates. Smallholders were the preferred source of labour. Yet the relationship was not between equals, and the independence of the smallholder was precarious. If he became insolvent and had to surrender his land to his powerful neighbour, the latter might find his labour problems

aggravated . . . The free peasantry was never eradicated in the Roman world, but the future lay largely with a dependent labour system.
Peter Garnsey, 'Non-slave labour in the Roman world', in Garnsey (ed.), *Non-Slave Labour in the Greco-Roman World*, Cambridge, Cambridge Philological Society, 1980, p. 43.

It is hard for subsistence farmers to survive and remain independent. **5**
Their margins are narrow. There is an easy slide into debt; small proprietors are readily converted into tenants of rich money-lending landowners.
Peter Garnsey, 'Peasants in ancient Roman society', *Journal of Peasant Studies*, 3 (1976), p. 225. Reprinted by permission of Frank Cass & Co.

The strength of the peasantry lay in the multifarious character of their **6**
resources, but this was not so much a matter of choice as of necessity, the required counterpoise to the low yields to be regularly expected from the sown crops.
J.K. Evans, 'Plebs rustica: the peasantry of classical Italy', *American Journal of Ancient History*, 5 (1980), p. 162.

PLEBS

A whole section of the poor in Rome, who attended the spectacles, **1**
never received the public dole of grain or cash at all. If we go one stage further in remembering that even the greatest of all spectacles, the games at the Circus Maximus, could be seen only by about 250,000 people (only about 50,000 could get into the Coliseum), then we begin to realize that of the million to a million and a half people who lived in the city, a substantial proportion of the really poor saw nothing of the blandishments that supposedly corrupted the Roman plebs.
C.R. Whittaker, 'The poor', in A. Giardina (ed.), *The Romans*, trans. L.G. Cochrane, Chicago, University of Chicago Press, 1993, pp. 272–3. Originally published in Italian in 1989. Copyright © 1993 by The University of Chicago. All rights reserved.

The Roman poor had to earn part of their living, and some had to **2**
earn the whole of it. The number of recipients of the grain dole was artificially limited, hence many free inhabitants of Rome had to buy all their own food . . . And even the *plebs frumentaria* needed cash. The grain ration of five *modii* a month was more than enough for a single man (though the *pistores* to whom it must have been taken for milling and baking presumably retained part of it), but insufficient for a family

... Money was also needed to pay for shelter, clothing and oil at least (for light and cleanliness as well as food). Nor is it likely that the poor man was *content* to wash down dry bread with free water from the public fountains; he will have *wanted* to buy wine and condiments.

P.A. Brunt, 'Free labour and public works at Rome', *Journal of Roman Studies*, 70 (1980), p. 94.

3   The growth of Clodius' gangs and the multiplication of *collegia* were contemporary with a growing imbalance between freedman and freeborn in the population of the city and its environs, this in turn due to the general distribution of free corn for which Cato and Clodius were responsible. But the imbalance of the population can have at most aggravated the existing dangers of violence, by providing the opportunity to recruit large gangs from the new proletariat.

A.W. Lintott, *Violence in Republican Rome*, Oxford, OUP, 1968, p. 88.

POLIS

1   What in fact was a polis? On purely etymological grounds, the term can be linked to *akropolis* or 'citadel', and probably derived from the earlier Mycenaean form *ptolis*. Classical writers used the word ambiguously, with *polis* sometimes referring to a 'city' (as opposed to its surrounding countryside) and other times referring to a larger and more formal entity, usually translated as 'state' or 'city-state', implying a discrete but small political unit that comprised a central town and its adjacent territory.

Philip Brook Manville, *The Origins of Citizenship in Ancient Athens*, Princeton, Princeton University Press, 1990, p. 36. Copyright © 1990 by Manville, P.B. Reprinted by permission of Princeton University Press.

2   For most historians, the expression 'the rise of the polis' is synonymous with both 'the rise of the city' and 'the rise of the state', and the sort of confusion Aristotle noted is deepened by the conventional translation of polis as 'city-state'. Classicists regularly point out that this is a poor translation, but few bother to ask themselves why.

Ian Morris, 'The early polis as city and state', in J. Rich & A. Wallace-Hadrill (eds), *City and Country in the Ancient World*, London and New York, Routledge, 1991, p. 25.

3   The truly remarkable aspect of the polis was the notion that the state should be autonomous from dominant-class interests. The ancient political thinkers recognised that the citizen body was composed of

very different but functionally interdependent groups, some of whom would inevitably be stronger and wealthier than others, but the mechanisms of the state itself were to be free from the control of any single element within the whole community. The ideal of the polis was almost a classless society, where the state and the citizens were identical, protecting one another's positions. The direct democracy found in Classical Athens was possible only in a society where such a notion of the state was widely accepted.

Ian Morris, *Burial and Greek Society: the rise of the Greek city-state*, Cambridge, CUP, 1987, pp. 216–17.

Of the actual processes of formation, written records present us with **4** one classic model, that of synoecism. Here too, as with the 'polis', the term is an irritatingly ambiguous one in Greek usage. It covers everything from the notional acceptance of a single political centre by a group of townships and villages whose inhabitants stay firmly put, to the physical migration of a population into a new political centre, which could be either an existing or a purpose-built city. The crucial element in all cases is the political unification.

Anthony Snodgrass, *Archaic Greece: the age of experiment*, London, Melbourne and Toronto, J.M. Dent & Sons, 1980, p. 34.

When it comes to redefining social and spatial relations, the religious **5** factor was at the heart of the debate. Within the territorial framework marked out by war and the exercise of power, previously separate neighbouring groups came to be organized in a new way as some were integrated, others incorporated as dependants, others opposed and excluded; and attitudes towards these operations and their implementation were determined by their respective implications vis-à-vis the religious cults. Participation in religious rituals guaranteed a mutual recognition of statuses and set the seal upon membership of the society, thereby defining an early form of citizenship. And it was in religious terms, through the gathering importance of rituals and the commitment to build sanctuaries for the deities who presided over this establishment of order, that the emerging society manifested its new cohesion and took its first collective – and hence political – long-term decisions. The religious space that was created in this was constituted the first civic space.

François de Polignac, *Cults, Territory and the Origins of the Greek City-State*, trans. J. Lloyd, Chicago and London, University of Chicago Press, 1995, pp. 152–3. First published in French in 1984. Copyright © 1995 by The University of Chicago. All rights reserved.

6 To the Germans, the *polis* can only be described in a handbook of constitutional law; the French *polis* is a form of Holy Communion; the English *polis* is a historical accident; while the American *polis* combines the practices of a Mafia convention with the principles of justice and individual freedom.

Oswyn Murray, 'Cities of Reason', in O. Murray & S. Price (eds), *The Greek City from Homer to Alexander*, Oxford, OUP, 1990, p. 3.

7 It was in the domain of foreign politics that the Greek city-state experienced failure. But failure here was fatal; for it meant the destruction of the city-state itself – the fine, sensitive mother of Greek freedom and life.

William Scott Ferguson, *Hellenistic Athens: an historical essay*, London, Macmillan, 1911, p. 6.

8 If the world had consisted of nothing but *poleis* (and perhaps a few remote tribal *ethne*) clustered, in Plato's simile, round the shores of the Mediterranean like frogs round a pond, then perhaps they could have reproduced themselves indefinitely without competition either between or within them forcing an evolution to another mode; tyrannies would no doubt have reappeared here and there, but only for a time and without developing the institutions of monarchical absolutism on the Near Eastern model; wars would have been won and lost, alliances formed and dissolved, democracies overthrown by oligarchies and oligarchies by democracies, and secessions, rebellions and *coups d'état* have succeeded or failed, but in a sort of perpetual Brownian motion without any fundamental institutional change. But the world did consist of other types of society too; and as it turned out, the form of social organisation which the *poleis* had evolved out of the confusion and depopulation which had followed the collapse of the Mycenaean system was positively disadvantageous in the wider environment which they themselves had helped to create.

W.G. Runciman, 'Doomed to extinction: the *polis* as an evolutionary dead-end', in Murray & Price (eds), *The Greek City*, p. 350.

POLITICS

See also DEMOCRACY

1 The Greeks were then – and this no one will dispute – the first to think systematically about politics, to observe, describe, comment and

eventually to formulate political theories . . . It was Greek writing provoked by the Athenian experience that the eighteenth and nineteenth centuries read, insofar as reading history played a role in the rise and development of modern democratic theories.
M.I. Finley, *Democracy Ancient and Modern*, London, Chatto & Windus, 1973, p. 14.

Democracy was cobbled together, thousands of years ago, by the **2** Athenians. It was at Athens, too, that political theory first appeared. The citizens of fifth-century B.C. Athens lived democracy, for the first time in the history of the world, and they thought about it. Democratic politics enabled all citizens, rich and poor, to express and pursue their own aims. Democratic politics also prompted citizens to construe their aims politically, and to reflect on their actions in terms of general, relatively abstract considerations. Political theory was part of democratic politics; self-understanding was political.
Cynthia Farrar, *The Origins of Democratic Thinking: the invention of politics in classical Athens*, Cambridge, CUP, 1988, p. 1.

It is not easy to understand how a people that know nothing about the **3** possibility of democracy could create democratic systems of government. It cannot have been an altogether probable development, or the Greeks would not have been the exception to the rule among advanced civilizations. For, whatever else may be said in their favor, there is nothing to suggest that the Greeks were from the beginning more 'gifted' than so many other peoples. Nor can the explanation lie in the special character of their culture, for this was itself clearly the outcome of the process that produced the conditions favorable to democracy.
Christian Meier, *The Greek Discovery of Politics*, trans. D. McLintock, Cambridge Mass. and London, Harvard University Press, 1990, p. 1. First published in German in 1980. Copyright © 1990 by the President and Fellows of Harvard College. All rights reserved.

RATIONALITY

Some years ago I was in the British Museum looking at the Parthenon **1** sculptures when a young man came up to me and said with a worried air, 'I know it's an awful thing to confess, but this Greek stuff doesn't move me one bit.' I said that was very interesting: could he define at all the reasons for his lack of response? He reflected for a minute or two. Then he said, 'Well, it's all so terribly *rational*, if you know what

I mean.' I thought I did know . . . To a generation whose sensibilities have been trained on African and Aztec art, and on the work of such men as Modigliani and Henry Moore, the art of the Greeks, and Greek culture in general, is apt to appear lacking in the awareness of mystery and in the ability to penetrate to the deeper, less conscious levels of human experience.

This fragment of conversation stuck in my head and set me thinking. Were the Greeks in fact quite so blind to the importance of nonrational factors in man's experience and behaviour as is commonly assumed both by their apologists and by their critics? That is the question out of which this book grew.

E.R. Dodds, *The Greeks and the Irrational*, Berkeley and Los Angeles, University of California Press, 1951, p. 1.

2   There is nothing surprising about the coincidence we have noted in the emergence of the philosopher and that of the citizen. Indeed, in its social institutions the city establishes the separation between nature and society that is the conceptual prerequisite for the exercise of rational thought. With the coming of the city, the political order was separated from the organisation of the cosmos. It was now seen as a human institution which was the subject of concerned inquiry and impassioned discussion.

Jean-Pierre Vernant, *Myth and Thought among the Greeks*, London, Boston, Melbourne and Henley, Routledge & Kegan Paul, 1983, pp. 357–8. First published in French in 1965.

3   Reason is not to be discovered in nature, it is immanent in language. It did not originate in techniques for operating upon things. It was developed from the organization and analysis of the various means of influencing men . . . Greek reason is the type of reason that makes it possible to act in a positive, deliberate, and methodical way upon men, but not to transform nature. In its limitations, as well as in the innovations it brought about, it appears truly as the product of the city.

Ibid., p. 366.

4   There was, from an economic point of view, no such rationalism in ancient farming as, for instance, in ancient science.

G. Mickwitz, 'Economic rationalism in Graeco-Roman agriculture', *English Historical Review*, 52 (1937), p. 589.

5   Nineteenth century thinkers assumed that in his economic activity man strove for profit, that his materialistic propensities would induce

him to choose the lesser instead of the greater effort and to expect payment for his labor; in short, that in his economic activity he would tend to abide by what they described as economic rationality, and that all contrary behavior was the result of outside interference . . .

Actually, as we now know, the behavior of man both in his primitive state and right through the course of history has been almost the opposite from that implied in this view.
Karl Polanyi, *The Great Transformation: the political and economic origins of our time*, Boston, Beacon Press, 1944, pp. 249–50.

The idea that efficiency, increased productivity, economic rationalism **6** and growth are good *per se* is very recent in human thinking . . . *We* might consider the Pont du Gard a fantastically expensive way of bringing fresh water to a not very important provincial town in southern Gaul; the Romans in Gaul ranked fresh water and the demonstration of power higher on the value–scale than costs. That was a rational view, too, though not economic rationalism.
M.I. Finley, 'Technical innovation and economic progress', in Finley, *Economy and Society in Ancient Greece*, B.D. Shaw & R. Saller (eds), London, Chatto & Windus, 1981, p. 179

The Finley/Mickwitz view is, in effect, anachronistic. What they have **7** done is to choose a model which does not even apply to present-day agriculture as a whole, measure the ancient economy by it, establish that the ancient economy does not answer to the model, and conclude that the ancient economy is primitive.
P.W. de Neeve, 'The price of land in Roman Italy and the problem of economic rationalism', *Opus*, 4 (1985), p. 94.

RELIGION

See also SACRIFICE, CHRISTIANITY, MACMULLEN

Classical Greek religion was at bottom a question of doing not **1** believing, of behaviour rather than faith.
Paul Cartledge, 'The Greek religious festivals', in P.E. Easterling & J.V. Muir (eds), *Greek Religion and Society*, Cambridge, CUP, 1985, p. 98.

Natural religion is associated with the soil. Lands may change in **2** respect of population and language, but the immigrants do not refuse their homage to the old gods of the country. The latter do not entirely disappear, even though they are supplanted and transformed. This was in all probability what occurred in the change of religion which took place in Greece in prehistoric times, and it is therefore our duty to seek for traces of the Minoan-Mycenaean religion in the Greek.

Martin P. Nilsson, *A History of Greek Religion*, trans. F.J. Fielden, Oxford, OUP, 2nd edn 1949, p. 22. First published in Swedish.

3   Greek religion, as set forth in popular handbooks, and even in more ambitious treatises, is an affair mainly of mythology, and moreover of mythology as seen through the medium of literature . . . Yet the facts of ritual are more easy definitely to ascertain, more permanent, and at least equally significant. What a people *does* in relation to its gods must always be one clue, and perhaps the safest, to what it *thinks*. The first preliminary to any scientific understanding of Greek religion is a minute examination of its ritual.

This habit of viewing Greek religion exclusively through the medium of Greek literature has brought with it an initial and fundamental error in method – an error which in England, where scholarship is mainly literary, is likely to die hard. For literature Homer is the beginning, though every scholar is aware that he is nowise primitive: for theology, or – if we prefer so to call it – mythology, Homer presents, not a starting-point, but a culmination, a complete achievement, an almost mechanical accomplishment, with scarcely a hint of *origines*, an accomplishment moreover, which is essentially literary rather than religious, sceptical and moribund already in its very perfection. The Olympians of Homer are no more primitive that his hexameters. Beneath this splendid surface lies a stratum of religious conceptions, ideas of evil, of purification, of atonement, ignored or suppressed by Homer, but reappearing in later poets and notably in Aeschylus. It is this substratum of religious conceptions, at once more primitive and more permanent, that I am concerned to investigate. Had ritual received its due share of attention, it had not remained so long neglected.

Jane Ellen Harrison, *Prolegomena to the Study of Greek Religion*, Cambridge, CUP, 1903, pp. vii–viii.

4   Among the Greeks, civilization was a mushroom growth. In contrast to the societies of the present day, it had sprung at a bound from darkness into light. The result was that, in spite of any veneer of civilized thought or habit which they might have acquired in their religion, the primitive was always lying just beneath the surface.

W.K.C. Guthrie, *The Greeks and their Gods*, London, Methuen, 1950, p. 18.

They are artists' dreams, ideals, allegories; they are symbols of some- 5
thing beyond themselves. They are Gods of half-hearted tradition, of
unconscious make-believe, of aspiration. They are gods to whom
doubtful philosophers can pray, with all a philosopher's due caution, as
to so many radiant and heart-searching hypotheses. They are not gods
in whom any one believes as a hard fact.
Gilbert Murray, *Four Stages of Greek Religion*, New York, Columbia
University Press, 1912, p. 97.

All this means that, for all its weight of tradition (not less evident 6
in ancient Greek religion than in other religions), Greek religion
remains fundamentally improvisatory. By which I mean that though
the response to experience crystallizes, on the one hand as ritual, on
the other as myth, and both involve repetition and transmission from
generation to generation, there is always room for new improvisations,
for the introduction of new cults and new observances. Greek religion
is not theologically fixed and stable, and it has no tradition of
exclusion or finality: it is an open, not a closed system.
John Gould, 'On making sense of Greek religion', in Easterling & Muir (eds),
Greek Religion and Society, pp. 7–8.

The reader will be struck first of all by the fact that pagan priests are 7
quite unlike their modern Christian counterparts. The priestly
officials discussed in this volume bear no significant resemblance to
the comforting image of the wise Christian pastor, guiding his flock
through the spiritual perils of the world: they did not play the part
(at least officially) of moral leaders; they were not involved with a
congregation that looked to them for advice and guidance. In political
terms too ancient pagan priests seem distinctively different. Unlike
the priests of Christianity and other modern world religions, who
can communally wield power independently of (and sometimes in
opposition to) the established political power in the state, pagan priests
never (or only in exceptional circumstances) stood apart from the
political order. There is hardly a sign of that – to us – familiar clash
between 'church' and 'state' – between priestly interests and the
dominant political hierarchy.
Mary Beard & John North (eds), *Pagan Priests: religion and power in the ancient
world*, London, Duckworth, and Ithaca, Cornell University Press, 1990,
pp. 1–2.

The origins of Roman religion lay in the earliest days of the city of 8
Rome itself. That, at least, was the view held by the Romans – who

would have been very puzzled that we should now have any doubt about where, when or how most of their priesthoods, their festivals, their distinctive rituals were established.

Mary Beard, John North & Simon Price, *Religions of Rome, Volume I: a history*, Cambridge, CUP, 1998, p. 1.

9   The Roman, as we have mentioned on several occasions, is scrupulously conservative. During the decay of the sacred science, he will obstinately maintain the traditional acts of the cult, even when he no longer understands them; moreover, with the calm conviction of the *maiestas* which attaches to the name, the usages, and the ideas of Rome, he observes a rigorous and absolute distinction between that which is *patrium* and that which is *peregrinum* or, to use the older term, *hostile*. On the other hand, he is, as we have also mentioned, an empiricist, ready to recognize and evaluate unfamiliar things which may prove to be powerful or useful. The result is that from the earliest times this most traditional of religions does not rule out innovations but rather tolerates, indeed welcomes them.

Georges Dumézil, *Archaic Roman Religion*, trans. P. Krapp, Chicago and London, University of Chicago Press, 1970, Volume I p. 125. First published in French in 1966 by Editions Payot. Translation Copyright © 1970 by The University of Chicago.

10   A system in which the emphasis falls primarily on the performance of ritual acts – not on the worshippers' belief , or religious emotions and experiences, or on theology or ethics – such a system inescapably makes it a primary value, though not necessarily the only value, that the known ritual should be successfully repeated. This in turn must imply some implicit respect for the past and for the tradition from which the ritual emerged. For the Romans of any generation, the real validation of their religion lay in the fact that it had worked: that their ancestors had won battles, survived crises, eaten dinners, begotten children and expanded their power by the practice of the self-same rites and ceremonies as they practised themselves.

J.A. North, 'Conservatism and change in Roman religion', *Papers of the British School at Rome*, 44 (1976), p. 1.

11   Most of the ceremonies discussed in the previous chapter were performed by special individuals on behalf of the state as a whole. What mattered was that they should be performed in the right way at the right time; the attendance of the Roman people as a whole at them was not necessary for their success, although, as a matter of fact, many of them drew large crowds of interested and devout spectators. Within the state there were smaller units – clubs, tribes, regiments, guilds, parishes and so on – each of which had its own patron gods and its own religious rites designed to ensure the continued prosperity of the group . . .

The smallest group within the community was the family. The family needs divine co-operation for the success of its day-to-day life just as much as the state, and the head of the family was responsible for taking the proper steps to ensure that co-operation. Normally, as in public religion, this was a matter of carrying out certain regularly recurring ceremonies.

R.M. Ogilvie, *The Romans and their Gods in the Age of Augustus*, London, Chatto & Windus, 1981, p. 100.

The Roman State religion, inseparably bound up with politics, was in **12** the hands of the governing nobles and could be manipulated by them in the interests of the entire body or for the benefit of one group in rivalry with another. Men who as magistrates celebrated the great games for the gods, performed the chief sacrifices, and took the auspices – which determined the will of the gods – served also as priests to interpret the gods on earth . . .

They feasted the gods, and often the people too, at banquets and sacrifices. They reported to the people signs and omens by which the gods had manifested their ill will and then allayed any fears that may have been aroused by putting on expiatory rites. Meanwhile the nobles, in contact with Greek rationalism, were themselves steadily developing skepticism toward the religion of their ancestors, but they were not deterred from exploiting religion for political purposes. The rival manipulation of religion by opposing groups in the nobility, each seeking to show that heaven was on its side, must have weakened the confidence of the people.

Lily Ross Taylor, *Party Politics in the Age of Caesar*, Berkeley and Los Angeles, University of California Press, 1949, pp. 76, 77–8.

It is easy to over-estimate the significance of the rationalism of the **13** late republic. First of all, the authors on whom we depend for our knowledge of the period, Cicero, Caesar, and Varro, were not necessarily typical even of the nobility. The great mass of the people were certainly much more directly in awe of the gods.

J.H.W.G. Liebeschuetz, *Continuity and Change in Roman Religion*, Oxford, OUP, 1979, p. 33.

14 Not only divination, but Roman religion as a whole, showed remarkable power of adaptation to changing conditions. In general, the success of the Roman state maintained a belief in the efficacy of an institution so intimately linked with all public action . . . On the other hand, the stresses and strains in the political system would be reflected in the religious institutions too . . . The late republic was such a period, when public religion was affected by the general breakdown of Roman institutions. This did not mean that the ancestral cults were rejected. On the contrary, the crisis itself came to be seen as a punishment for neglect of religion and a religious renewal as an essential part of political reconstruction. Needless to say, the religious renewal included, as it had done in earlier times, a good deal of innovation. Ibid., pp. 38–9.

15 Far from being *merely* a literary device, Cicero's rhetoric about his opponent's enmity of the gods gained its force from the ideological principle we have outlined: that the good politician enjoyed divine support, while his adversary was necessarily in a relationship of hostility with the gods.

This principle also helps us to understand those incidents (often dismissed as fraud) in which assemblies were cancelled or interrupted by the declaration of bad omens. The first important point here is that in Rome all formal political activity took place in an explicitly religious context. Assemblies were preceded by religious ritual to ascertain that the gods approved their being held, and magistrates, when conducting political business with the people, always had to occupy specifically religious ground: that is, they stood in a *templum*, not necessarily a 'temple' in our sense, but any specially consecrated area, such as the platform for speakers in the Forum.

In this religious context, the principle of opposition between those politicians with divine support and those in a position of enmity with the gods once again operated – as the logic underlying the religious hindrance of assemblies. Imagine Cicero again. Suppose he had just learnt that an assembly was to be convened by one of his arch-enemies, with the aim of introducing legislation that was, to his mind, misguided or even dangerous. It would appear to him axiomatic that the gods also disapproved of the proposals and would regard any assembly convened to enact such legislation as in conflict with their will. The proper links between the gods and political activity were thus ruptured; and it would seem inevitable to Cicero that divine disapproval would be displayed and ill omens be sighted. The holding of the assembly was already, in religious terms, incorrect.

Did Roman politicians consciously rehearse this reasoning when they held up proceedings of the assembly by declaring a bad omen? We cannot know. But it is misleading and ethnocentric of us to put it all down to a combination of clever fraud by the declarer and simple-minded acceptance by the assembly. It is easy to be sceptical about other people's religions.

Mary Beard & Michael Crawford, *Rome in the Late Republic*, London, Duckworth, 1985, pp. 32–3. Reprinted by permission of Gerald Duckworth & Co. Ltd.

The Roman people were constantly craving for new forms of **16** religion in the hope of obtaining spiritual bread in place of the stone with which the 'Establishment' supplied them; but every time the 'Establishment' gave admittance to a new cult, it sterilised it by changing the bread to stone as a condition for sanctioning its entry.

Arnold J. Toynbee, *Hannibal's Legacy: the Hannibalic War's effects on Roman life, Volume II: Rome and her neighbours after Hannibal's exit*, Oxford, OUP, 1965, p. 378.

Neither the Jews nor the Christians had a monopoly on holiness. **17** Piety of whatever kind can be expected to bring in its train persons and places whose apparent closeness to the divine implies the workings of an other-worldly power. This is no less true of polytheism than monotheism, although the language of holiness in the great literary texts of the so-called Judaeo-Christian tradition has tended to obscure that important fact. Holiness among the pagans is richly attested across the diverse cults of the ancient world.

G.W. Bowersock, *Hellenism in Late Antiquity*, Ann Arbor, University of Michigan Press, 1990, p. 15.

From the triumph of Christianity, it is natural but not certainly **18** right to reason backwards: Christianity in its now familiar outline, Christianity as it was 'supposed to be', prevailed because it was intrinsically better. It was freely espoused by people who could see its superiority. But that view should not involve the quite crude error of supposing the now familiar outline to have been already clear in the period of our study. In fact, of course, the Church was undergoing constant change in its early history as in its later. The marked prominence of exorcism in its outer face, and of demonology in the inner, faded rapidly away during the fourth century . . .

Crude error avoided, there remain several further points of doubt. First, is it possible to define, almost a priori, major human wants to which answer must, or can only easily, be made through religion? So, if nothing in all the variety of paganism answered some of these wants, but Christianity did, the rise of the latter could be explained. As one illustration . . . no pagan cult held out promise of afterlife for the worshiper as he knew and felt himself to be. Resurrection in the flesh was thus a truth proclaimed to the decisive advantage of the Church. In making any such assertion, however, much care would be needed against attributing to the third century social and spiritual needs that were created rather than answered by Christianity.

Second, is it possible to weigh the impact of two adventitious factors, the destructive political and economic forces at work upon the more prominent parts of paganism after 250 and the constructive dynamic of Constantine's reign in favour of the Church? Together, one might argue, these factors over three-quarters of a century coincided with, and were very nearly enough to account for, the great changes in the Church's fortunes. But the argument must be tested.

Ramsay MacMullen, *Paganism in the Roman Empire*, New Haven and London, Yale University Press, 1981, pp. 136–7.

REPUBLIC, ROMAN

See also MOMMSEN

1   During the years 220 to 150 B.C., effective political control at Rome rested in the hands of twenty or fewer noble families, who owed this virtual monopoly partly to their adroit control of the elections. Their power was based on birth and family tradition, political alliance, and above all on patronage, economic, legal, and political. Although occasionally constrained by popular action, the nobles in the main skilfully controlled the People, and the chief domestic struggles raged less between nobles and commons than within the ranks of the nobility itself, which would naturally tend to fall into rival groups.

H.H. Scullard, *Roman Politics 220–150 B.C.*, Oxford, OUP, 1973, p. xvii.

2   The entire Roman people, both the ruling circle and the mass of voters whom they ruled was, as a society, permeated by multifarious relationships based on *fides* and on personal connections . . . These relationships determined the distribution of political power. To maintain their rights citizens and subjects alike were constrained to seek the protection of powerful men, and the beginner in politics had need of a powerful protector to secure advancement. Political

power was based on membership of the senate, which was composed of the magistrates elected by the people. Thus the most powerful man was he who by virtue of his clients and friends could mobilise the greatest number of votes.

Matthias Gelzer, *The Roman Nobility*, trans. R. Seager, Oxford, Basil Blackwell, 1969, p. 139. First published in German in 1912.

Modern analogies are notoriously unsafe, but if we have any in **3** America for the Roman election campaign they are to be found not in our contests every four years between Republicans and Democrats but in the preparatory maneuvering and the final decision at the national nominating convention within one of our great parties. The groups that form about candidates for the nomination emphasize personalities and make few pretences of providing programs, and the final result depends largely on the strength of the friends whose support each of the candidates can muster. A Roman politician would have been completely lost in the complicated organization of an American presidential election, but he could have learned the ropes fairly easily in the type of organization leading up to a nominating convention.

Lily Ross Taylor, *Party Politics in the Age of Caesar*, Berkeley and Los Angeles, University of California Press, 1949, p. 8.

Neither optimates nor *populares* were organized parties with a perma- **4** nent life. At most times the Senate was still divided into factions, actuated by private feuds, competing for offices or disputing on transitory questions of the moment. But these factions tended to close ranks when the authority or interests of the whole order were imperilled. There was an optimate party only when there was a popular threat to senatorial control. *Populares* came forward only at intervals, generally to carry some particular measure.

P.A. Brunt, *Social Conflicts in the Roman Republic*, London, Chatto & Windus, 2nd edn 1978, p. 95.

In the light of recent work it is time to abandon the once established **5** presuppositions of a hereditary 'nobility', of aristocratic *factiones*, and of an all-embracing network of dependence and clientship. We might then be able to see the public life of the classical Republic in a rather different light: as an arena in which those who sought and held office competed before the crowd by advertisement of their glorious descent if they could; by the exercise of rhetoric in defence of citizens; by reports and demonstrations of military victory. They also fought out their most bitter rivalries before juries constituted by the citizen assemblies. Their ability to legislate depended on the tribal assembly; and the necessary persuasion was applied, often in open conflict and debate, by the means of speeches, which were made not only, or even primarily, in the 'sacred Senate', but in the open space of the Forum, before the ever-available crowd consisting of whoever was already there, or whoever turned up. It was this crowd which, however imperfectly, symbolized and represented the sovereignty of the Roman People.

Fergus Millar, 'The political character of the classical Roman republic, 200–151 B.C.', *Journal of Roman Studies*, 74 (1984), p. 19.

6   The popular will of the Roman people found expression in the context, and only in the context, of divisions within the oligarchy. Democratic politics in Rome was consequently a function of the degree and type of competition in progress between oligarchic families, groups or individuals. It is simply a fact that the ruling class accepted the arbitration of popular voting in certain extremely important circumstances, just as they accepted that the power and success of families and individuals should be limited by the rotation of office, regular succession to commands, and so on. These conventions or restraints lay at the heart of the system; as they weakened, so the system collapsed.

J.A. North, 'Democratic politics in Republican Rome', *Past & Present* (1990), p. 18.

7   To an outside observer, then, the Roman constitution and community appears as a self-regulating device, kept in being by a system of checks and balances that not only prevented disintegration from within but made the community better able to cope with threats from without. To the Romans it looked different. First, as members of the community they assigned value to the system: anything that tended to upset the balance was undesirable and vicious; and as the system was a closed one, concerned with a single body politic, all virtues and vices would be seen in terms of that community. Secondly, they saw the community as a living body, a person. Both factors help to explain why they saw politics and history in moral terms.

Barbara Levick, 'Morals, politics, and the fall of the Roman Republic', *Greece & Rome*, 29 (1982), p. 60. Reprinted by permission of Oxford University Press and the Classical Association.

8   To explain the fall of the Roman Republic, historians invoke a variety

of converging forces or movements, political, social and economic, where antiquity was prone to see only the ambition and the agency of individuals.

Ronald Syme, *The Roman Revolution*, Oxford, OUP, 1939, p. 502.

According to Burke 'a state without the means of some change is **9** without the means of its conservation'. At Rome there were too many checks and balances in the constitution, which operated in practice only in the interest of the ruling class. Reformers had to use force, or at least to create conditions in which the senate had reason to fear its use.

P.A. Brunt, 'The Roman mob', in M.I. Finley (ed.), *Studies in Ancient Society*, London and Boston, Routledge & Kegan Paul, 1974, p. 80. First published in *Past and Present*, 35 (1966).

The maxims of ancient politics contain, in general, so little humanity **10** and moderation, that it seems superfluous to give any particular reason for the acts of violence committed at any particular period. Yet I cannot forbear observing, that the laws, in the later period of the Roman commonwealth, were so absurdly contrived, that they obliged the heads of parties to have recourse to these extremities. All capital punishments were abolished: however criminal, or, what is more, however dangerous any citizen might be, he could not regularly be punished otherwise than by banishment. And it became necessary, in the revolutions of party, to draw the sword of private vengeance; nor was it easy, when laws were once violated, to set bounds to these sanguinary proceedings. Had Brutus prevailed over the *triumvirate*, could he, in common prudence have allowed Octavius and Antony to live, and have contented himself with banishing them to Rhodes or Marseilles, where they might still have plotted new commotions and rebellions? His executing C. Antonius, brother to the *triumvir*, shows evidently his sense of the matter. Did not Cicero, with the approbation of all the wise and virtuous of Rome, arbitrarily put to death Catiline's accomplices, contrary to law, and without any trial or form of process? . . .

Thus one extreme produces another. In the same manner as excessive severity in the laws is apt to beget great relaxation in their execution; so their excessive levity naturally produces cruelty and barbarity.

David Hume, 'Of the populousness of ancient nations' [1752], in *Essays: moral, political, and literary I*, T.H. Green & T.H. Grose (eds), London, Longman, Green & Co., 1875, pp. 408–9.

11   If we look beyond the ambitions and machinations of the great figures of the late Republic, the main cause of its fall must in my view be found in agrarian discontents; it was the soldiers, who were of peasant origin, whose disloyalty to the Republic was fatal. The rôle of the *urban* mob was more restricted. Still, it was their clamour that gave Pompey his extraordinary command in 67 and set in motion the events that led to his alliance with Caesar in 59. And the violence in the city from 58 to 52, which was itself one result of that alliance, produced such chaos that it finally brought Pompey and the senatorial leaders together again, and helped to sever his connection with Caesar; hence the civil wars in which the Republic foundered.

Popular leaders sometimes proclaimed the sovereignty of the people. But the people who could actually attend meetings at Rome were not truly representative and were incapable of governing an empire. The only workable alternative to the government of the few was the government of one man. The interventions of the people in affairs led on to monarchy.

Brunt, 'The Roman mob', p. 101.

12   During the late Republic violence was used to force measures through an assembly, to influence the outcome of an election or trial, and to intimidate or even kill political opponents. Although a number of constitutional means were devised to check it and nullify its effects, these were not proof against persistent violence on a large scale. Moreover the declaration of emergency, the *senatus consultum ultimum*, required co-operation from the majority to be effective. The Romans of the Republic seem genuinely to have considered it an essential constituent of *libertas* that a man should be allowed to use force in his personal interest to secure what he believed to be his due. So, when a conflict could not be resolved constitutionally, it was not surprising that the frustrated party employed violence, and this in turn could not be countered except by further partisan violence. This vicious circle continued until the military force which was finally summoned to break it moved the conflict to the higher plane of civil war.

A.W. Lintott, *Violence in Republican Rome*, Oxford, OUP, 1968, pp. 204–5.

13   A system in which a man might have just one year in which to make his mark was bound to involve, even in periods of consensus, a high level of competition. Its very structure would tend to diminish the scrupulousness of politicians: the *methods* by which glory is achieved are of secondary importance if the competition is intense.

Yet the late Republic witnessed an escalation in even the high level of competition embedded within the Roman political structure. There were two main reasons for this.

First, the value of the prizes to be won grew in absolute terms. Election to office might now lead to a military command in, say, the eastern Mediterranean, where victory would be likely to bring immense wealth and immense prestige. The gap between the successful and the non-successful politician widened; failure became even more devastating, and winning – no matter how – more important.

Secondly, the reforms of Sulla made the intensity of competition for high office even greater in the final phase of the Republic . . . More men than ever before, entering the quaestorship, would have had their hopes of a political career raised; more than ever before would have found the higher echelons of that career impossible to reach. This kind of career 'blockage' (only partially relieved by the early death of some of those involved) had obvious consequences.

As the competition became more intense (and as the stakes in that competition grew), more members of the Roman elite were prepared to resort to illicit tactics to secure the offices they wanted. The *institutions* of the middle Republic may have remained intact, but they were by-passed as ambitious politicians found that violence was a more effective way of achieving their goals – magistracies or the passing of contentious laws.

Mary Beard & Michael Crawford, *Rome in the Late Republic*, London, Duckworth, 1985, pp. 69–70. Reprinted by permission of Gerald Duckworth & Co. Ltd.

Romans and Italians in the tens and hundreds of thousands turned to **14** individuals to provide them with what the state had failed to offer. To repeat Syme's words, men 'were ceasing to feel allegiance to the state'; or in Weberian terms, conquest and the state itself were also no longer 'value-rational'. Roman armies marched against other Roman armies and against Rome itself as readily as against the armies of Mithridates. Politics had ceased to be instrumentally useful to the populace, and the ultimate solution proved to be the end not only of popular participation but of politics itself.

M.I. Finley, *Politics in the Ancient World*, Cambridge, CUP, 1983, p. 121.

RHETORIC

1   Oratory became the vehicle of power. Such a role was not wholly
     new, for no one could read the Homeric poems without sensing the
     power recognized even then to come from the persuasive spoken
     word. However, after the 450s, in Athens and elsewhere, the formal
     sovereignty of Council and Assembly and lawcourts, and the size of
     the audience involved in each institution, directed a massive and
     continuing intellectual investment, essential for any public figure, into
     the techniques of effective persuasion.
     J.K. Davies, *Democracy and Classical Greece*, Sussex, Harvester Press, 1978,
     p. 124.

2   Rhetoric does not play the part in our lives that it did in ancient
     Greece. Nowadays the words 'success' or 'a successful man' suggest
     more immediately the world of business, and only secondarily that of
     politics. In Greece the success that counted was first political and
     secondly forensic, and its weapon was rhetoric, the art of persuasion.
     Following the analogy, one might assign to rhetoric the place now
     occupied by advertising. Certainly the art of persuasion, often by
     dubious means, was no less powerful then, and, as we have our
     business schools and schools of advertising, so the Greeks had their
     teachers of politics and rhetoric: the Sophists.
     W.K.C. Guthrie, *A History of Greek Philosophy, Volume II: the fifth-century
     enlightenment*, Cambridge, CUP, 1969, p. 50.

3   The tendency of orators to say whatever they believed might please
     their audience was considered reprehensible by elite political philo-
     sophers, who thought a speaker's responsibility was to say what is
     true and necessary, not what is pleasant. But at the practical level
     of discourse in the courtroom and the Assembly, the orator had to
     conform to his audience's ideology or face the consequences: losing
     votes or being ignored.
     Josiah Ober, *Mass and Elite in Democratic Athens: rhetoric, ideology and the power
     of the people*, Princeton, Princeton University Press, 1989, p. 43. Copyright ©
     1989 by Ober, J. Reprinted by permission of Princeton University Press.

4   Along with drama in the theater and gossip in the streets, public
     oratory, in the courts and the Assembly, was the most important form
     of ongoing verbal communication between ordinary and elite
     Athenians.
     Ibid., p. 45.

ROMANIZATION

See also IMPERIALISM

Romanization was, then, a complex process with complex issues. It **1**
does not mean simply that all the subjects of Rome became wholly and
uniformly Roman. The world is not so monotonous as that. In it two
tendencies were blended with ever-varying results. First Romanization
extinguished the difference between Roman and provincial through all
parts of the Empire but the east, alike in speech, in material culture, in
political feeling and religion. When the provincials called themselves
Roman or when we call them Roman, the epithet is correct. Secondly,
the process worked with different degrees of speed and success in
different lands. It did not everywhere and at once destroy all traces of
tribal or national sentiments or fashions. These remained, at least
for a while and in certain regions, not in active opposition, but in latent
persistence, capable of resurrection under proper conditions. In such a
case the provincial had become a Roman, but he could still undergo
an atavistic reversion to the ways of his forefathers.
F. Haverfield, *The Romanization of Roman Britain*, Oxford, OUP, 4th edn
1923, p. 22.

Romanization has thus been seen not as a passive reflection of change, **2**
but rather as an active ingredient used by people to assert, project
and maintain their social status. Furthermore, Romanization has
been seen as largely indigenous in its motivation, with emulation of
Roman ways and styles being first a means of obtaining or retaining
social dominance, then being used to express and define it while its
manifestations evolved.
Martin Millett, *The Romanization of Britain: an essay in archaeological
interpretation*, Cambridge, CUP, 1990, p. 212.

'Right! For a start, we're going to build an aqueduct.' **3**
'An aqueduct? But Chief Cassius Ceramix, we don't need an aque-
duct. The river flows right through our village and our fields.'
'Then we'll redirect the course of the river! Aqueducts are more
Roman!'
Goscinny & Uderzo, *Asterix and the Big Fight*, trans. A. Bell & D. Hockridge,
London, Sydney and Auckland, Hodder Dargaud, 1971. First published in
French in 1966.

All right . . . all right . . . apart from the better sanitation and medicine **4** and education and irrigation and public health and roads and fresh-water system and baths and public order . . . what *have* the Romans done for *us*?

Graham Chapman et al., *Monty Python's Life of Brian*, London, Methuen, 1979, p. 20.

5   [The empire] did not become a single, uniform culture shared by all of its members; rather, it embraced a number of distinct local cultures governed by a small aristocracy, most of its members being only partially Romanized, with deep local roots flourishing beneath the veneer of a common identity as a class. It seems doubtful, also, that the Roman Empire ever became a nation even in the more limited sense of a people who perceived themselves and each other all to be members of a single shared community. Although these various circumstances – the absence of a model of national identity for Roman subjects, Rome's heavy reliance on local élites for adminis-tration, and the paucity of resources for communication outside traditional lines of authority – minimized sources of conflict within the empire, they also limited the formation of a larger, national identity and solidarity.

Gary B. Miles, 'Roman and modern imperialism: a reassessment', *Comparative Studies in Society and History*, 32 (1990), p. 656.

ROME, EARLY

See also NIEBUHR

1   In my experience the most commonly advanced justification for neglecting the early centuries of Roman history is that the evidence is too uncertain. The written accounts were all produced centuries after the events they purport to describe, and there is no way of ascertaining the truth of most of what they say. In the absence of any contemporary sources, so the argument runs, the history of Rome before the Punic Wars cannot be written. There is enough truth in this formulation to make it plausible, but one of the purposes of this book is to show that the situation is not nearly as bad as that.

T.J. Cornell, *The Beginnings of Rome: Italy and Rome from the Bronze Age to the Punic Wars (c. 1000–264 BC)*, London and New York, Routledge, 1995, p. xv.

2   The dreadful, inescapable fact is that there was no written history of

138

Rome before about 200 B.C. Every one of the *auctores* on whose work Livy and Dionysius (etc.) depend for their narratives was writing after that date. So two questions have to be squarely faced. First, how much of what Livy and Dionysius (etc.) present to us was *created* by their predecessors? And second, even assuming that what they offer represents what Fabius Pictor knew in 200 B.C., how much of *that* was accurately remembered or recorded from centuries before?

T.P. Wiseman, 'What do we know about early Rome?', *Journal of Roman Archaeology*, 9 (1996), pp. 311–12.

Much of what we read in the surviving sources about early Rome   **3** must be derived from oral tradition – that is to say, stories passed down by word of mouth from one generation to the next. This general point can be asserted with some confidence, simply because of the nature and form of the stories themselves. The legends of the Horatii and Curiatii, the dramatic narratives of Coriolanus, Cincinnatus and Verginia, and the whole saga of tales surrounding the rise and fall of the Tarquins, cannot possibly have been based to any great extent on documentary evidence; and while some elements may be of late literary origin, the majority certainly predate the earliest Roman literature. That the famous legends of early Rome were handed down orally is not only inherently probable, but virtually guaranteed by the absence of any serious alternative. It is also likely enough that many of them go back a long way. The most outstanding example is the foundation legend itself: that the story was already well known in the archaic period is proved by the famous bronze statue of a she-wolf, an archaic masterpiece which may be earlier than 500 BC.

Cornell, *Beginnings of Rome*, pp. 10–11.

Already in the fifth century BC, Etruscans and Latins were familiar   **4** with the she-wolf as a symbol of defiance, and with stories that involved wild beasts suckling human children. A story of a she-wolf suckling twins was known in fourth-century Praeneste, and evidently applied to her neighbour and successful rival, Rome. But Remus and Romulus are not yet identifiable . . . Provisionally, at least, it looks as if Remus and his twin brother are creations of the late fourth century BC.

T.P. Wiseman, *Remus: a Roman myth*, Cambridge, CUP, 1995, p. 76.

The burden of proof lies as heavily on those who wish to deny as on   **5** those who wish to affirm. Where there is no evidence either way the proper course is to suspend judgement. It is quite wrong to dismiss the

story of (e.g.) Verginia as fiction, simply because it cannot be shown to be based on fact. It cannot be shown to be fiction either.
Cornell, *Beginnings of Rome*, p. 11.

6   So what are we to conclude from all this? First, that Cornell is systematically optimistic about the likelihood of authentic history being transmitted in the literary tradition. Second, that it is also possible, and not (I think) intellectually disreputable, to be systematically pessimistic about it.
Wiseman, 'What do we know about early Rome?', p. 315.

SACRIFICE

See also RELIGION

1   Sacrifice lay at the heart of the majority of Greek religious rituals. But since it could take varying forms, it would be more appropriate to talk of sacrifices in the plural. However, one form in particular, which may be defined as 'bloody animal sacrifice of alimentary type', predominated within the collective civic practice of the ancient city. For this simultaneously gave expression to the bonds that tied the citizens one to another and served as a privileged means of communication with the divine world. In return the gods authorized and guaranteed the functioning of the human community, maintaining it in its proper station between and at a due distance from themselves and the animal kingdom respectively.
Louise Bruit Zaidman & Pauline Schmitt Pantel, *Religion in the Ancient Greek City*, trans. P. Cartledge, Cambridge, CUP, 1992, pp. 29–30. First published in French in 1989 by Armand Colin.

2   The myth connects the ritual of sacrifice to primordial events that have made men what they are, mortal creatures living on earth in the midst of countless ills, eating grain from the fields they have worked, and accompanied by female spouses. In other words, men have become a race of beings completely separated from those to whom at the outset they were very close, living together and sitting at the same tables to share the same meals – the Blessed Immortals, residing in heaven and fed on ambrosia, towards whom now rises the smoke of sacrificial offerings.
Jean-Pierre Vernant, 'At man's table: Hesiod's foundation myth of sacrifice', in M. Detienne & J.-P. Vernant, *The Cuisine of Sacrifice among the Greeks*,

trans. P. Wissing, Chicago and London, University of Chicago Press, 1989, p. 24. Copyright © 1989 by The University of Chicago. All rights reserved. First published in French in 1979.

Hunting behaviour became established and, at the same time, transfer- **3** able through ritualization. In this way it was preserved long after the time of the primitive hunter. This cannot be explained simply by the psychological mechanisms of imitation and imprinting, whereby customs are inherited. These rituals were indispensable because of the particular thing they accomplished. The only prehistoric and historic groups obviously able to assert themselves were those held together by the ritual power to kill. The earliest male societies banded together for collective killing in the hunt. Through solidarity and cooperative organization, and by establishing an inviolable order, the sacrificial ritual gave society its form.

Walter Burkert, *Homo Necans: the anthropology of ancient Greek sacrificial ritual and myth*, trans. P. Bing, Berkeley, Los Angeles and London, University of California Press, 1983, p. 35. First published in German in 1972.

SCIENCE AND PHILOSOPHY

Science is a modern category, not an ancient one: there is no one term **1** that is exactly equivalent to our 'science' in Greek. The terms *philosophia* (love of wisdom, philosophy), *episteme* (knowledge), *theoria* (contemplation, speculation) and *peri physeos historia* (inquiry concerning nature) are each used in particular contexts where the translation 'science' is natural and not too misleading. But although these terms may be used to refer to certain intellectual disciplines which we should think of as scientific, each of them *means* something quite different from our own term 'science'.

G.E.R. Lloyd, *Early Greek Science: Thales to Aristotle*, London, Chatto & Windus, 1970, p. xv.

It may surprise, and even enrage, some readers that there is a volume **2** on astrology in a series dedicated to the history of science. But this recategorisation of the subject is necessary to jolt us out of our preconceptions. It leads to questions about what 'science' means in the context of a history of the ancient world . . .

Little produced in antiquity could be accepted as scientific by modern standards, but there was a form of proto-science which could be seen to lie beneath the edifice of modern science. So, once the highlights, from Democritean atomic theory to the discovery of the

Fallopian tubes, had been set out, interest centred on seeing how the rules of enquiry developed the beginnings of a scientific culture. Astrology has always been a very poor relation in studies of ancient science. Because the same word *astronomia*, or *astrologia*, was used until the sixth century more or less indiscriminately, and because the two subjects were closely intertwined at one level, astrology had to be mentioned. Astrological sources had to be used in the study of astronomy, one of the glories of ancient science. But it was rarely of interest in its own right, except to specialists outside the history of science, and until quite recently it was seen as an embarrassing lapse on the past of astronomers like Ptolemy that he should write on astrology as well, and appear to see the two as part of a single enquiry.

Tamsyn Barton, *Ancient Astrology*, London and New York, Routledge, 1994, p. 5.

3 The earliest philosopher was no longer a shaman. His role was to teach, to establish a school. What had been secrets for the shaman were divulged by the philosopher to a group of disciples. He extended what used to be the privilege of one exceptional individual to all who desired to enter his brotherhood.

Jean-Pierre Vernant, *Myth and Thought among the Greeks*, London, Boston, Melbourne and Henley, Routledge & Kegan Paul, 1983, p. 355. First published in French in 1965.

4 The dominant ideology among those who investigated nature was that of the life of pure research, and in view of the positive preference for non-utilitarian over utilitarian studies expressed by such writers as Plato and Aristotle, it is hardly surprising that the Greeks were often slow to consider, or entirely failed to notice, whether their theoretical knowledge could be put to practical use.

Lloyd, *Early Greek Science*, p. 136.

5 Verdenius observed that there were three ways in which the shackles of philosophy prevented science from flourishing: (a) the Greek scientist was more interested in his own philosophical speculations than in experimentation and these speculations were not considered hypotheses, to be tested experimentally; (b) he was more concerned in the reason for phenomena than in describing them; (c) more attention was paid to the 'qualitative' aspect of things than to the quantitative one. Any experiments carried out were usually intended as confirmation of preconceived theories, and moreover the experimental

design was often too oversimplified to warrant the occasionally far-reaching conclusions drawn from it.

H.W. Pleket, 'Technology and society in the Graeco-Roman world', *Acta Historiae Neerlandica*, 2 (1967), Brill, Leiden, The Netherlands, p. 2; summarising W.J. Verdenius, 'Science grecque et science moderne', *Revue Philosophique*, 152 (1962).

In other areas of the life sciences, too, the claim of Greek work to be **6** more than recorded popular notions must chiefly rest on the same two elements we have identified – of critical analysis and of research. Yet we must both refine these two criteria and mark the limitations of the Greek performance, when they are applied. To begin with, not only is learning from experience a universal feature of human behaviour, but trial and error procedures are common in a wide range of contexts some of which are relevant to the acquisition of knowledge about what we should call natural phenomena. Research implies a more deliberate enquiry, often one carried out to test a well-defined idea or theory. But if we allow, as we surely should, that research may have practical, not just theoretical ends – for example in medicine – then the distinctions between those who first tried out trepanning, or hellebore, to see whether they would help in therapy, and those (like Galen) who investigated the nervous system in detail by dissection, are matters of degree rather than of kind, a question of how systematic and how sustained the investigation was.

When we turn to the Greek performance in research, the actual practice of many writers falls far short of the ideals they profess when they describe their aims and methods. To listen to some Hippocratic writers, the practice of medicine depended on the most wide-ranging and meticulous collection of data and the scrupulous avoidance of preconceived opinions. Yet not only are their theoretical preoccupations often much in evidence, but their observations in some fields are unimpressive, not to say slap-dash.

G.E.R. Lloyd, *Science, Folklore and Ideology: studies in the life sciences in ancient Greece*, Cambridge, CUP, 1983, pp. 205–6.

SLAVES AND SLAVERY

See also LABOUR, FREEDMEN

It is now time to try to add all this up and form some judgement about **1** the institution. This would be difficult enough to do under ordinary circumstances; it has become almost impossible because of two extraneous factors imposed by modern society. The first is the confusion of the historical study with moral judgements about slavery. We condemn slavery, and we are embarrassed for the Greeks, whom we admire so much; therefore we tend either to underestimate its role in their life, or we ignore it altogether, hoping that somehow it will quietly go away. The second factor is more political, and it goes back at least to 1848, when the *Communist Manifesto* declared that 'The history of all hitherto existing society is the history of class struggles. Free man and slave, patrician and plebeian, lord and serf, guild-master and journeyman, in a word, oppressor and oppressed, stood in constant opposition to one another.' Ever since, ancient slavery has been a battleground between Marxists and non-Marxists, a political issue rather than a historical phenomenon.

M.I. Finley, 'Was Greek civilization based on slave labour?', in Finley, *Economy and Society in Ancient Greece*, B.D. Shaw & R. Saller (eds), London, Chatto & Windus, 1981, p. 111.

2   Slavery existed throughout the history of antiquity side by side with free labor as a constant factor of the changing social and economic order. Both by masters and by slaves it was regarded as an inevitable and unavertable condition. In his discussion of the origins of the state at the beginning of the *Politics*, Aristotle gives the connections between master and slave, husband and wife, father and children as the three fundamental social expressions of the relationship between rulers and ruled in any organized society. His decision that the master-slave relation is consistent with nature stands in opposition to another philosophic explanation which regarded slavery as expedient, but justified only by man-made law, not by nature. Neither Aristotle nor those he opposed conceived the possibility of the abolition of slavery, the discussion being merely an academic one regarding the genesis of the institution. This attitude of complete acceptance of slavery, despite the continuance of the debate as to its genesis in nature or through human agency, is characteristic of the literary attitude toward it as an institution throughout antiquity.

W.L. Westermann, *The Slave Systems of Greek and Roman Antiquity*, Philadelphia, American Philosophical Society, 1955, p. 1.

3   Only with the development of capitalism did wage labour emerge as the characteristic form of labour for others. *Labour power* then became one of the main commodities in the market-place. With slavery, in contrast, the *labourer himself* is the commodity. The slave is in that

respect unique among types of labour despite overlapping with, for example, the most oppressive kinds of serfdom or with convict labour. The slave and the free wage-labourer thus stand at the extreme poles of labour for others, but historically the important contrast is rather between slaves and other types of compulsory labour. As institutionalized systems of organizing labour, other kinds of involuntary labour preceded chattel slavery, and both preceded (and then coexisted with) free hired labour.

M.I. Finley, *Ancient Slavery and Modern Ideology*, London, Chatto & Windus, 1980, pp. 68–9.

Only a handful of human societies can properly be called 'slave **4** societies', if by slave society we mean a society in which slaves play an important part in production and form a high proportion (say over 20%) of the population. There are only two well established cases from antiquity: classical Athens and Roman Italy.

Keith Hopkins, *Conquerors and Slaves: sociological studies in Roman history I*, Cambridge, CUP, 1978, p. 99.

An Athenian had to be decidedly poor not to have a slave. The **5** crippled client of Lysias (24.6) excuses his continuing to work at his trade while claiming public support because he is unable as yet (*oupo*) to acquire a slave to take his place. Few if any hoplites could have been without slaves. We cannot say how much farther down the social scale slave ownership went but it seems inescapable that the majority of Athenian households had one or more servile members and that, whatever the percentages between slave and free, to have slave help was considered the norm.

M.H. Jameson, 'Agriculture and slavery in classical Athens', *Classical Journal*, 73 (1977), pp. 122–3.

Some ordinary peasants may have had a slave, male or female, who **6** lived as part of the family and shared in all its activities; but we should not underestimate how difficult it would have been for a peasant family, living always close to the margin – and this would include not just the poorest but the many who had holdings of a few acres – and typically 'underemployed', to solve its problems of subsistence by adding to the household yet more permanent and alien mouths to feed.

Ellen Meiksins Wood, *Peasant-Citizen and Slave: the foundations of Athenian democracy*, London and New York, Verso, 1988, p. 63.

145

7   We can appreciate Greek slavery as due both to that vitality which demanded that a man have a complete and active life even at the expense of others, and also to that way of thinking which looks on power not as the aimless discharge of brute force but rather as a rational instrument to bring about order . . . These forces fundamental to Hellenism succeeded in wresting the miraculous creation of the *polis* and its civilization from the poverty of the land, the inclemency of its climate and the opposition of a hostile world. Slavery and its attendant loss of humanity were part of the sacrifice which had to be paid for this achievement.

Joseph Vogt, *Ancient Slavery and the Ideal of Man*, trans. T. Wiedemann, Oxford, Basil Blackwell, 1974, p. 25. First published in German in 1965.

8   Nor does my critique of the moralistic approach imply an end to moral judgments. I return to the rhetorical question I posed earlier, about Wallon: What difference did it make to him whether Athens had 100,000, 200,000 or 400,000 slaves? Was the evil less if there were only 100,000? I see no validity in an ethical system that holds such a question to be meaningful, any more than in Vogt's belief that detailed research will one day produce a moral calculus with which to determine whether slavery 'was a beneficial growth or a malignant cancer on the ancient body politic'. Slavery is a great evil: there is no reason why a historian should not say that, but to say only that, no matter with how much factual backing, is a cheap way to score a point on a dead society to the advantage of our own: 'retrospective indignation is also a way to justify the present'. The present-day moralistic approach has taken a different turn. It starts from the high evaluation of ancient culture and then tries to come to terms with its most troublesome feature, slavery. Anyone who clings to the cause of neo-classicism or classical humanism has little room for manoeuvre, except in the way he prefers to abate the nuisance of ancient slavery.

Finley, *Ancient Slavery and Modern Ideology*, p. 64.

9   The literature of the Athenians proves that they not only cultivated, but counted on finding, moral virtues in their slaves, which is not consistent with the worst form of slavery. Neither, in Greece, did slavery produce that one of its effects by which, above all, it is an obstacle to improvement – that of making bodily labour dishonourable. Nowhere in Greece, except at Sparta, was industry, however mechanical, regarded as unworthy of a freeman, or even of a citizen; least of all at Athens, in whose proudest times a majority of the Demos consisted of free artisans. Doubtless, however, in Greece as elsewhere,

slavery was an odious institution; and its inherent evils are in no way lessened by the admission, that as a temporary fact, in an early and rude state of the arts of life, it may have been, nevertheless, a great accelerator of progress.
John Stuart Mill, 'Grote's History of Greece II', in *Collected Works Vol. VII*, J.M. Robson (ed.), Buffalo, University of Toronto Press, 1978, p. 315.

It seems to me that, seeing all this, if we could emancipate ourselves **10** from the despotism of extraneous moral, intellectual and political pressures, we would conclude, without hesitation, that slavery was a basic element in Greek civilization.
Finley, 'Was Greek civilization based on slave labour?', p. 111.

Take away the barbarian slaves, and one would have been left with a **11** very different Classical Greek world, not only materially but mentally and even spiritually.
Paul Cartledge, *The Greeks: a portrait of self and others*, Oxford, Oxford University Press, 1993, p. 128.

The distinction between free and slave was one of the most funda- **12** mental and determining antitheses in the structures of thought and moral values of the Athenians (and probably of other Greeks). This polarity played a significant part in the Athenians' formation of their identities and ideals as free and independent men, and, as Greeks, more fully free and advanced than all foreigners. It also profoundly affected their attitudes and moral judgements over a whole range of economic, social and sexual matters. In these senses, then, slavery was undoubtedly a fundamental feature of Athenian society.
N.R.E. Fisher, *Slavery in Classical Greece*, Bristol, Bristol Classical Press, 1993, p. 108.

The underlying cause of the revolts of the Helots, as of servile revolt **13** everywhere, was the simple fact that they wanted to be free. But the Helots were only *able* to revolt outright because their ethnic and political solidarity provided the Messenians with the appropriate ideological inspiration and organizational cohesion, and because their numerical, geographical and international situation gave them (and Sparta's enemies) the requisite room for manoeuvre and ultimately justified hope of success.

These conditions did not obtain for the chattel slaves of Classical Greece. That they did not to our knowledge revolt is not therefore a sign that they were mostly happy with their unsought lot but rather a mark of the success with which their owners conducted a conscious and unremitting class struggle against them.

P.A. Cartledge, 'Rebels and *sambos* in classical Greece: a comparative view', in P.A. Cartledge & F.D. Harvey (eds), *Crux: studies presented to G.E.M. de Ste Croix on his 75th birthday*, London, Duckworth, 1985, p. 46.

14 It seems that the life of the slave alternated between rewards and punishments which depended on the proclivities of individual slave-owners. Immediate rewards such as holidays and privileges of a deeper significance such as the capacity to establish and maintain a family or to aspire towards and achieve manumission were offset by slaves' periodic subjection to physical pain and suffering. It follows from this state of affairs that the slave was never able to take anything for granted, so that in consequence his submission was guaranteed: rewards and privileges provided incentives towards compliant industry, punishment added the spur when necessary and quite literally beat down the slave's independence.

K.R. Bradley, *Slaves and Masters in the Roman Empire: a study in social control*, Tournai, Latomus, 1984, p. 140.

15 This type of slave can therefore be considered without peer as the most important technological invention of antiquity . . . We may ask ourselves whether there has ever existed, before the computer or the robot, a mechanism more perfectly intelligent and automatic than the slave. Of course it needs to be regulated by *monitores* [instructors] and *vilici* [bailiffs], but what complex instrument does not need to be supervised?

Andrea Carandini, 'Quando la dimora dello strumento è l'uomo', in Carandini, *Schiavi in Italia: gli strumenti pensanti dei Romani fra tarda Repubblica e medio Impero*, Rome, Nuova Italia Scientifica, 1988, pp. 302–3. Trans. N. Morley.

16 Considerations of efficiency, productivity, profitability, played little part if any in the creation of a slave society in Greece or Rome.

Finley, *Ancient Slavery and Modern Ideology*, p. 92.

17 If great improvements are seldom to be expected from great proprietors, they are least of all to be expected when they employ slaves for their workmen. The experience of all ages and nations, I believe, demonstrates that the work done by slaves, though it appears to cost only their maintenance, is in the end the dearest of any. A person who can acquire no property can have no other interest but to eat as much and to labour as little as possible.

Adam Smith, *An Inquiry into the Nature and Causes of the Wealth of Nations* [1776], R.H. Campbell & A.S. Skinner (eds), Oxford, OUP, 1976, pp. 387–8.

The slave mode of production was by no means devoid of technical progress; as we have seen, its extensive ascent in the West was marked by some significant agricultural innovations, in particular the introduction of the rotary mill and the screw press. But its dynamic was a very restricted one, since it rested essentially on the annexation of labour rather than the exploitation of land or the accumulation of capital; thus unlike either the feudal or capitalist modes of production which were to succeed it, the slave mode of production possessed very little objective impetus for technological advance, since its labour-additive type of growth constituted a structural field ultimately resistant to technical innovations . . . The boundaries of the Roman agrarian economy were soon reached, and rigidly fixed. **18**

Perry Anderson, *Passages from Antiquity to Feudalism*, London, New Left Books, 1974, p. 79.

The qualitative performance of slave labour is the essential point from which to proceed to a consideration of its efficiency and profitability, and hence of the choices available to the employers of labour in antiquity. This is a subject bedevilled by dogma and pseudo-issues, most of them growing out of moral judgements. There is a long line of writers, of the most varied political coloration, who assert that slave labour is inefficient, at least in agriculture, and ultimately unprofitable. This suggestion would have astonished Greek and Roman slave-owners, who not only went on for many centuries fondly believing that they were making substantial profits out of their slaves but also spending those profits lavishly. **19**

M. I. Finley, *The Ancient Economy*, London, Hogarth Press, 2nd edn 1985, p. 83.

One of the main functions of slavery was that it allowed the elite to increase the discrepancy between rich and poor without alienating the free citizen peasantry from their willingness to fight in wars for the further expansion of the empire; slavery also allowed the rich to recruit labour to work their estates in a society which had no labour market; and it permitted ostentatious display, again without the direct exploitation of the free poor. **20**

Hopkins, *Conquerors and Slaves*, p. 14.

21   To Marxist historians the periodization of history into ancient, medieval and modern is arbitrary and futile. As the modes of production are the all–important element, five eras are distinguishable in history: the archaic, prestate period of primitive communism; the period of slavery; the feudal era; the capitalist era; and the socialist era. Slavery was not only a necessary step in the development of humanity, but was also at a certain point, an element of progress (notwithstanding all the pain and suffering which were the lot of slaves) making possible the transition from a more primitive stage to a more advanced one. Slavery was the only possible way of centralizing the means of production on a large scale in a pretechnological society.

Zvi Yavetz, *Slaves and Slavery in Ancient Rome*, New Brunswick and Oxford, Transaction, 1988, p. 123. Reprinted by permission of Transaction Publishers. Copyright © 1988 by Transaction, Inc.; all rights reserved.

22   The history of nations knows not a few revolutions. But those revolutions differ from the October Revolution in that all of them were one–sided revolutions. One form of exploitation of the working people was replaced by another form of exploitation, but exploitation itself remained . . . The revolution of the slaves eliminated the slave-owners and abolished the slave form of exploitation of the toilers. But in their place it set up the serf owners and the serf form of exploitation of the toilers. One set of exploiters was replaced by another set of exploiters.

Joseph Stalin, *Speech delivered at the First All-Union Congress of Collective-Farm Shock Brigades, 19th February 1933*, in Stalin, *Works, Volume 13*, London, Lawrence & Wishart, 1955, p. 245.

23   The Roman slave wars were not revolutionary mass movements in any sense, but to a large extent historical accidents precipitated by a combination of circumstances that never again reappeared in the long history of slavery in the Roman world.

Keith R. Bradley, *Slavery and Rebellion in the Roman World, 140 B.C.–70 B.C.*, Bloomington and Indianapolis, Indiana University Press, and London, Batsford, 1989, p. 126.

24   'Decline' is a dangerous word. Slavery is not a moral category, comparable to good manners or honesty; it is an institution performing various functions, in particular that of providing an important part of the labour supply. So long as that labour is needed, slavery cannot decline *tout court*; it has to be replaced. I believe the impression to be correct that the Roman Empire eventually saw a slow, quantitative decline in slaves, though recent research shows that

the amount of the drop was far less than used to be thought (and is still too often repeated). If so, a changeover was presumably taking place in the status and organization of labour. But where? in which sector or sectors of the labour force? 'Location' is as central to the decline of slavery as it was to its establishment.
Finley, *Ancient Slavery and Modern Ideology*, pp. 126–7.

But if we accept that there was some growth in tenancy as the Empire **25** progressed, was the change so great and what are the implications of this for the employment of slaves? To start with, slaves as tenants or quasi-*coloni* and absentee landlords or tenants-in-chief were not a new development of the Later Roman Empire. Tenancy of all types, including that by slaves, was a norm rather than an exception, side by side with villa-based production, that had a long history stretching back to the Republic. One did not evolve from the other. Neither was tenancy linked necessarily to a shortage of slaves.
C. R. Whittaker, 'Circe's Pigs: from slavery to serfdom in the Later Roman world', in M.I. Finley (ed.), *Classical Slavery*, London, Frank Cass & Co., 1987, p. 92.

SOCRATES

He was a critic of Athens and of her democratic institutions, and **1** in this he may have borne a superficial resemblance to some of the leaders of the reaction against the open society. But there is no need for a man who criticises democracy and democratic institutions to be their enemy, although both the democrats he criticises, and the totalitarians who hope to profit from any disunion in the democratic camp, are likely to brand him as such. There is a fundamental difference between a democratic and a totalitarian criticism of democracy. Socrates' criticism was a democratic one, and indeed of the kind that is the very life of democracy.
Karl Popper, *The Open Society and its Enemies*, London, Routledge & Kegan Paul, 3rd edn 1957, p. 189.

Plato, his most gifted disciple, was soon to prove the least faithful. He **2** betrayed Socrates, just as his uncles had done. These, besides betraying Socrates, had also tried to implicate him in their terrorist acts, but they did not succeed, since he resisted. Plato tried to implicate Socrates in his grandiose attempt to construct the theory of the arrested society; and he had no difficulty in succeeding, for Socrates was dead.
Ibid., p. 194.

3 The regime of philosopher kings is usually ridiculed and regarded as totalitarian, but it contains much of what we really want. Practically everyone wants reason to rule, and no one thinks a man like Socrates should be ruled by inferiors or have to adjust what he thinks to them.
Allan Bloom, *The Closing of the American Mind*, New York, Simon & Schuster, 1987, p. 266.

4 Plato's hero lived and died by his principles. The historical, like the Platonic, Socrates would have found it repugnant to plead a principle in which he did not believe; free speech for him was the privilege of the enlightened few, not of the benighted many. He would not have wanted the democracy he rejected to win a moral victory by setting him free.

His martyrdom, and the genius of Plato, made him a secular saint, the superior man confronting the ignorant mob with serenity and humor. This was Socrates' triumph and Plato's masterpiece. Socrates needed the hemlock, as Jesus needed the Crucifixion, to fulfil a mission. The mission left a stain forever on democracy. That remains Athens' tragic crime.
I.F. Stone, *The Trial of Socrates*, London, Jonathan Cape, 1988, p. 230.

SPARTA

1 Ancient Sparta: a militaristic and totalitarian state, holding down an enslaved population, the helots, by terror and violence, educating its young by a system incorporating all the worst features of the traditional English public school, and deliberately turning its back on the intellectual and artistic life of the rest of Greece. Such, at least, is the picture, if any, which mention of the name consciously or unconsciously conjures up in the minds of most people in this country today. The liberal democratic tradition that dominates modern English thought has very naturally tended to idealize Sparta's great rival, democratic Athens; and its consequent distrust of Sparta was reinforced by reaction against a very different set of political ideas, particularly prominent in Germany, where admiration of Sparta reached a fantastic conclusion under the Nazis; to some writers, at that time, Sparta was the most purely Nordic state in Greece, and an example of National Socialist virtues. Two hundred years ago, however, an ordinary educated Englishman would most probably have viewed the Spartan constitution as a prototype of the British limited monarchy in all its perfection; his French contemporary might have been one of those who revered her, with Rousseau and others, primarily as an egalitarian, more or less communistic, republic. Two hundred years before that, she appeared in still other guises; as the ideal aristocratic republic, for example, practically indistinguishable from Venice.

Elizabeth Rawson, *The Spartan Tradition in European Thought*, Oxford, OUP, 1969, p. 1.

Classical Sparta was renowned for the skill and courage of her army **2** and for the stability and excellence of her constitution. Both, it was thought, she owed to the genius of one man, Lykourgos, who, far back in her history, had created all those institutions which made Sparta and the Spartans what they were. There was a large element of myth in this simple picture; Lykourgos adapted as much as he created and much of what he produced had been altered or even superseded long before fifth- or fourth-century scholars began to study their contemporary 'Lykourgan' Sparta; Lykourgos himself is a shadowy, possibly even a mythical figure – those same scholars found less evidence for his life than for his works; and the antiquity of his system had been grossly exaggerated. And yet the picture had substantial elements of truth in it . . . In a world where individual law-givers abounded by revolution by committee is unknown, the chances are that Sparta owed her new look to a single hand.

W.G. Forrest, *A History of Sparta 950–192 BC*, London, Hutchinson, 1968, p. 40.

Two overlapping and mutually reinforcing aspects of the 'Spartan **3** mirage' have played havoc with our evidence for early Spartan political history. The first in point of time and significance was the 'Lykourgos legend', which held that Sparta was the paradigm of a state owing all its institutions to the legislative enactments of a single lawgiver – in this case to the wondrously omniprovident Lykourgos, for whom dates ranging (in our terms) from the twelfth to the eighth centuries were offered. The second distorting aspect of the 'mirage' was the theory of the 'mixed constitution', developed perhaps in the fifth century but not apparently applied to Sparta until the fourth. This theory contended that the best, because most stable, form of state was either one which combined ingredients from each of the basic constitutional types (monarchy, aristocracy/oligarchy, democracy) in a harmonious whole (the 'pudding' version) or one in which the different elements acted as checks and balances to each other (the 'seesaw' version). The combined effect – and, no doubt, the object – of the 'Lykourgos legend' and the theory of the 'mixed constitution' was to suggest that Sparta had achieved an internal political equilibrium considerably earlier than could in fact have been the case.

Paul Cartledge, *Sparta and Lakonia: a regional history 1300–362 B.C.*, London, Boston and Henley, Routledge & Kegan Paul, 1979, pp. 131–3.

4   The major determining fact about Sparta, which in the last analysis affects every other aspect, is the existence of a large subject population of helots and Messenians . . . To this permanent threat, the peculiar Spartan training, the *agoge*, and Spartan discipline in general are designed to provide and answer.

David M. Lewis, *Sparta and Persia*, Leiden, Brill, 1977, pp. 27, 29.

5   Being equal meant sharing a common, well defined life-cycle, including: (1) a common, formalised, compulsory upbringing designed to inculcate obedience, valour, discipline and professional military skill; (2) a single vocation or profession, that of a hoplite soldier or officer; (3) economic security and complete freedom from economic concerns, all productive and ancillary services being provided by two distinct categories of dependants, helots and *perioikoi*; (4) a public (rather than private) life in an all-male community, with maximum conformity and anti-individualism.

Structurally, however, the system then generated two further, unavoidable, closely interrelated inequalities apart from those inherent in each child at birth. One was the inequality, not very tangible but none the less real, that followed from inequality of performance, whether in the *agoge* or in games and hunting or in war. The other arose from the need for leadership and elites, not only at the top (kings, ephors and council of elders), but also in the smaller military units, and, because of the Spartan *agoge*, in the age-classes beginning at a remarkably early age. Xenophon's 'love of victory' (*philonikia*) produced losers as well as winners, a self-evident fact which is often overlooked by modern scholars, who then write as if everyone passed through every stage a prizewinner.

M.I. Finley, 'Sparta and Spartan society', in Finley, *Economy and Society in Ancient Greece*, B.D. Shaw & R. Saller (eds), London, Chatto & Windus, 1981, p. 27.

6   The female citizen population of Sparta – or so it has seemed to non-Spartan males from at least the sixth century B.C. – enjoyed the extraordinary and perhaps unique distinction of both being 'in society' and yet behaving in a (to them) socially unacceptable manner.

Paul Cartledge, 'Spartan wives: liberation or licence?', *Classical Quarterly*, 31 (1981), p. 85. Reprinted by permission of Oxford University Press and the Classical Association.

Leading Spartiates ignored the economic problems of poorer citizens,   **7**
and the unity and identity of purpose among the *homoioi* created
by the seventh-century compromise over landownership finally broke
down. The rich became richer, while poorer families lost their citizen
status and Spartiate numbers continued their rapid decline. After her
defeat at Leuktra Sparta had insufficient manpower to prevent the
Thebans from liberating Messenia or to regain it afterwards. From
being the leading power in sixth-century Greece, a position created
and sustained by her large population among whom land was shared
with a modicum of fairness such that each family possessed at least an
adequate sufficiency, Sparta declined by the second quarter of the
fourth century to the level of a second-rate *polis* with a minute citizen
body rent by socio-economic divisions.
Stephen Hodkinson, 'Inheritance, marriage and demography: perspectives
upon the success and decline of classical Sparta', in A. Powell (ed.), *Classical
Sparta: techniques behind her success*, London, Routledge, 1989, p. 114.

STATE

See also ADMINISTRATION, TAXES

There is a strong temptation to describe all such distributions and   **1**
subventions as emanating from the abstract 'state', but the temptation
must be firmly resisted. The 'state' did not exist as an abstraction
for the citizens. It was not the 'state' which distributed money to
Athenians who wished to attend performances at the theatre during
the festivals of Dionysus, in the same way as Social Security pays out
sickness benefits; what happened was that the Athenians redistributed
among themselves part of the revenues of the community.
M.M. Austin & P. Vidal-Naquet, *Economic and Social History of Ancient Greece:
an introduction*, trans. M.M. Austin, London, Batsford, 1977, p. 120. First
published in French in 1972 by Armand Colin.

Even in peacetime it is illuminating to look at government through   **2**
the eyes of those subject to it. What did it do? It took one's money
away. That was the apparent object of its existence, that was certainly
the bulk of its business.

Ramsay MacMullen, *Roman Government's Response to Crisis*, New Haven and London, Yale University Press, 1976, p. 197.

3   There were two kinds of service that the Roman state needed to have done and could not perform for itself. One was the provision of supplies – for religious ritual, for the army, for secular civic purposes (e.g. public buildings), all needed so that the state should perform its proper minimal duties. Of course, these supplies had to be paid for, as soon as the state as such was more than the circle of aristocratic families composing its governing class. And so the state needed money to pay for the essential state services. With the state machinery minimal, both sides of the public ledger were at least to some extent in private hands. What must be repeated . . . is that this is perfectly simple and neither surprising nor – from any moral standpoint – reprehensible. Just as some modern states regard all (and all modern states regard some, and indeed an increasing number) of the economic operations of society as their proper sphere, even though practical considerations temper whatever the ideal happens to be, so the early Roman Republic did not regard economic operations as, in principle, in its sphere at all – even though, for reasons that nobody bothered to expound in theoretical form, some were traditionally exercised.
E. Badian, *Publicans and Sinners: private enterprise in the service of the Roman Republic*, Oxford, Basil Blackwell, 1972, p. 15.

4   The later Roman empire was before all things a bureaucratic state. Civil servants played a vital role in all departments of government, in the drafting and circulation of laws and ordinances and the administration of justice, in the recruitment and supply of the armies, and above all in the operation of the vast and complicated fiscal machine . . . Without its civil servants the whole complicated machinery of government which held the vast empire together would have collapsed.
A. H. M. Jones, *The Later Roman Empire 284–602*, Oxford, Basil Blackwell, 1964, p. 512.

TAXES

See also STATE, EUERGETISM

1   Direct and regular taxes on the property of citizens and especially their persons were usually avoided; they were felt to be degrading. Tyrants

resorted to them occasionally, but cities with republican-type constitutions abolished them as far as possible. By contrast there was no hesitation in taxing non-citizens . . . But if regular taxes on citizens and their property were felt to be unacceptable, the city had all the same to make use of the wealth of its members. Here a convenient way round was available, in that it was an accepted principle in Greek cities that the wealthier citizens had a moral obligation to spend their wealth for the public good. This obligation, although unwritten, was strongly felt and consequently impossible to avoid altogether.

M.M. Austin & P. Vidal-Naquet, *Economic and Social History of Ancient Greece: an introduction*, trans. M.M. Austin, London, Batsford, 1977, p. 121. First published in French in 1972 by Armand Colin.

The ancient world never achieved the notion of an income tax. Even **2** if they had thought of it, their accounting methods were too primitive to distinguish income from capital.

A.H.M. Jones, 'Taxation in antiquity', in Jones, *The Roman Economy: studies in ancient economic and administrative history*, P.A. Brunt (ed.), Oxford, Basil Blackwell, 1974, p. 175.

The first proposition is that the Romans' imposition of taxes paid in **3** money greatly increased the volume of trade in the Roman empire (200 B.C.–A.D. 400). Secondly, in so far as money taxes were levied on conquered provinces and then spent in other provinces or in Italy, then the tax-exporting provinces had to earn money with which to pay their taxes by exporting goods of an equal value.

Keith Hopkins, 'Taxes and trade in the Roman Empire (200 B.C.–A.D. 400)', *Journal of Roman Studies*, 70 (1980), p. 101.

Even at local levels, the Roman imposition of money taxes and their **4** expenditure outside the region where they were levied had a serious impact on simple cultivators; they were forced to produce, and to sell, more food in order to pay taxes. The impact was greatest in those regions in which simple cultivators had paid little or no tax in money before the Roman conquest. There, cultivators were forced to produce and sell a surplus which they had not previously produced, or which they had previously consumed themselves (afterwards they simply went without).

Ibid., p. 101.

We can locate a few cases in which provinces appear to have paid **5** tax in money, a few in which they were paid in kind, and one case

where the two forms appear together. But we cannot fill in the many
blanks by generalising from particular examples, or by appealing to a
supposed uniformity of practice imposed by Augustus.
Richard Duncan-Jones, *Structure and Scale in the Roman Economy*, Cambridge,
CUP, 1990, p. 197.

6   The effect of rising rates of taxation was thus that increasing areas of
marginal lands ceased to yield an adequate profit to their owners, and
finally became a burden instead of an asset. Owners of such land
naturally spent less and less on improving or maintaining their estates,
and tried to put up the rents, thereby driving their tenants into
overworking their land, and leaving them no margin for necessary
maintenance work. The evil effects of over-taxation were most evident in areas where there was much marginal land, and the assessment
took no account of variations in quality.
A.H.M. Jones, 'Over-taxation and the decline of the Roman empire', in *The
Roman Economy*, p. 87. First published in *Antiquity*, 33 (1959).

7   It would be naive to accept without question the complaints of
taxpayers, or even the apologies of a government which is introducing
a new form of taxation . . . Taxpayers have rarely been ready to admit
that the claims of the government are modest and reasonable. The
volume of their complaints, moreover, is usually governed not so
much by the relation of the sum demanded to their capacity to pay, as
by its relation to what they are accustomed to pay.
Ibid., p. 82.

TECHNOLOGY

See also TRANSPORT

1   Paradoxically, there was both more and less technical progress in the
ancient world than the standard picture reveals. There was more,
provided we avoid the mistake of hunting solely for great radical
inventions and we also look at developments within the limits of
the traditional techniques. There was less – far less – if we avoid the
reverse mistake and look not merely for the appearance of an
invention, but also for the extent of its employment.
M.I. Finley, 'Technical innovation and economic progress in the ancient
world', in Finley, *Economy and Society in Ancient Greece*, B.D. Shaw &
R. Saller (eds), London, Chatto & Windus, 1981, p. 176.

The superior productiveness of modern compared with ancient   2
labour depends, perhaps, principally on the use of these instruments.
We doubt whether all the exertions of all the inhabitants of the
Roman Empire, if exclusively devoted to the manufacture of cotton
goods, could, in a whole generation, have produced as great a quantity
as is produced every year by a portion of the inhabitants of Lancashire;
and we are sure that the produce would have been greatly inferior in
quality. The only moving powers employed by the Greeks or Romans
were the lower animals, water, and wind. And even these powers they
used very sparingly.
Nassau Senior, *Political Economy*, London, Richard Griffin & Co., 3rd edn
1854, p. 70.

It is probably fair to say that during most periods of the Graeco-   3
Roman era the climate of opinion was not entirely favourable to
technological progress. By and large the ancient world before the
Christian era was a backward-looking, pessimistic society which
tended to regard human history as a steady process of decline from a
golden age which it put firmly in a dim, distant past.
David W. Reece, 'The technological weakness of the ancient world', *Greece
and Rome*, 16 (1969), p. 34. Reprinted by permission of Oxford University
Press and the Classical Association.

The most important factors which are known to operate in a modern   4
industrial society in which mechanisation takes place ... (i) an
expanding market for the products of industry, served by a good
system of land and sea communications; (ii) close co-operation
between pure science and technology; (iii) plenty of capital and easy
ways of raising it; (iv) new and improved sources of power; (v) social
self-consciousness.
K.D. White, 'Technology and industry in the Roman empire', *Acta Classica*,
2 (1959), p. 82.

Every great culture produces, and gradually modifies, a technology   5
appropriate to its hierarchy of values.
L. White Jnr, 'Technological development in the transition from antiquity to
the Middle Ages', in *Tecnologia, Economia e Società nel Mondo Romano*, Como,
New Press, 1980, p. 235.

A further problem with most histories of technology is that only those   6
items that led to modern western 'high' technology are considered really
interesting. Anything military or mechanical is always valued above the

ingenuity of ordinary ceramics, textiles or basketwork, despite the greater benefit of the latter to a larger number of people. Likewise, almost everything is judged in terms of saving time and labour, which are unlikely to have been conceptualised, let alone commoditised, in anything like the same manner in pre-industrial societies.

Kevin Greene, 'The study of Roman technology: some theoretical constraints', in E. Scott (ed.), *Theoretical Roman Archaeology: first conference proceedings*, Aldershot, Avebury, 1993, p. 41.

7   It is undeniable that a horse wearing a padded collar pulling a cart with fully-turning front undercarriage would make progress along an uneven winding track, but does the technical equipment involved make that better than the performance of a lightly equipped horse and rigid vehicle operating on a straight, low-gradient Roman road whose hard surface offered much lower rolling resistance?

Kevin Greene, 'Technology and innovation in context: the Roman background to mediaeval and later developments', *Journal of Roman Archaeology*, 7 (1994), p. 33.

TRADE AND EXCHANGE

See also INDUSTRY, ECONOMY

1   The scale of inter-regional trade was very small. Overland transport was too expensive, except for the cartage of luxury goods. And even by sea, trade constituted only a very small proportion of gross product. That was partly because each region in the Mediterranean basin had a roughly similar climate and so grew similar crops. The low level of long-distance trade was also due to the fact that neither economies of scale nor investment in productive techniques ever reduced unit production costs sufficiently to compensate for high transport costs. Therefore, no region or town could specialize in the manufacture of cheaper goods; it could export only prestige goods, even overseas. And finally, the market for such prestige goods was necessarily limited by the poverty of most city-dwellers and peasants.

Keith Hopkins, 'Introduction', in P. Garnsey, K. Hopkins & C.R. Whittaker (eds), *Trade in the Ancient Economy*, London, Chatto & Windus/Hogarth Press, 1983, pp. xi–xii.

2   From time to time the world meets with situations that change commerce. Today the commerce of Europe is principally carried on

from north to south. However, the difference in climates makes people have a great need for each other's commodities. For example, the beverages of the South carried to the North form a kind of commerce scarcely pursued by the ancients. Thus the capacity of ships formerly measured by hogsheads of grain is measured today by casks of liquor.

As the ancient commerce that is known to us was from one Mediterranean port to another, it was almost entirely in the South. But, as peoples of the same climate have almost the same things, they do not need commerce with one another as much as do peoples of differing climates. Therefore, commerce in Europe was less extensive formerly than it is at present.

Montesquieu, *The Spirit of the Laws* [1748], trans & eds A.M. Cohler, B.C. Miller & H.S. Stone, Cambridge, CUP, 1989, p. 356.

In the systems of the past we do not find simple exchange of goods, **3** wealth and produce through markets established among individuals. For it is groups, and not individuals, which carry on exchange, make contracts, and are bound by obligations; the persons represented in the contracts are moral persons – clans, tribes, and families; the groups, or the chiefs as intermediaries for the groups, confront and oppose each other. Further, what they exchange is not exclusively goods and wealth, real and personal property, and things of economic value. They exchange rather courtesies, entertainments, ritual, military assistance, women, children, dances and feasts; and fairs in which the market is but one element and the circulation of wealth but one part of a wide and enduring contract.

Marcel Mauss, *The Gift* [1925], trans. I. Cunnison, Glencoe, The Free Press, 1954, p. 8. Reprinted by permission of Presses Universitaires de France and Routledge.

Polanyi's typology consisted of three forms of economic process: **4** reciprocity, redistribution and (market) exchange. Reciprocity, he defined as exchange or interaction between individuals or groups of broadly similar standing. Redistribution, by contrast, designates the role of some central agent or agency in handling exchange between individuals or groups. Polanyi implied that this agent or agency was appropriating some portion of that handled. Market exchange in his view involved everybody, each person finding his own level in which to interact within this all-embracing system.

Richard Hodges, *Primitive and Peasant Markets*, Oxford, Basil Blackwell, 1988, p. 10, summarising Karl Polanyi, 'The economy as instituted process', in K. Polanyi, C.W. Arensberg & H.W. Pearson (eds), *Trade and Market in the Early Empires: economies in history and theory*, Glencoe, The Free Press, 1957, pp. 250–6.

5   In many economies trade and commerce are associated with the market place. Yet, while in conventional economic analysis the market stands for a certain kind of exchange which functions independently of the culture by which it is surrounded, the ancient *agora* was firmly embedded in the value-system of the *polis*.
Sitta von Reden, *Exchange in Ancient Greece*, London, Duckworth, 1995, p. 105.

6   Business in the Greek city, it is agreed, was in the hands of a body of people who, though permanently resident in the city, were foreigners, and did not possess full civic status or political rights: and these resident aliens, furthermore, were first and foremost traders and manufacturers. How, then, is it possible to believe that the citizens themselves took an active part in the commerce and industry of the cities? How, indeed, can it be supposed that external commerce played a large part at all in the life of the Greek state? . . . If trade was in the hands of non-citizens that was because the citizens were not anxious to take an active part in it themselves.
Johannes Hasebroek, *Trade and Politics in Ancient Greece*, trans. L.M. Fraser & D.C. MacGregor, London, Bell, 1933, p. 22. First published in German in 1928.

7   The policy of isolation and exclusion, then, was not directed against commercial competition; nor was the opening of a market to the outside world designed to further the interests of citizen traders or to benefit national production. When a city abandoned its policy of isolation and involved itself in inter-city commerce, it had only two motives – the motives which governed its whole outlook upon commerce: the maintenance of necessary supplies, and the fiscal exploitation of such traffic as touched its shores.
Ibid., pp. 124–5.

8   The Greeks were well aware that imports and exports must, in the long run, somehow, balance . . . What then did they make to pay for these necessary imports? To this question we can unfortunately make no very satisfactory answer; but we can make certain things clear enough for the purposes of the present argument. We know that they exported olives and olive-oil; but we have no idea in what quantities

– that is, for what proportion of imports this sufficed. Also that they exported pottery . . .

A.W. Gomme, 'Traders and manufacturers in Greece', in Gomme, *Essays in Greek History and Literature*, Oxford, Basil Blackwell, 1937, p. 45.

Taken all together, the foreign trade was almost wholly a trade in luxuries and had no real importance for the economic life of the Empire. Of far greater moment was the internal trade of the Empire, the trade of Italy with the provinces and of the provinces with Italy. As in the Hellenistic period, it was mostly a trade in products of prime necessity.

9

M.I. Rostovtzeff, *The Social and Economic History of the Roman Empire*, rev. P.M. Fraser, Oxford, OUP, 2nd edn 1957, p. 67.

It is, however, hardly correct to affirm that Rome and Italy paid for the imported goods with the tribute which Rome received from the provinces. We have no statistics; but what can be gathered about the industrial productivity of Italy shows that the largest part of the import was covered by a corresponding export.

10

Ibid., pp. 69–70.

Has too much energy been wasted proving the self-evident fact that the rich sold or otherwise disposed of the produce of their estates for profit, whether directly themselves or through their own agents? Whereas what requires definition is the extent to which they made use of entrepreneurs also. I suspect that few middlemen were used.

11

C.R. Whittaker, 'Late Roman trade and traders', in Garnsey, Hopkins & Whittaker, *Trade in the Ancient Economy*, p. 179.

The diffusion of Dressel 1 amphorae (the main carriers of Italian wine) in the second and first centuries BC constitutes the most spectacular evidence of the export of agricultural produce from Italy in the ancient world.

12

André Tchernia, 'Italian wine in Gaul at the end of the Republic', in Garnsey, Hopkins & Whittaker, *Trade in the Ancient Economy*, p. 87.

Wine is used to obtain slaves in Europe and the Aegean, and the slaves are used to make the wine. One comes to exchange an amphora for a slave (but the modern era will know even worse cases). Italian wine now floods the throats, not only of the Italians but also of indigenous aristocracies. The quantity of wine exported is enormous, not in terms of absolute consumption . . . but in terms of maritime

13

commerce . . . As in any market to which access is largely forbidden (Carthage has now been destroyed, and for the people of Transalpine Gaul there is the interdict of 129), those in command are the astute producers rather than the still ignorant consumers. Thus we find ourselves before a true and proper monopoly . . .

The monopolistic protectionism, made possible also by the anti-bureaucratic fluidity of a variegated imperialism, not yet crystallised into an imperial state, sought to prevent a widening of the supply [of wine], which would have brought about the collapse of the overvaluation of wine and of Italian land, as a result of competition.

Andrea Carandini, 'L'economia italica fra tarda repubblica e medio impero considerata dal punto di vista di una merce: il vino', in *Amphores Romaines et Histoire Économique: dix ans de recherche*, Rome, École Française de Rome, 1989, p. 511. Trans. N. Morley.

14 It has been argued that pottery distributions can be used to help us evaluate the force and direction of commercial currents in the Roman world. This is not to claim that pottery was intrinsically important, but since it survives in the archaeological record it may be all that remains to indicate interaction concerned mainly with more valuable perishable commodities. Amphorae are different: they provide us not with an *index* of the transportation of goods, but with direct witness of the movement of certain foodstuffs which were of considerable economic importance, and which were an essential part of Roman culture.

D.P.S. Peacock & D.F. Williams, *Amphorae and the Roman Economy: an introductory guide*, London and New York, Longman, 1986, p. 2.

15 In sum, supplying the city of Rome involved food and goods of very high aggregate value (enough food for minimum subsistence alone was worth 65 million HS per year at farm-gate wheat prices). This food was transported in ships, each of which cost a lot (say 300,000 HS per 400 tonnes). The total capital value of ships involved in supplying the city of Rome alone probably equalled over 100 million HS, that is the minimum fortunes of 100 senators. The sums involved, especially in large ships, were so substantial that it was likely to have involved those Romans with substantial capital to invest and to put at risk . . . The total risk capital invested in trade and transport to Rome, and in the rest of the Mediterranean, was very large. It did not equal investment in land, either in size or in status, but because it was more risky, it was also probably more profitable to those who succeeded.

Keith Hopkins, 'Models, ships and staples', in P. Garnsey & C.R. Whittaker (eds), *Trade and Famine in Classical Antiquity*, Cambridge, Cambridge Philological Society, 1983, p. 102.

Jean Samuel Depont, Cicero, Tacitus, and Pliny have this in common, **16** that they exhibit an attitude which might be described as one of moral disdain for traders and men of commerce, and attach high value to agriculture, above all as a nonoccupation, a gentlemanly pursuit. Here are spokesmen from two sophisticated and complex civilizations, eighteen centuries apart but comparable in that both were preindustrial economies and stratified societies – which is to say, differences of status were marked and keenly noticed, frequently commented upon by the wealthy few, the persons who comprised the political and social elite. But the Roman evidence fails us in one particular in which the French is explicit: we do not have even one example of a Roman senator who, like Depont, deprecated traders but can be shown nevertheless to have trade in his own background: that is, condemns the very source of his family's wealth. And yet, if there were senators whose fortunes derived from *mercatura*, their adoption of a disdainful attitude is precisely what we might expect, owing to the familiar tendency for new members of any elite to assimilate and espouse the values and attitudes characteristic of their new station: it is difficult to think of a more eloquent spokesman for and dedicated defender of traditional senatorial values than M. Tullius Cicero, a *novus homo*.

John H. D'Arms, *Commerce and Social Standing in Ancient Rome*, Cambridge Mass. and London, Harvard University Press, 1981, p. 7. Copyright © 1981 by John H. D'Arms.

All this clearly proves that the economic life of the Roman empire was **17** continued into the Merovingian epoch throughout the Tyrrhenian basin; for there is no doubt that what was happening in Gaul happened also in Africa and in Spain.

All the features of the old economic life were there: the preponderance of Oriental navigation, the importation of Oriental products, the organization of the ports, of the *tonlieu* and the impost, the circulation and the minting of money, the lending of money at interest, the absence of small markets, and the persistence of a constant commercial activity in the cities, where there were merchants by profession. There was, no doubt, in the commercial domain as in other departments of life, a certain retrogression due to the 'barbarization' of manners, but there was no definite break with what had been the economic life of the Empire. The commercial activities of the Mediterranean continued with singular persistence.

Henri Pirenne, *Mohammed and Charlemagne*, trans. B. Miall, London, George Allen & Unwin, 1939, p. 116. First published in French, 10th edn 1937.

18   These glimpses of late Roman trade suggest two working hypotheses. First, the arrival of the 'barbarians' in the late fourth and fifth centuries damaged, but did not destroy, the commerce of the central and western Mediterranean: Rome continued to import oil and wine (and many other things) after the Gothic invasion; under the Vandals, Carthage may actually have experienced a boom in trade with the East; Luni was still receiving foreign goods in the sixth century . . . Secondly, however, the situation had changed completely by about 600: Carthage had virtually ceased trading with the East and at Luni imported luxuries disappeared.

Richard Hodges & David Whitehouse, *Mohammed, Charlemagne and the Origins of Europe: archaeology and the Pirenne thesis*, London, Duckworth, and Ithaca, Cornell University Press, 1983, p. 32.

TRANSPORT AND COMMUNICATION

1   Diocletian's tariff of prices gives us accurate information on the cost of transport. The authorised charge per miles for a wagon load of 1,200 lbs. is 20 denarii, for a camel load of 600 lbs. 8 denarii, for a donkey load 4 denarii. A *modius* of wheat, which is priced at 100 denarii, weighs 20 lbs., so that a wagon would carry 60 *modii* and a camel 30. A wagon load of wheat, therefore, costing 6,000 denarii, would be doubled in price by a journey of 300 miles, a camel load by a journey of 375 miles. Maritime rates are much cheaper, especially for long journeys.

A.H.M. Jones, *The Later Roman Empire 284–602*, Oxford, Basil Blackwell, 1964, p. 841.

2   Ancient fleets encountered a fair number of obstacles to sailing that remained largely unchanged until the appearance of the steamship. These were natural or human conditions, which determined both the times of sailing and the sea routes used.

Owing to general climatic conditions in the Mediterranean, there are two long seasons: what the Greeks called *cheimon* on the one hand, and *theios* on the other, the 'bad season' and the 'good season', each implying more than 'winter' and 'summer' respectively. Furthermore, the ends of these seasons did not coincide precisely with the ends of

the four seasons as determined by astronomy. *Cheimon* was characterized by unstable weather, making the prediction of storms or their
degree of violence impossible. During this period, sailing on the open
seas was not possible; only coastal sailing could be undertaken, and
even so, large-scale, commercial shipping was avoided. It was the time
the Romans quite typically called the *mare clausum*, the sea is closed
– and some texts add, 'to regular sailings'.

Jean Rougé, *Ships and Fleets of the Ancient Mediterranean*, Middletown, Conn.,
copyright © 1981 by Susan Frazer, translator; Wesleyan University Press by
permission of University Press of New England, pp. 15–16. First published in
French in 1975.

The ancient mariners of the Mediterranean can claim credit for most   **3**
of the major discoveries in ships and sailing that the western world
was to know until the age of steam. The details of this achievement –
the arrangements they hit upon for rowing war galleys, the rigs they
devised for merchantmen, the ways they worked out for assembling a
hull, and the like – make up a highly technical and specialized subject,
yet one that has an intimate connection with ancient man's day-to-day
experience. It is no accident that the west's first epic poet chose to sing
of a storm-tossed captain, its first historian and first dramatist to
highlight a crucial naval battle.

Lionel Casson, *Ships and Seamanship in the Ancient World*, Princeton,
Princeton University Press, 1971, p. vii. Copyright © 1971 by Casson, L.
Reprinted by permission of Princeton University Press.

Thalassocracy, thus, requires political and economic systems that can   **4**
consciously aim at naval control of sea lanes for the transport of useful
supplies and also of armies toward that end. Sea power must be able
to facilitate and protect a state's commerce and deny that of opposing
states, though in classical times the limited seakeeping qualities of
galleys severely restricted this role. Instead of viewing sea power as an
important element in the course of ancient history, we must expect it
to be a spasmodic factor, though at points it does indeed become a
critical force.

Chester G. Starr, *The Influence of Sea Power on Ancient History*, Oxford, OUP,
1989, pp. 5–6. Copyright © 1989 by Oxford University Press, Inc. Used by
permission of Oxford University Press, Inc.

The various forms of communication were complementary to each   **5**
other rather than competitive, and sometimes specialised in different
traffic. However, towards the end of the Roman period, movement

was tending to be by water, not by road. This brought about the decline of towns that were route centres, but not situated on rivers, with a consequent shift in urban life.

Raymond Chevallier, *Roman Roads*, trans. N.H. Field, London, Batsford, 1976, p. 200. First published in French in 1972 by Armand Colin.

6   The emperor typically lived and died in central Italy. This meant that Egypt was not well placed for hearing of any change at an early stage. Nevertheless journeys to Alexandria of 6 and 7 days from Puteoli were recorded, though only as exceptional events. Typical delays in Egyptian awareness of change of emperor turn out to have been much longer, suggesting that even urgent news in practice travelled slowly to provinces overseas.

The most direct route from Rome to the Egyptian interior involved one journey by sea and another by river. Occasionally the two stages can be separated. Galba's accession was known in Alexandria by 6 July, within 27 days of Nero's death on 9 June AD 68. The news had reached parts of the Thebaid within 14 days, but was still unknown in other parts on 8 August, 33 days later.

Richard Duncan-Jones, *Structure and Scale in the Roman Economy*, Cambridge, CUP, 1990, pp. 7–8.

7   The figure of Phidippides may dominate the modern idea of Greek news-carrying, but he represents only one aspect, albeit the most picturesque, of Greek systems for the dissemination of news. Organised systems of news, in which one can include the assembly, the herald and the official dispatch, were created in the Greek polis, but unofficial sources of news were equally significant, whether travellers, traders and partisans, or gossip and rumour. Instead of creating systems for gathering and disseminating news, poleis relied on individuals to provide them with the news they needed, and on their citizens to find their own sources of news.

Sian Lewis, *News and Society in the Greek Polis*, London, Duckworth, 1996, p. 155.

8   Access to information is a crucial determinant of political power generally, and the amount of information available to a government concerning the institutions, activities and affairs of potentially hostile neighbours exercises a decisive influence on the ability of a state to conduct its foreign relations effectively . . .

It is natural to think of information primarily in positive terms, as items of definite knowledge, which is after all the dictionary definition. But there is value in also giving consideration to an alternative, 'negative' definition derived from the discipline of information theory: information as 'the reduction of uncertainty, the elimination of possibilities'. Although uncertainty is clearly not a problem unique to antiquity, the scope for uncertainty then was clearly much greater than in the modern world.

A.D. Lee, *Information and Frontiers: Roman foreign relations in late antiquity*, Cambridge, CUP, 1993, pp. 1–2.

TYRANNY

A tyrant was roughly what we should call a dictator, a man who **1** obtained sole power in the state and held it in defiance of any constitution that had existed previously. This might be done by mere force for the sake of personal power, but the common justification of dictatorship, then as now, was the dictator's ability to provide more effective government. There are times when it can plausibly be asserted that the existing machinery of state is unable to cope with a crisis arising from external pressure or internal tension, and it was mainly at such times that support could be found in a Greek city for the strong rule of a single tyrant. Such occasions might also be manufactured, and even when the need was genuine the tyrant was likely to go beyond what was called for by the immediate crisis: personal ambition and public necessity cannot be neatly disengaged, nor is it ever easy for an autocrat to resign.

A. Andrewes, *The Greek Tyrants*, London, Hutchinson, 1956, p. 7.

But tyranny nowhere endured. After it had performed the services **2** which the popular classes expected of it, after it had powerfully contributed to material prosperity and to the development of democracy, it disappeared with an astonishing rapidity . . . The people regarded tyranny only as an expedient. They used it as a battering ram with which to demolish the citadel of the oligarchs, and when their end had been achieved they hastily abandoned the weapon which wounded their hands.

G. Glotz, *The Greek City*, trans. N. Mallinson, London, Kegan Paul, Trench & Trubner, 1929, pp. 115–16.

The new and dominating element in Greek society in the seventh and **3** sixth centuries was the emergence of rich men . . . The People did not come into it. The age was the age of dynasts.

G.L. Cawkwell, 'Early Greek tyranny and the people', *Classical Quarterly*,

45 (1995), p. 86. Reprinted by permission of Oxford University Press and the Classical Association.

WAR

1 The total character of contemporary wars, whether foreign or civic, has helped us to discern that ancient war has a reality, a manner of being, a practice and a mode of behaviour that are as wide as society itself. We have rediscovered the function of war on the community level, with its institutions, its rites, its ideology representing the reactions aroused in any given society by the natural, if not permanent threat of the foreigner . . . Since experience has taught us that war can no longer be considered as a pathological phenomenon alien to the normal course of events, we can no longer justify treating the military history of the Greeks and Romans as an isolated chapter of ancient history for the satisfaction of the intellectual foibles of some retired colonel.

Yvon Garlan, *War in the Ancient World*, trans. J. Lloyd, London, Chatto & Windus, 1975, pp. 20–1. First published in French in 1972.

2 We may observe, that the ancient republics were almost in perpetual war, a natural effect of their martial spirit, their love of liberty, their mutual emulation, and that hatred which generally prevails among nations that live in close neighbourhood.

David Hume, 'On the populousness of ancient nations' [1752], in *Essays: moral, political, and literary I*, T.H. Green & T.H. Grose (eds), London, Longmans, Green & Co., 1875, p. 400.

3 For the Greeks of the classical period, war is natural. Organised in little cities, equally jealous of their independence, equally anxious to affirm their superiority, they see in war the normal expression of the rivalry which presides over relations between states; peace, or rather truces, is registered as a dead time in the ever-renewed story of conflicts.

   Moreover the spirit of struggle which opposes the cities to one another is only one aspect of a much vaster force, at work in all human relationships and even in nature itself. Between individuals and between families as between states, in the games, the judicial process, the debates of the assembly as on the field of battle, the Greeks recognised, under the different names of Polemos, Eris, Neikos, this same force of competition which Hesiod places at the roots of the world and Heraclitus celebrates as father and king of the universe.

This agonistic conception of man, of social relations, of natural forces, has deep roots not only in the heroic ethos proper to the epoch, but in the institutional practices where we can recognise the prehistory of this 'political' war which is carried on by the cities.

Jean-Pierre Vernant, 'Introduction', in Vernant (ed.), *Problèmes de la Guerre en Grèce Ancienne*, Paris, Mouton, 1968, p. 10. Trans. N. Morley.

If war was indeed a central occupation of the ancient state, if war was **4** always one of the possible options, then the search for the origins of an individual war is foredoomed so long as it remains stuck in a narrative of preceding events. Thucydides demolished that approach in his brief phrase about the 'truest cause' of the Peloponnesian War. Given Athenian expansion and Spartan fear of it, war between the two was inevitable, and it was a minor matter whether it broke out in one year rather than another, over one incident rather than another.

M.I. Finley, 'War and empire', in *Ancient History: evidence and models*, London, Chatto & Windus, 1985, p. 75.

Part 2

KEY WRITERS

BROWN, PETER (1935–)

It is only too easy to present the study of history in a modern **1**
university system as if it were a discipline for the mind alone, and so to
ignore the slow and erratic processes which go to the enrichment
of the imagination. Yet it is precisely this imaginative curiosity
about the past that is a unique feature of western civilization. Since
the eighteenth century, we westerners have taken pleasure, and even
thought to derive wisdom, from a persistent attempt to project
ourselves into the thoughts and feelings of men and women whose
claim to our respect was precisely that they were sensed to be
profoundly different from ourselves. This unique respect for the
otherness of the past and of other societies did not begin in archives;
nor was it placed in the centre of European culture by antiquarians. It
began among dreamers and men of well-stocked imagination. The
tap-roots of the western historical tradition go deep into the rich and
far from antiseptic soil of the Romantic movement. By the standards
of a well-run History Department, the Grand Old Men of the
historical tribe were wild and woolly.

'Learning and imagination', in *Society and the Holy in Late Antiquity*, London,
Faber & Faber, 1982, p. 3.

Late antiquity

On the most straightforward level, nothing is quite what it appears **2**
in the Later Roman Empire. This is the first and most lasting
attraction to that age of change. Seldom were the externals of
traditional Roman life so strenuously maintained: seldom did the
aristocracy feel so identified with their inherited classical tradition and
with the myth of Eternal Rome. Seldom had the authority of the
Roman Emperors been supposed to reach so far – into the definition
of their subjects' beliefs, into what oaths they swore when gambling,
into the 'irrepressible avarice' that might lead a man, if undeterred by
beheading, to sell edible dormice above the market price. When we
enter a museum, we peer at the fourth-century ivories to catch some
hint of the profound changes that raced beneath their surface: the
smooth, neo-classical faces stare us down.

And yet we know that the surface of ancient life was being betrayed
at every turn: it was being abandoned in the clothes men wore, in the
mosaics they walked on, in the beliefs they held, or in the beliefs of the
women they married, in the very sounds that filled their streets and
churches with the strange chants of Syria. Like bizarre reflections of a

building in troubled water, the façade of Greco-Roman life shifts and dissolves.
Religion and Society in the Age of St Augustine, London, Faber & Faber, 1971, p. 11.

3   It is as if a lunar landscape whose outlines once stood out with unearthly clarity in standard accounts of the political and administrative changes of the age has taken on softer tints, because it is now bathed in an atmosphere heavy with hopes and fears rooted in the religious and cultural traditions of the participants.
Power and Persuasion in Late Antiquity: towards a Christian empire, Madison, University of Wisconsin Press, 1992, p. viii. Reprinted by permission of the University of Wisconsin Press.

4   The reader should labor under no illusion. Power, not persuasion, remains the most striking characteristic of the later Roman Empire in all its regions.
Ibid., p. 7.

Early Christianity

5   At some time – or, more precisely, over a certain period – the secular traditions of the senatorial class, traditions which one might have assumed to be intimately bound up with the fate of their pagan beliefs, came to be continued by a Christian aristocracy. To understand this 'sea change', it is necessary to consider the 'Romans of Rome' in themselves, apart from the public crises which they had weathered so effectively; and to see whether the Christianization of their class was not part of a long-term development, as elusive but, ultimately, as decisive as any change of taste.
'Aspects of the Christianization of the Roman aristocracy', *Journal of Roman Studies*, 51 (1961), p. 4.

6   It was through the hard business of living his life for twenty-four hours in the day, through catering for the day-to-day needs of his locality, through allowing his person to be charged with the normal hopes and fears of his fellow men, that the holy man gained the power in society that enabled him to carry off the occasional *coup de théâtre*. Dramatic interventions of holy men in the high policies of the Empire were long remembered. But they illustrate the prestige that the holy man had already gained, they do not explain it. They were rather like the cashing of a big cheque on a reputation.

'The rise and function of the holy man in late antiquity', *Journal of Roman Studies*, 61 (1971), pp. 80–1.

Above everything the holy man is a man of power. In Theodoret's **7** account, the Syrian countryside is shown dotted with figures of supernatural δυναμις quite as palpable, as localized and as authenticated by popular acclamation, as were the garrison posts and the large farmhouses. To visit a holy man was to go where power was. The *Historia Religiosa* is a study of power in action – χαρις ενεργουσα. Hence the emphasis even on the detail of the stylized gestures by which this power was shown. Theodoret's accounts of his holy men in action are as precisely delineated as a Late Antique artist's formal representation of the gestures of Christ as He performs His miracles. The scene is grouped around the hand of the holy man – an ancient and compact symbol of power. Hence a certain monotony in the account, and even a misleading *sprezzatura*. There are few long miracle stories. That this is so is due to no Hellenic humanism on the bishop's part, but rather to his serious preoccupation with the absorbing topic of power. The miracle is felt to be secondary: for it was merely a proof of power – like good coin, summarily minted and passed into circulation to demonstrate the untapped bullion of power at the disposal of the holy man.
Ibid., p. 87.

For all the creaking rigidities of our ancient sources, and for all the **8** intellectual skills demanded of a modern scholar in rendering them intelligible, it would be deeply inhumane to deny that, in these centuries, real men and women faced desperate choices, endured privation and physical pain, courted breakdown and bitter disillusionment, and frequently experienced themselves, and addressed others, with a searing violence of language. It is disturbing to read of Saint Eupraxia, a noble girl, and so better fed and more vigorous than her fellow-nuns in a great Egyptian monastery, sleeping on hard ashes to tame her body at the time when her periods first began. The very matter-of-fact manner in which monastic sources report bloody, botched attempts at self-castration by desperate monks shocks us by its lack of surprise . . . The historian's obligation to the truth forces us to strive to make these texts intelligible, with all the cunning and serenity that we would wish to associate with a living, modern culture. But the reader must remain aware that understanding is no substitute for compassion. This book will have failed in its deepest purpose if the elaborate, and strictly necessary, strategies involved in the recovery of a distant age were considered to have explained away, to have diminished or, worse still, to have stared through the brutal cost of commitment in any age, that of the Early Church included.

The Body and Society: men, women and sexual renunciation in early Christianity, New York, Columbia University Press, 1988, p. xviii.

9   *Paideia* continued to provide the bishops of the fifth century with what they needed most – the means of living at peace with their neighbors. The newly edited letters of Firmus, bishop of Caesarea . . . make this plain. Their interest lies in the fact that they are so uninteresting. They show how a bishop, whom we know to have been an active participant in the ecclesiastical maneuvering associated with the Council of Ephesus, maintained his alliances in the old manner. Firmus appealed to the natural friendship that should bind together those associated with Greek *paideia*. Later Byzantines, who copied these letters into anthologies, appreciated them for what they were: gems of old-world civility. A neighboring bishop, Eugenios, received a hunting dog whose beauty rivalled that of Helen of Troy. The two wines that Eugenios had sent to Firmus required a Homer to do justice to their bouquet. Basil's poorhouse at Caesarea, the famous Basileias, is mentioned in only one letter, in which Firmus declared his determination that it should not serve as a refuge for work-shy peasants fleeing from the estates of their owners. Bishops such as Firmus cast the spell of *paideia* over what had remained a potentially faction-ridden community.

Power and Persuasion, pp. 122–3.

BURCKHARDT, JACOB (1818–97)

On history

1   The philosophy of history is a centaur, a contradiction in terms, for history co-ordinates, and hence is unphilosophical, while philosophy subordinates, and hence is unhistorical.

Reflections on History, London, George Allen & Unwin, 1943, p. 15. First published in German in 1906, taken from lectures delivered 1868–71.

2   All genuine records are at first tedious, because and in so far as they are alien. They set forth the views and interests of their time *for their time,* and come no step to meet us. But the shams of today are addressed to us, and are therefore made amusing and intelligible, as faked antiques generally are. This is especially true of the historical novel, which so

many people read as if it were history, slightly rearranged but true in essence.
Ibid., p. 27.

The word 'amateur' owes its evil reputation to the arts. An artist must   **3** be a master or nothing, and must dedicate his life to his art, for the arts, of their very nature, demand perfection.

In learning, on the other hand, a man can only be a master in one particular field, namely as a specialist, and in some field he *should* be a specialist. But if he is not to forfeit his capacity for taking a general view, or even his respect for general views, he should be an amateur at as many points as possible, privately at any rate, for the increase of his own knowledge and the enrichment of his possible standpoints. Otherwise he will remain ignorant in any field lying outside his own speciality and perhaps, as a man, a barbarian.
Ibid., p. 30.

Having considered the constant interaction of the world forces and   **4** the accelerated historical processes, we may pass on to world movements concentrated in individuals. We have now to deal with great men.

In doing so, we are fully aware of the ambiguity in the idea of greatness, and must, as a matter of course, abandon any attempt at scientific system.

Our starting-point might be ourselves – jejune, perfunctory, many-minded. Greatness is all that we are *not*. To the beetle in the grass the hazel-bush (if he so much as notices it) may seem great, just because he is a beetle . . .

All kinds of illusions and difficulties lie in wait for us here. Our judgement and feeling may change fundamentally with our age and mental development, may be at odds between themselves and with the judgement and feeling of everybody else, simply because our starting-point, like that of everybody else, is our own littleness.

Further, we discover in ourselves a feeling of the most spurious kind, namely a need to submit and wonder, a craving to drug ourselves with some seemingly majestic impression, and to give our imaginations full play. Whole peoples may justify their humiliation in this way, risking the danger that other peoples and cultures will come to show them that they have worshipped false idols.

Finally, we are irresistibly drawn to regard those figures of the past and present as great whose activity dominates our individual existence and without whose lives we could not imagine our own . . . In short,

we run the risk of confusing power and greatness and taking our own persons far too seriously.
Ibid., pp. 172–3.

5   At our universities, the historians like to dump the Ancient History course in the lap of the philologists, and vice versa. Here and there it is treated like a poor old relation whom it would be a disgrace to let go to ruin entirely. But with the public at large antiquity is completely out of fashion, and the 'culture' which is supported by this public even feels hatred for it. Various faults of antiquity serve as a pretext. The real reason is conceit about modern communication and transport and the inventions of our century; then, too, there is the inability to distinguish technical and material greatness from the intellectual and moral kinds; and finally, the prevalent views about refinement of manners, philanthropy and the like.

Judgements on History and Historians, trans. H. Zohn, Boston, Beacon Press, 1958, pp. 26–7. First published in German in 1929, taken from lectures delivered 1865–85.

On classical antiquity

6   If history is ever to help us solve even an infinitesimal part of the great and grievous riddle of life, we must quit the regions of personal and temporal foreboding for a sphere in which our view is not forthwith dimmed by self. It may be that a calmer consideration from a greater distance may yield a first hint of the true nature of life on earth, and, fortunately for us, ancient history has preserved a few records in which we can closely follow growth, bloom and decay in outstanding historical events and in intellectual, political and economic conditions in every direction. The best example is Athens.

Reflections on History, p. 21.

7   Attic drama . . . casts floods of light on the whole life of Attica and Greece.

Firstly, the performance was a social occasion of the first magnitude, an αγων in the supreme sense of the word, the poets contesting with each other, a fact which certainly very soon brought amateurs into the ranks of the competitors. Further, as to its subject-matter and treatment, we are faced here with that mysterious rise of drama 'from the spirit of music'. The protagonist remains an echo of Dionysus, and the entire content is pure myth, avoiding history, which often tries to force its way in. It is dominated by the steady determination to present

humanity only in typical, and not in realistic figures, and, connected with this, the conviction of the inexhaustibility of the golden age of gods and heroes.
Ibid., pp. 69–70.

In Athens, then, intellect comes out free and unashamed, or at any rate **8**
can be discerned throughout as if through a light veil, owing to the simplicity of economic life, the voluntary moderation of agriculture, commerce and industry, and the great general sobriety. Citizenship, eloquence, art, poetry and philosophy radiated from the life of the city.
Ibid., p. 108.

By an optical illusion, we see happiness at certain times, in certain **9**
countries, and we deck it out with analogies from the youth of man, spring, sunrise and other metaphors. Indeed, we imagine it dwelling in a beautiful part of the country, a certain house, just as the smoke rising from a distant cottage in the evening gives us the impression of intimacy among those living there.

Whole epochs, too, are regarded as happy or unhappy. The happy ones are the so-called high epochs of man, For instance, the claim to such happiness is seriously put forward for the Periclean Age, in which it is recognized that the life of the ancient world reached its zenith in the State, society, art and poetry. Other epochs of the same kind, e.g. the age of the good emperors, have been abandoned as having been selected from too one-sided a standpoint . . .

Judgements of this kind are characteristic of modern times and only imaginable with modern historical methods.
Ibid., pp. 205–6.

Among all the fields of learning in the world there prevails, like a funda- **10**
mental chord that keeps sounding through, the history of the ancient world, i.e. of all those peoples whose lives have flowed into ours.

It would be idle to assume that after four centuries of humanism everything had been learned from the ancient world, all experiences and data had been utilized, and there were no longer anything to be gained there, so that one could content oneself with a knowledge of more modern times or, possibly, make a pitying or reluctant study of the Middle Ages and spend the time saved on more useful things.

We shall never be rid of antiquity as long as we do not become barbarians again. Barbarians and modern American men of culture live without consciousness of history.
Judgements on History and Historians, p. 24.

11   Once it is understood that there never were, not ever will be, any
happy, golden ages in a fanciful sense, one will remain free from
the foolish overvaluation of some past, from senseless despair of
the present or fatuous hope for the future, but one will recognize
in the contemplation of historical ages one of the noblest under-
takings. It is the story of the life and suffering of mankind viewed as a
whole.

And yet antiquity has a great specific importance for us; our
concept of the state derives from it; it is the birthplace of our religions
and of the most permanent part of our civilization. Of its creations
in form and writing a great deal is exemplary and unequalled. Our
accounting with it in affinity as well as in contrast is infinite.

However, let us regard antiquity as merely the first act of the drama
of man, to our eyes a tragedy with immeasurable exertion, guilt, and
sorrow. And even though we are descended from peoples who were
still slumbering in a state of childhood alongside the great civilized
peoples of antiquity, yet we feel ourselves the true descendants of the
latter, because their *soul* has passed over into us; their work, their
mission, and their destiny live on in us.
Ibid., pp. 24–5.

12   It is hard for us to give a fair judgement between Athens and Sparta,
because we owe an infinitude to Athens and nothing to Sparta, and
because Sparta did not hold on to any venerable primitive piety in the
face of rapid Athenian progress, but from the beginning maintained a
depraved rule of force over subjugated fellow Hellenes. We do not
know, however, whether *without* such an adversary Athens would
not soon have degenerated in other ways.
Ibid., p. 31.

13   Rome is everywhere the conscious or tacit premise of our views
and thought; if in the essential intellectual points we are now no
longer part of a specific people and country but belong to Western
civilization, this is a consequence of the fact that at one time the world
was Roman, universal, and that this ancient common culture has
passed over into ours.
Ibid., p. 31.

14   Incidentally, apropos of latifundia, we have no right to shoot off our
mouths, at a time when the whole farm-owning class is undermined
by usurers, the bankrupt are in the majority, the Jews are in the
saddle, and the peasants retreat to the cities. Not does it behove us to

consider the Roman Empire especially unhappy because of its lack of competitive factory industries with 'free' workers.
Ibid., p. 41.

CAMERON, AVERIL (1940–)

Although written texts are also themselves historical documents **1** in their own right, many ancient historians, it would be fair to say, continue to regard historiography in the more traditional sense as being necessary, perhaps, but not of particular interest to themselves – even sometimes as a sort of sub-genre, less intrinsically important than the discovery of new information or the establishment of new 'facts'. Defined in this way, it must always run the risk of appearing simply a preliminary to the modern historian's real task of adjudicating between the sources.
'Introduction', in Cameron (ed.), *History as Text: the writing of ancient history*, London, Duckworth, and Chapel Hill, University of North Carolina, 1989, p. 2.

For history is a matter of interpretation. In order to write history – to **2** generate a text – the historian must interpret existing texts . . . But he will interpret, or 'read', his texts in accordance with a set of other texts, which derive from the cultural code within which he works himself; and he will go on to write his text, that is, his history, against the background of and within the matrix of this larger cultural text. Thus history-writing is not a simple matter of sorting out 'primary' and 'secondary' sources; it is inextricably embedded in a mesh of text.
Ibid., pp. 4–5.

We have therefore a seemingly strange situation – one in which a **3** debate about the 'position' of women is carried on on the basis of texts that are in the main highly misogynistic, and yet in which it has also been thought possible to argue for a kind of early Christian feminism. My purpose here is to show how the misogynistic rhetoric of the early Christian texts became established; I would also want to argue that at least some of the statements made in pagan and Christian sources alike about the attraction of Christianity for women are simply the product of an easy rhetorical convenience, like the claim often made by even the most sophisticated of the Fathers that they were able to speak directly to the 'simple'. The question of how women really fared in the early Christian world is a second-order question, to be approached only after we have first examined the rhetoric of the texts.

'Virginity as metaphor: women and the rhetoric of early Christianity', in *History as Text*, pp. 184–5.

4   The relation of Christian discourse to classical discourse is not to be seen in terms of linear progression from the one to the other. Nor is it a simple one. It remained convenient to be able to decry classical rhetoric even while drawing heavily on it.
Christianity and the Rhetoric of Empire: the development of Christian discourse, Berkeley, Los Angeles and London, University of California Press, 1991, p. 85.

5   Christian discourse presents a paradox: sprung from a situation of openness and multiplicity, its spread produced a world with no room for dissenting opinion.
Ibid., p. 222.

FINLEY, M.I. (1912–86)

1   Very few ancient historians are introspective: one must infer their most fundamental presuppositions from their substantive accounts, since they refuse to discuss methodological questions.
'Epilogue', in *Ancient History: evidence and models*, London, Chatto & Windus, 1985, p. 105.

2   A critical enquiry, professional historiography, is thus a potential danger to the 'sublime and powerful unhistoricity' of tradition. It is also terribly complicated: it piles up data, documents, events beyond number, it impedes what Professor Barnes happily called 'structural amnesia', it offers too many partial explanations (when it does not refuse to explain it altogether), it may undermine a common inter-pretation of the past and therefore the social bonds that are fortified by a common identification with the past. It threatens to render the past unstable.
'The ancestral constitution', in *The Use and Abuse of History*, London, Chatto & Windus, 1975, p. 58.

3   The long tradition, normally not expressed overtly but implied in the treatment, that sources written in Greek or Latin occupy a privileged status and are immune from the canons of judgement and criticism that are applied to all other documentation, is unwarranted and constitutes a major stumbling-block to any proper historical analysis. One example is the touching faith in the oral tradition of the Greeks

and Romans, which no one shares who has to deal with oral traditions in other societies, and which does not stand up to scrutiny the moment other evidence is available. Defective sources cannot be 'rescued' by hard thinking alone, not even those written in the ancient classical languages.

'Epilogue', in *Ancient History: evidence and models*, p. 104.

The use of theory

The relationship between trade and politics in classical Greece still   4
seems to be treated most of the time as if there were no conceptual problems, as if, in Rostovtzeff's language, it is only a question of facts. And that means, necessarily, that the concepts and generalizations which are constantly being brought to bear, expressly or tacitly, are modern ones, even when they hide beneath the mask of 'common sense'.

'Classical Greece', in Finley (ed.), *Second International Conference of Economic History, Volume I: trade and politics in the ancient world*, New York, Arno, 1979, p. 13.

Historians, one hears all the time, should get on with their proper   5
business, the investigation of the concrete experiences of the past, and leave the 'philosophy of history' (which is a barren, abstract and pretty useless activity anyway) to the philosophers. Unfortunately the historian is no mere chronicler, and he cannot do his work at all without assumptions and judgements, without generalizations, in other words. In so far as he is unwilling to discuss generalizations explicitly – which means that he does not reflect on them – he runs grave risks.

'Generalizations in ancient history', in *The Use and Abuse of History*, p. 61.

The barest bones of any historical narrative, the events selected and   6
arranged in a temporal sequence, imply a value judgement (or judgements). The study and writing of history, in short, is a form of ideology.

'Progress in historiography', in *Ancient History: evidence and models*, p. 5.

My aim is not a plea for the end of theoretical concerns. In historical   7
study that can lead only to a heaping up of discrete data, of raw material for the historian and not to history itself. The difficult discrimination that has to be made is between appropriate social theory and political ideology in the narrow sense.

Ancient Slavery and Modern Ideology, London, Chatto & Windus, 1980, p. 64.

8   The ability of the ancients to invent and their capacity to believe are persistently underestimated. How else could they have filled the blatant gaps in their knowledge once erudite antiquarians had observed that centuries had elapsed between the destruction of Troy and the 'foundation' of Rome, other than by inventing an Alban king-list to bridge the gap?

'The ancient historian and his sources', in *Ancient History: evidence and models*, p. 9.

Models and ideal types

9   The ancient historian cannot be a cliometrician in a serious way, but he can resort to a second-best procedure through the use of non-mathematical models, thereby controlling the subject of his discourse by selecting the variables he wishes to study.

'"How it really was"', in *Ancient History: evidence and models*, p. 60.

10   Except among economic historians, however, model-construction is a rare procedure among historians, especially so, I suspect, among ancient historians . . . Indeed, the signs are unmistakable that the reverse is taking place precisely in the field that Weber mentioned, the history of cities. Instead of efforts to establish clear patterns of city behaviour through the employment of simplifying assumptions, there has emerged in recent decades a spate of pseudo-historical histories of ancient cities and regions in which every statement or calculation to be found in an ancient text, every artefact finds a place, creating a morass of unintelligible, meaningless, unrelated 'facts' (which I write in inverted commas because many of the so-called facts are pure guesses or outright fictions) . . . The old problem of establishing canons of selection and of settling who determines them has been 'settled' by abolishing selection altogether. Everything now goes in, as if in answer to the familiar question in children's examinations. 'Tell all you know about X'.

Ibid., p. 61.

11   It is in the nature of models that they are subject to constant adjustment, correction, modification or outright replacement. Non-mathematical models have few if any limits to their usefulness; whereas cliometric models are restricted to quantitative data, there is virtually nothing that cannot be conceptualized and analysed by non-mathematical models – religion and ideology, economic institutions and ideas, the state and politics, simple descriptions and

developmental stages . . . Without [a hypothesis], however, there can be no explanation; there can be only reportage and crude taxonomy, antiquarianism in its narrowest sense.
Ibid., p. 66

The model of a 'consumer city' and indeed the whole analysis I have   12
attempted of the ancient economy would not be in the least affected or impaired by the discovery of a few more textile workshops in Pompeii or a few members of the senatorial aristocracy who actively engage in commerce and manufacture. There can be no dispute over the existence of exceptional men, even of exceptional cities. No historical or sociological model pretends to incorporate all known or possible instances. In the absence of meaningful quantitative data, the best that one can do is judge whether or not a model, a set of concepts, explains the available data more satisfactorily than a competing model.
The Ancient Economy, London, Hogarth Press, 2nd edn 1985, p. 194.

FOUCAULT, MICHEL (1926–84)

Power, knowledge and history

Each society has its regime of truth, its 'general politics' of truth: that   1
is, the types of discourse which it accepts and makes function as true; the mechanisms and instances which enable one to distinguish 'true' and 'false' statements; the means by which each is sanctioned; and the techniques and procedures accorded value in the acquisition of truth; the status of those who are charged with saying what counts as true.
Power/Knowledge: selected interviews and other writings, 1972–1977, New York, Pantheon, 1980, p. 131.

It is true that History existed long before the constitution of the   2
human sciences; from the beginnings of the Ancient Greek civiliza- tion, it has performed a certain number of major functions in Western culture: memory, myth, transmission of the Word and of Example, vehicle of tradition, critical awareness of the present, decipherment of humanity's destiny, anticipation of the future, or promise of a return. What characterized this History – or at least what may be used to define it in its general features, as opposed to our own – was that by ordering the time of human beings upon the world's development . . . or inversely by extending the principle and movement of a human destiny to even the smallest particles of nature . . . it was conceived of

as a vast historical stream, uniform in each of its points, drawing with it in one and the same current, in one and the same fall or ascension, or cycle, all men, and with them things and animals, every living or inert being, even the most unmoved aspects of the earth. And it was this unity that was shattered at the beginning of the nineteenth century, in the great upheaval that occurred in the Western *episteme*: it was discovered that there existed a historicity proper to nature . . . Moreover, it became possible to show that activities as peculiarly human as labour or language contained within themselves a historicity that could not be placed within the great narrative common to things and to men.

The Order of Things: an archaeology of the human sciences, trans. A. Sheridan, London, Tavistock, 1970, p. 367. First published in French as *Les mots et les choses* in 1966.

3   History constitutes, then, for the human sciences, a favourable environment which is both privileged and dangerous. To each of the sciences of man it offers a background, which establishes it and provides it with a fixed ground and, as it were, a homeland; it determines the cultural areas − the chronological and geographical boundaries − in which that branch of knowledge can be recognised as having validity; but it also surrounds the sciences of man with a frontier that limits them and destroys, from the outset, their claim to validity within the element of universality.
Ibid., p. 371.

4   I understand the unease of all such people. They have probably found it difficult enough to recognize that their history, their economics, their social practices, the language that they speak, the mythology of their ancestors, even the stories that they were told in their childhood, are governed by rules that are not all given to their consciousness; they can hardly agree to being dispossessed in addition of that discourse in which they wish to be able to say immediately and directly what they think, believe or imagine; they prefer to deny that discourse is a complex, differentiated practice, governed by analysable rules and transformations, rather than be deprived of that tender, consoling certainty of being able to change, if not the world, if not life, at least their 'meaning', simply with a fresh word that can come only from themselves, and remain for ever close to the source.
The Archaeology of Knowledge, trans. A. Sheridan, London, Tavistock, 1972, pp. 210–11. First published in French in 1969.

Sexuality

It seemed to me, therefore, that the question that ought to guide my inquiry was the following: how, why and in what forms was sexuality constituted as a moral domain? Why this ethical concern that was so persistent despite its varying forms and intensity? Why this 'problematization'? **5**
The History of Sexuality, Volume II: the use of pleasure, trans. R. Hurley, London, Viking, 1986, p. 10. First published in French in 1984 by Editions Gallimard.

The interiority of Christian morality is often contrasted with the exteriority of a pagan morality that would consider acts only in their concrete realization, in their visible and manifest form, in their degree of conformity with rules, and in the light of opinion or with a view to the memory they leave behind them. But this traditionally accepted opposition may well miss the essential details of both. What is called Christian interiority is a particular mode of relationship with oneself, comprising precise forms of attention, concern, decipherment, verbalization, confession, self-accusation, struggle against temptation, renunciation, spiritual combat, and so on. And what is designated as the 'exteriority' of ancient morality also implies the principle of an elaboration of self, albeit in a very different form. **6**
Ibid., p. 63.

For the Greek moralists of the classical epoch, moderation was prescribed to both parties in matrimony; but it depended on two distinct modes of relation to self, corresponding to the two individuals. The wife's virtue constituted the correlative and the proof of a submissive behaviour; the man's austerity was part of an ethics of self-delineating domination. **7**
Ibid., p. 184.

FRANK, TENNEY (1876–1939)

I have also kept constantly in mind the needs of college classes, which, till very recently, have had to depend upon elementary books or upon histories emanating from Europe. The latter, though usually well written, do not seem to meet our needs. The older peoples of Europe are more interested than we are in the imperialistic problems of Rome, in the government of widely scattered provinces, and in the survival of late Roman institutions which they have inherited. We **1** are naturally more concerned with Rome's earlier attempts at developing an effective government while trying to preserve democratic institutions.

A History of Rome, London, Jonathan Cape, 1923, p. v.

2   That our constitution is a peculiar combination of democratic and aristocratic principles in conjunction with strong executive power is largely due to the enthusiasm of eighteenth century essayists for the republican constitution of Rome. Our laws of inheritance, our acceptance of the legal parity of men and women, our respect for property rights and for contracts are essentially Roman; and it is largely due to the precepts and examples of Republican Rome that modern governments have so persistently searched for a way to combine liberty and law, to follow after justice as against privilege, to accept the principles of equity as axiomatic, and to persist against every discouragement in extending the domain of a sane and intelligent democracy.

Ibid., pp. 584–5.

3   The Gracchan reforms did not save Rome from the deserved penalties of her misdeeds. The more important measures were obstructed, those that passed were either modified by the senate or administered with so little of the spirit of the author that their benefits were largely neutralized and their evils exaggerated . . . Of immediate interest to economists as a result of these contests are the elevation of the capitalist-mercantile class to a position of power in the state and in its financial enterprises, the closing of Italian lands for colonization, which directed capital into other channels, and the acceptance of the policy of state-charity for the poor of Rome which placed industry in the city at a discount for all time.

An Economic History of Rome, London, Jonathan Cape, 2nd edn 1927, pp. 139–40.

4   The simple economy of the primitive household may have existed in the mountains of Italy in Cicero's day, but few traces of it can be found. The Roman farmstead was often meant to be 'self-sufficient', to provide for all its needs and to possess slaves who could perform the technical as well as the ordinary work. When, however, this was the case, the self-sufficiency was not a mark of primitive conditions – as in our own frontier life – but rather of an elaborate capitalistic economy in which the fastidious landlord could afford to satisfy his every whim.

In the cities we find an industrial system which in many respects resembles that of early nineteenth-century New England where the native artisans of inland towns not yet connected by steam power produced most of the articles needed by each town. However, many of the Roman cities were now growing large and the number of wealthy men who demanded and could pay for luxuries and delicacies far exceeded that of our early Republic. To gratify these an extensive commerce had long existed, and in some lines of production industries aiming at a world market had already arisen.
Ibid., p. 271.

The surplus capital of the Romans, as we have noticed, had for 5 centuries followed the expanding armies inland. Time and again when the population of the city became dense and there were signs of a drift toward the sea or toward commercial outlets, a new advance on the border had required military colonization, and the familiar call of the land that Romans were accustomed to heed turned men inland once more. It is a situation that reminds one strongly of the opening of the American frontiers, which permitted our once flourishing merchant marine to decay and temporarily stemmed the current of New England industries.
Ibid., p. 277.

This Orientalizing of Rome's populace has a more important bearing 6 than is usually accorded it upon the larger question of why the spirit and acts of imperial Rome are totally different from those of the republic, if indeed racial characteristics are not wholly a myth. There is to-day a healthy activity in the study of the economic factors – unscientific finance, fiscal agriculture, inadequate support of industry and commerce, etc. – that contributed to Rome's decline. But what lay behind and constantly reacted upon all such causes of Rome's disintegration was, after all, to a considerable extent, the fact that the people who built Rome had given way to a different race. The lack of energy and enterprise, the failure of foresight and common sense, the weakening of moral and political stamina, all were concomitant with the gradual diminution of the stock which, during the earlier days, had displayed these qualities.
'Race mixture in the Roman empire', in D. Kagan (ed.), *Decline and Fall of the Roman Empire: why did it collapse?*, Boston, D.C. Heath & Co., 1962, pp. 54–5. Originally published in *American Historical Review*, 21 (1916).

GIBBON, EDWARD (1737–94)

1   Diligence and accuracy are the only merits which an historical writer may ascribe to himself; if any merit indeed can be assumed from the performance of an indispensable duty.
The History of the Decline and Fall of the Roman Empire [1776–88], D. Womersley (ed.), Harmondsworth, Penguin, 1994; Chapter I, Vol. 1 p. 5.

2   The policy of the emperors and the senate, as far as it concerned religion, was happily seconded by the reflections of the enlightened, and by the habits of the superstitious, part of their subjects. The various modes of worship, which prevailed in the Roman world, were all considered by the people, as equally true; by the philosophers, as equally false; and by the magistrates, as equally useful. And thus toleration produced not only mutual indulgence, but even religious concord.
Ibid., Chapter II, Vol. I p. 56.

3   Under the Roman empire, the labour of an industrious and ingenious people was variously, but incessantly employed, in the service of the rich. In their dress, their table, their homes, and their furniture, the favourites of fortune united every refinement of conveniency, of elegance, and of splendour; whatever could soothe their pride, or gratify their sensuality. Such refinements, under the odious name of luxury, have been severely arraigned by the moralists of every age; and it might perhaps be more conducive to the virtue, as well as happiness of mankind, if all possessed the necessaries, and none the superfluities, of life. But in the present imperfect condition of society, luxury, though it may proceed from vice or folly, seems to be the only means that can correct the unequal distribution of property. The diligent mechanic, and the skilful artist, who have obtained no share in the division of the earth, receive a voluntary tax from the possessors of land; and the latter are prompted, by a sense of interest, to improve those estates, with whose produce they may purchase additional pleasures. This operation, the particular effects of which are felt in every society, acted with much more diffusive energy in the Roman world. The provinces would soon have been exhausted of their wealth, if the manufactures and commerce of luxury had not insensibly restored to the industrious subjects, the sums which were exacted from them by the arms and authority of Rome.
Ibid., Chapter II, Vol. I p. 80.

The labours of these monarchs were over-paid by the immense reward **4** that inseparably waited on their success; by the honest pride of virtue, and by the exquisite delight of beholding the general happiness of which they were the authors. A just, but melancholy reflection embittered, however, the noblest of human enjoyments. They must often have recollected the instability of a happiness which depended on the character of a single man. The fatal moment was perhaps approaching, when some licentious youth, or some jealous tyrant, would abuse, to the destruction, that absolute power, which they had exerted for the benefit of their people. The ideal restraints of the senate and the laws might serve to display the virtues, but could never correct the vices, of the emperor. The military force was a blind and irresistible instrument of oppression; and the corruption of Roman manners would always supply flatterers eager to applaud, and ministers prepared to serve, the fear or the avarice, the lust or the cruelty, of their masters.

Ibid., Chapter III, Vol. I pp. 103–4.

Our curiosity is naturally prompted to inquire by what means the **5** Christian faith obtained so remarkable a victory over the established religions of the earth. To this inquiry an obvious but satisfactory answer may be returned; that it was owing to the convincing evidence of the doctrine itself, and to the ruling providence of its great Author. But as truth and reason seldom find so favourable a reception in the world, and as the wisdom of Providence frequently condescends to use the passions of the human heart, and the general circumstances of mankind, as instruments to execute its purpose, we may still be permitted, though with becoming submission, to ask, not indeed what were the first, but what were the secondary causes of the rapid growth of the Christian Church.

Ibid., Chapter XV, Vol. I p. 447.

In the cruel reigns of Decius and Diocletian, Christianity had been **6** proscribed, as a revolt from the ancient and hereditary religion of the empire; and the unjust suspicions which were entertained of a dark and dangerous faction, were, in some measure, countenanced by the inseparable union, and rapid conquests, of the Catholic Church. But the same excuses of fear and ignorance cannot be applied to the Christian emperors, who violated the precepts of humanity and of the gospel. The experience of ages had betrayed the weakness, as well as folly, of Paganism; the light of reason and of faith had already exposed, to the greatest part of mankind, the vanity of idols; and the declining

sect, which still adhered to their worship, might have been permitted to enjoy, in peace and obscurity, the religious customs of their ancestors. Had the pagans been animated by the undaunted zeal, which possessed the minds of the primitive believers, the triumph of the church might have been stained with blood; and the martyrs of Jupiter and Apollo might have embraced the glorious opportunity of devoting their lives and fortunes at the foot of their altars. But such obstinate zeal was not congenial to the loose and careless temper of polytheism. The violent and repeated strokes of the orthodox princes, were broken by the soft and yielding substance against which they were directed; and the ready obedience of the Pagans protected them from the pains and penalties of the Theodosian Code. Instead of asserting, that the authority of the gods was superior to that of the emperor, they desisted with a plaintive murmur, from the use of those sacred rites which their sovereign had condemned . . . If the pagan wanted patience to suffer, they wanted spirit to resist; and the scattered myriads, who deplored the ruin of the temples, yielded, without a contest, to the fortune of their adversaries.
Ibid., Chapter XXVIII, Vol. II pp. 87–8.

7   An ingenious philosopher [Montesquieu] has calculated the universal measure of the public impositions by the degrees of freedom and servitude; and ventures to assert that, according to an invariable law of nature, it must always increase with the former, and diminish in a just proportion to the latter. But this reflection, which would tend to alleviate the miseries of despotism, is contradicted at least by the history of the Roman empire: which accuses the same princes of despoiling the senate of its authority, and the provinces of their wealth. Without abolishing all the various customs and duties on merchandise, which are imperceptibly discharged by the apparent choice of the purchaser, the policy of Constantine and his successors preferred a simple and direct mode of taxation, more congenial to the spirit of an arbitrary government.
Ibid., Chapter XVII, Vol. I pp. 632–3.

8   Odoacer was the first Barbarian who reigned in Italy, over a people who had once asserted their just superiority above the rest of mankind. The disgrace of the Romans still excites our respectful compassion, and we fondly sympathise with the imaginary grief and indignation of their degenerate posterity. But the calamities of Italy had gradually subdued the proud consciousness of freedom and glory.
Ibid., Chapter XXXVI, Vol. II p. 407.

I should have consulted my own ease, and perhaps I should have acted **9**
in stricter conformity to the rules of prudence, if I had still persevered
in patient silence. But Mr Davis may, if he pleases, assume the merit of
extorting from me the notice which I had refused to more honourable
foes. I had declined the consideration of their *literary Objections*; but
he has compelled me to give an answer to his *criminal Accusations*.
Had he confined himself to the ordinary, and indeed obsolete charges
of impious principles, and mischievous intentions, I should have
acknowledged with readiness and pleasure that the religion of Mr
Davis appeared to be very different from mine. Had he contented
himself with the use of that style which decency and politeness have
banished from the more liberal part of mankind, I should have smiled,
perhaps with some contempt, but without the least mixture of anger
or resentment. Every animal employs the note, or cry, or howl, which
is peculiar to its species; every man expresses himself in the dialect the
most congenial to his temper and inclination, the most familiar to the
company in which he has lived, and to the authors with whom he is
conversant; and while I was disposed to allow that Mr Davis had made
some proficiency in ecclesiastical studies, I should have considered
the difference of our language and manners as an insurmountable
bar of separation between us. Mr Davis has overleaped that bar, and
forces me to contend with him on the very dirty ground which he
has chosen for the scene of our combat. He has judged, I know not
with how much propriety, that the support of a cause, which would
disdain such unworthy assistance, depended on the ruin of my moral
and literary character. The different misrepresentations, of which he
has drawn out the ignominious catalogue, would materially affect my
credit as an historian, my reputation as a scholar and even my honour
and veracity as a gentleman. If I am indeed incapable of understanding
what I read, I can no longer claim a place among those writers
who merit the esteem and confidence of the public. If I am capable
of wilfully perverting what I understand, I no longer deserve to live in
the society of those men, who consider a strict and inviolable
adherence to truth as the foundation of every thing that is virtuous or
honourable in human nature.
A Vindication of Some Passages in the fifteenth and sixteenth chapters of the
History of the Decline and Fall of the Roman Empire [1779], Oxford, OUP, 1961,
p. 6.

GROTE, GEORGE (1794–1871)

1   It is that general picture which an historian of Greece is required first to embody in his own mind, and next to lay out before his readers:– a picture not merely such as to delight the imagination by brilliancy of colouring and depth of sentiment, but also suggestive and improving to the reader. Not omitting the points of resemblance as well as of contrast with the better-known forms of modern society, he will especially study to exhibit the spontaneous movement of Greek intellect, sometimes aided but never borrowed from without, and lighting up a small portion of a world otherwise clouded and stationary. He will develop the action of that social system, which, while ensuring to the mass of freemen a degree of protection else-where unknown, acted as a stimulus to the creative impulses of genius, and left the superior minds sufficiently unshackled to soar above religious and political routine, to overshoot their own age, and to become the teachers of posterity.

A History of Greece, London, John Murray, new edn 1869, Vol. I pp. iv–v.

2   The same comparison reappears a short time afterwards, where [Herodotus] tells us that 'the Athenians, when free, felt themselves a match for Sparta, but while kept down by any man under a despotism, were feeble and apt for submission'. Stronger expressions cannot be found to depict the rapid improvement wrought in the Athenian people by their new democracy. Of course this did not arise merely from suspension of previous cruelties, or from better laws, or better administration. These indeed were essential conditions, but the active transforming cause here was, the principle and system of which such amendments formed the detail: the grand and new idea of the sovereign People, composed of free and equal citizens – or liberty and equality, to use words which so profoundly moved the French people half a century ago. It was this comprehensive political idea which acted with electric effect upon the Athenians, creating within them a host of sentiments, motives, sympathies, and capacities, to which they had before been strangers. Democracy in Grecian antiquity possessed the privilege, not only of kindling an earnest and unanimous attachment to the constitution in the bosoms of the citizens, but also of creating an energy of public and private action, such as could never be obtained under an oligarchy, where the utmost that could be hoped for was a passive acquiescence and obedience.

Ibid., Vol. IV pp. 104–5.

HOPKINS, KEITH (1934–)

Let me admit straight away that I am not an ideal advocate for **1**
conventional ancient history.
'Rules of evidence', *Journal of Roman Studies*, 68 (1978), p. 182.

There are obviously many types of history. But should not all **2**
historians consider inference and generalization carefully, and perhaps
take the reader into their confidence about the interstitial processes
between reading sources and writing history? One useful guide may
be to see the historian as holding a balance between at least four
protagonists: first, the actors, their acts, beliefs, values, intentions and
justifications; secondly, the social structure which reflects, restricts
and also shapes the actors' acts, thoughts and feelings; thirdly, the
sources, which record the acts and emotions of actors, but which also
have biases and intentions of their own; and finally, the audience of
readers to whom the historian with his own biases must interpret a
dead culture. I realise that such a specification makes history writing
difficult; it can also make it exciting.
Ibid., p. 183.

Aesthetic and intellectual pleasures are compatible with high scholar- **3**
ship. One writes history in some degree surely to portray, to evoke a
lost world and to make it live in the mind of the reader. There may
well be other objectives, but that should be one of them.
Ibid., p. 185.

All history is contemporary history and reflects not only the prejudices **4**
of the sources but current concerns and concepts. The achievements
of the Roman world need to be interpreted with empathetic understanding of what the Romans themselves thought and with concepts
that we ourselves use. Modern historians might well take this for
granted, but many ancient historians have allowed themselves to be
isolated from mainstream ancient history. Several factors have contributed: the rigours of learning classical languages, the organization of
universities, convention and tradition. Whatever the causes, the results
are clear: a wide gulf between the ways in which modern and ancient
historians write their history.
Conquerors and Slaves: sociological studies in Roman history I, Cambridge, CUP,
1978, p. ix.

History is a conversation with the dead. We have several advan- **5**
tages over our informants. We think we know what happened

subsequently; we can take a longer view, clear of ephemeral detail; we can do the talking; and with all our prejudices, we are alive. We should not throw away these advantages by pretending to be just collators or interpreters of our sources.
Ibid., p. x.

6 Historical interpretations do not necessarily get better; many simply change. Even so, one of the persistent problems in each generation is how to choose between competing fictions. That is where sociological methods can be helpful. And that is why these two books make use of sociological concepts and arguments, set out explicit hypotheses, and seek to support these arguments with models, figures and coordinates, as well as with quotations from the sources. They are all attempts to reveal how Romans thought and to measure the links between factors; they are attempts to limit the arena within which elusive and competing truths may probably be found.
Ibid., p. x.

7 Unfortunately there is hardly any sound evidence with which this generalisation can be validated; yet it seems more attractive than any alternative I can think of. There are several pieces of evidence, each insufficient or untrustworthy in itself, which seem collectively to confirm it. I call this the wigwam argument: each pole would fall down by itself, but together the poles stand up, by leaning on each other; they point roughly in the same direction, and circumscribe truth.
Ibid., pp. 19–20.

8 Methodologically I am trying a new tack by experimenting at length with lies, whereas most Roman history is purportedly aimed at the discovery of truths, through establishing facts or describing events which are known to have occurred. This article is built around a single source, which is an inventive fiction, a pack of lies, an anonymous accretive novella, composed and revised, as I suspect, over centuries, as a vehicle for comedy and manners . . . My objective here is to illustrate my underlying contention that the social history which can be squeezed from 'real histories' and from fiction may be broadly similar, and that, for the interpretation of culture, there is little justification for privileging one above the other.
'Novel evidence for Roman slavery', Past & Present, 138 (1993), pp. 3–4.

JONES, A.H.M. (1904–70)

The chief problem of ancient economic history is one that I hesitate **1**
to confess before a mixed audience – an audience, that is to say,
containing modern historians and perhaps even economists – lest
ancient history should be brought into disrepute. However, it is
unlikely that I shall long be able to conceal the ignominious truth, that
there are no ancient statistics.
Ancient Economic History, London, H.K. Lewis, 1948, p. 1.

I do not therefore despair of ancient economic history. It can never **2**
be science comparable to modern economic history, yielding more
or less accurately measured quantitative results. But one can hope to
discern in general outline the economic trends which prevailed in
different areas in successive periods, the main sources of wealth and
its distribution among different classes, the relative importance of
agriculture, manufacture and trade, and the general lines on which
these activities were organized. And one can hope to discover these
things, not by attempting to apply to the ancient world a technique
which is. owing to the nature of the evidence, inapplicable, but by
analysing from an economic angle the evidence which is available.
Ibid., pp. 10–11.

Many modern historians, it seems to me, have too readily assumed **3**
that Roman citizens obeyed the law, and that everything was done as
the imperial government directed. My own impression is that many, if
not most, laws were intermittently and sporadically enforced, and that
their chief evidential value is to prove that the abuses which they were
intended to remove were known to the central government. The laws,
in my view, are clues to the difficulties of the empire, and records of
the aspirations of the government and not its achievement.
The Later Roman Empire 284–602, Oxford, Basil Blackwell, 1964, p. viii.

MACMULLEN, RAMSAY (1928–)

Romans, of course, not only built bridges but beat their wives. **1**
Enemies of the Roman Order: treason, unrest, and alienation in the Empire,
Cambridge Mass., Harvard University Press, 1966, p. v. Copyright © 1966
by the President and Fellows of Harvard College. All rights reserved.

Paganism

2   Was every one of these many gods just an invention? And did the whole structure of belief that we have surveyed thus rest at last on pure delusion? A challenge to be taken seriously. As superstition, so-called by some, much of that whole survives today; much (a little changed) receives attention daily in the newspaper, for readers who see stars. Historians, however, moved by some natural persuasion or by the dictates of their craft, pretend a terrible impiety. They must pretend, not that the gods lived and ruled, but that they did not exist – yet served.

Paganism in the Roman Empire, New Haven and London, Yale University Press, 1981, p. 49.

3   Metaphors have their uses, also their deceits. Paganism died, agreed – like the last stegosaurus or like a coral reef? . . .

     Upon those upper parts [of paganism] our account has naturally focused, because they were the most visible in the surviving record. They were also the most fragile. Like a coral reef, to live and grow further, they required conditions favourable within quite narrow limits. When conditions changed, life and growth must end. The more substantial, older, primitive parts of the pyramid of beliefs, however, lying at a level below the reach of our inquiry, died more slowly – just when, no record declares.

Ibid., pp. 131, 136.

Epigraphy

4   Modern scholars of the Roman world will say that this or that activity or behaviour was prominent, vital, declining or the like according to the frequency of epigraphic attestation. That assumes, however, that the body of all inscriptions against which attestation is measured does not itself rise or fall – a false assumption. So administrative, economic, social, and religious history need to be rewritten . . .

'The epigraphic habit in the Roman empire', *American Journal of Philology*, 103 (1982), p. 244. Copyright © 1982 The Johns Hopkins University Press.

5   Apparently the rise and fall of the epigraphic habit was controlled by what we can only call the sense of audience. In the exercise of the habit, people (I can only suppose) counted on their world still continuing in existence for a long time to come, so as to make nearly permanent memorials worthwhile; and they still felt themselves

members of a special civilization, proud (or obliged) to behave as such. Later, in not bothering any more to record on stone their names or any other claim to attention, perhaps they expressed their doubts about the permanence or importance of that world. Perhaps. At least I cannot see in the evidence anything less than the sign of some very broad psychological shift.
Ibid., p. 246.

Social history

Sometimes it is possible to catch people of the past doing their own   **6**
generalizing for us. They may do this in fiction, when authors try to present a situation that would easily be believed by their readers, and weave in details felt to be applicable throughout their own world. Or they may do this in predictions, as astrologers, dream-diviners, and seers: to stay in business, such practitioners had to deal in probabilities. Or again, we can apply a sort of 'association test' to written sources of all kinds, through the study of pairs of words or pairs of ideas: 'rich and honored,' 'rustic and cloddish,' 'paupers and criminals.'

Such, amongst others, are the devices that must be resorted to in any attempt to understand social feelings and the sense of place in antiquity. But the task is very difficult.
Roman Social Relations 50 BC to AD 284, New Haven and London, Yale University Press, 1974, pp. x–xi.

No doubt in some nineteenth-century commentary on Cicero's   **7**
speeches there is a learned essay on displays of feeling by Romans; but I have not discovered it. The history of manners is in our century entirely out of fashion. Without knowledge of manners, however, we cannot picture people in action in the mind's eye, and our reconstruction of event and motive will be to that extent false.
'Romans in tears', *Classical Philology*, 75 (1980), p. 254. Reprinted by permission of University of Chicago Press.

The necessary numbers cannot be developed from available sources to   **8**
prove a striving quality x per cent greater among Romans or a saving quality y per cent greater among the Protestant bourgeoisie than among other contemporary groups. We must be content with the observed phenomena (whether or not, results): the troops under arms or the capital accumulated.
'Roman elite motivation: three questions', *Past & Present*, 88 (1980), pp. 9–10.

Let me at the start divide the historian's facts or data into two   **9**

kinds, for convenience termed 'irrational' and 'sensible'. By the first, I mean whatever data lie inside the mind, apart from reasoning itself: therefore, passion, emotion, prejudice, mood, personality, ideals. By the sensible, I mean whatever data lie outside the mind . . . The characteristic weight and ease of handling that we discover in sensible data carry over into those debates by which historians, using such material, determine the truths they can agree on. Of course the material may be totally lacking, or reports of it erroneous, hence controversy and uncertainty; but to the extent that it is available, conflicting interpretations can always be resolved.
Ibid., pp. 12–13.

10 What Veyne is trying to do, and in the field of ancient history today no one does it better, is to invite our serious attention to the irrational. But he must do it through tricks not normally employed by historians, offering for instance a purely imaginary street scene with its hooting mob, and merely asserting what is pleasant or unpleasant, unsupported by the usual scholarly citations.

But these and similar tricks are needed because, in the effort to make clear why people in the past behaved as they did, plain prose suffices to replicate sensible motives in the reader's mind, but not the irrational ones. The latter must rather be stimulated through the novelist's, playwright's or poet's skill. They must be evoked through a street scene, by Veyne, or through a scene in a theatre, by John Chrysostom. Language must be used that touches, stirs, or makes the spine tingle. Only then will the written account yield those moments of marvellous illumination in which at last the reader realizes: '*That's* how it was! *Now* I can see!'.

If advances in our understanding of the sensible evidence from the past appear to be so hard-won nowadays and so seldom on a satisfactory scale, our concentration rather on the irrational would involve a radical change in the nature of serious historiography. Let us return to a problem already touched on: historians' disagreements. Would one reconstruction, one richly worded evocation, have to be pitted against another? And judges of 'what really happened' (in Ranke's famous phrase) would somehow have to compare them, and somehow empathetically decide which one felt more likely to be true? And would not scholars have to adopt approaches very hard to contemplate: the consulting of their own emotions as they study the past; the reading of fiction, even of anthropology; the use of adjectives and other touches of colour in their arguments?
Ibid., p. 15.

The necessary effort of historical imagination is not easily made, at the **11** remove of two thousand years. Across so great an interval, of course very little of the heat of human affairs can ever be felt; yet the heat of feelings is what accounts for most of human behaviour, after all. Or so it seems to me. On the other hand, across the interval, nothing of the folly is lost; and the more rational the observer, the greater his impatience with the sort of persons I have been examining.
'Hellenizing the Romans (2nd century B.C.)', *Historia*, 40 (1991), p. 437.

MARX, KARL (1818–83)

On history

The history of all hitherto existing society is the history of class **1** struggles.

Freeman and slave, patrician and plebeian, lord and serf, guild-master and journeyman, in a word, oppressor and oppressed, stood in constant opposition to one another, carried on an uninterrupted, now hidden, now open fight, a fight that each time ended, either in a revolutionary re-constitution of society at large, or in the common ruin of the contending classes.

In the earlier epochs of history, we find almost everywhere a complicated arrangement of society into various orders, a manifold gradation of social rank. In ancient Rome we have patricians, knights, plebeians, slaves; in the Middle Ages, feudal lords, vassals, guild-masters, journeymen, apprentices, serfs; in almost all of these classes, again, subordinate gradations.

The modern bourgeois society that has sprouted from the ruins of feudal society has not done away with class antagonisms. It has but established new classes, new conditions of oppression, new forms of struggle in place of the old ones.

Our epoch, the epoch of the bourgeoisie, possesses, however, this distinctive feature: it has simplified the class antagonisms. Society as a whole is more and more splitting up into two great hostile camps, into two classes directly facing each other: Bourgeoisie and Proletariat.
Karl Marx & Frederick Engels, *Manifesto of the Communist Party* [1848], in *Selected Works in One Volume*, London, Lawrence & Wishart, 1968, pp. 35–6.

Hegel remarks somewhere that all facts and personages of great **2** importance in world history occur, as it were, twice. He forgot to add: the first time as tragedy, the second as farce.
The Eighteenth Brumaire of Louis Bonaparte [1852], in *Selected Works*, p. 93.

3   Men make their own history, but they do not make it just as they please; they do not make it under circumstances chosen by themselves, but under circumstances directly encountered, given and transmitted from the past. The tradition of all the dead generations weighs like a nightmare on the brain of the living. And just when they seem engaged in revolutionising themselves and things, in creating something that has never yet existed, precisely in such periods of revolutionary crisis they anxiously conjure up the spirits of the past to their service and borrow from them names, battle-cries and costumes in order to present the new scene of world history in this time-honoured disguise and this borrowed language. Thus Luther donned the mask of the Apostle Paul, the revolution of 1789 to 1814 draped itself alternately as the Roman Republic and the Roman Empire, and the revolution of 1848 knew nothing better to do than to parody, now 1789, now the revolutionary tradition of 1793 to 1795.
Ibid.

Historical materialism

4   One thing is clear: the Middle Ages could not live on Catholicism, nor could the ancient world on politics. On the contrary, it is the manner in which they gained their livelihood which explains why in one case politics, in the other case Catholicism, played the chief part.
Capital Vol. I, trans. B. Fowkes, London, New Left Books, 1976, p. 176 n. 35.

5   In direct contrast to German philosophy which descends from heaven to earth, here it is a matter of ascending from earth to heaven. That is to say, not of setting out from what men say, imagine, conceive, not from men as narrated, thought of, imagine, conceived, in order to arrive at men in the flesh; but setting out from real, active men, and on the basis of their real life-process demonstrating the development of the ideological reflexes and echoes of this life-process. The phantoms formed in the brains of men are also, necessarily, sublimates of their material life-process, which is empirically verifiable and bound to material premises. Morality, religion, metaphysics, and all the rest of ideology as well as the forms of consciousness corresponding to these, thus no longer retain the semblance of independence. They have no history, no development; but men, developing their material production and their material intercourse, alter, along with this their actual world, also their thinking and the products of their thinking. It is not consciousness that determines life, but life that determines consciousness.

Marx and Engels, *The German Ideology* [1845–6], in *Marx-Engels Collected Works Volume V*, London, Lawrence & Wishart, 1976, pp. 36–7.

We must begin by stating the first premise of all human existence and, **6** therefore, of all history, the premise, namely, that men must be in a position to live in order to be able to 'make history'. But life involves before everything else eating and drinking, housing, clothing and various other things. The first historical act is thus the production of the means to satisfy these needs, the production of material life itself. Ibid., pp. 41–2.

In the social production of their existence, men inevitably enter into **7** definite relations, which are independent of their will, namely rela- tions of production appropriate to a given stage in the development of their material forces of production. The totality of these relations of production constitutes the economic structure of society, the real foundation, on which arises a legal and political superstructure and to which correspond definite forms of social consciousness. The mode of production of material life conditions the general process of social, political and intellectual life. Preface to *A Contribution to the Critique of Political Economy* [1859], in *Selected Works*, p. 173.

On classical antiquity

The real meaning of Aristotle's definition [of man, as a political **8** animal] is that man is by nature citizen of a town. This is quite as characteristic of classical antiquity as Franklin's definition of man as a tool-making animal is characteristic of Yankeedom. *Capital I*, p. 444 n.7.

The materials and means of labour, a proportion of which consists of **9** the products of previous work, play their part in every labour process in every age and in all circumstances. If, therefore, I label them 'capital' in the confident knowledge that 'semper aliquid haeret', then I have proved that the existence of capital is an eternal law of nature of human production and that the Xinghiz who cuts down rushes with a knife he has stolen from a Russian so as to weave them together to make a canoe is just as true a capitalist as Herr von Rothschild. I could prove with equal facility that the Greeks and Romans celebrated communion because they drank wine and ate bread. *Capital Vol. I*, pp. 998–9.

10   In encyclopedias of classical antiquity one can read such nonsense as this: In the ancient world capital was fully developed 'except for the absence of the free worker and of a system of credit'. Mommsen too, in his History of Rome, commits one blunder after another in this respect.
Ibid., p. 271 n.2.

11   Because a form of production that does not correspond to the capitalist mode of production can be subsumed under its forms of revenue (and up to a certain point this is not incorrect), the illusion that capitalist relationships are the natural conditions of any mode of production is further reinforced.
Capital Vol. III, trans. D. Fernbach, London, New Left Books, 1981, p. 1015.

12   Do we never find in antiquity an inquiry into which form of landed property etc. is the most productive, creates the greatest wealth? Wealth does not appear as the aim of production, although Cato may well investigate which manner of cultivating a field brings the greatest rewards, and Brutus may even lend out his money at the best rates of interest. The question is always which mode of property creates the best citizens. Wealth appears as an end in itself only among the few commercial peoples – monopolists of the carrying trade – who live in the pores of the ancient world, like the Jews in medieval society.
Grundrisse [1857–8], trans. M. Nicolaus, London, New Left Books, 1973, p. 487.

13   The Roman slave was held by chains; the wage-labourer is bound to his owner by invisible threads.
Capital Vol. I, p. 719.

14   It is well known that Greek mythology is not only the arsenal of Greek art but also its foundation. Is the view of nature and of social relations on which the Greek imagination and hence Greek [mythology] is based possible with self-acting mule spindles and railways and locomotives and electrical telegraphs? What chance has Vulcan against Roberts & Co., Jupiter against the lightning-rod and Hermes against the Crédit Mobilier? All mythology overcomes and dominates and shapes the forms of nature in the imagination and by the imagination; it therefore vanishes with the advent of real mastery over them. What becomes of Fama alongside Printing House Square? Greek art presupposes Greek mythology . . . Hence, in no way a social development which excludes all mythological, all mythologizing relations to nature; which therefore demands of the artist an imagination not dependent on mythology.

From another side: is Achilles possible with powder and lead? Or the *Iliad* with the printing press, not to mention the printing machine? Do not the song and the saga and the muse necessarily come to an end with the printer's bar, hence do not the necessary conditions of epic poetry vanish?

But the difficult lies not in understanding that the Greek arts and epic are bound up with certain forms of social development. The difficulty is that they still afford us artistic pleasure and that in a certain respect they count as a norm and as an unattainable model.
Grundrisse, pp. 110–11.

MEYER, EDUARD (1855–1930)

If the serfdom of the aristocratic epoch of antiquity, of the Homeric **1** period, corresponds to the economic relations of the Christian middle ages, just so *the slavery of the following epoch stands on the same level as the free labor of the modern age.*
'Die Sklaverei im Altertum', in *Kleine Schriften zur Geschichtstheorie und zur wirtschaftsliche und politischen Geschichte des Altertums*, Halle, 2nd edn 1922, Vol. I, pp. 169–212 n.38.

The later period of antiquity was in essence entirely modern. **2**
'Die wirtschaftliche Entwicklung des Altertums', in *Kleine Schriften*, Halle, 1922, Vol. I., p. 89.

Naturally modern research wishes to know far more about many **3** things than can be gleaned from Thucydides. We may be sorry or even critical that he set himself such narrow boundaries. In fact, one cannot apply an absolute standard here, only the subjective judgement of the historian; the way he views his craft can be the only decisive factor. The historian can, in this respect, claim the right not to be judged differently from the artist. He has fulfilled his task if he has successfully and without falsification described the historical process as it appears to him after conscientious research and sifting of facts. He has fulfilled his task if he has succeeded in creating the same impression in the reader as he himself has gained. Under these circumstances he cannot be reproached, even if the reader does not agree with his views.
Forschungen zur Alten Geschichte II: Zur Geschichte des 5. Jahrhunderts v. Chr. [1899], Hildesheim, Georg Olms, 1966, p. 378; trans. M. Smith.

4   Aristophanes' view that Pericles brought about war for personal
motives, because he could otherwise not have maintained his position,
has often enough been reiterated and will be repeated many more
times yet. In 1866 just such a view was expressed by Bismarck's
conservative and radical opponents and would have become mainstream, had that war proceeded like the Peloponnesian war.
Ibid., p. 302.

5   In Sparta, as elsewhere in the Peloponnese, there certainly existed,
especially amongst the young, a strong inclination towards war with
Athens. The reasons for this are well known: the propagandist
character of the Attic democracy, which must have had an attractive
and exciting effect everywhere, even if the Attic government kept
entirely in the background, just as all dissatisfied elements in the
Attic empire looked hopefully towards Sparta; the contrast between
lifestyles, education and military training, which meant that
Peloponnesian warriors, who had grown up with strict standards of
discipline, looked down contemptuously at the 'galleon-slaves'; and
above all the natural contrast between a population of farmers and
nobility, and a nation of shopkeepers and traders, which was felt to
create exploitation and material dependence everywhere.

   In our century the same contrast has developed between all
continental nations of Europe and America and the English. That
lasting peace could nevertheless have existed, is shown, however,
by this particular analogy. Moods alone do not lead to war where
reasonably stable conditions exist. They become a powerful driving
force, however, when an external spark is added, when serious
political differences appear and when the fortunes of war seem
favourable.
Ibid., p. 312.

MOMIGLIANO, ARNALDO (1908–87)

1   What do we want to know about the origins of Rome? Indeed why
should we want to know anything about them at all? Nobody, except
the specialist, cares very much about the origins of the Greeks or of
the Germans. Even the Nazis were unable to whip up a widespread
interest in German origins. But it seems to be part of our cultural
heritage to want to know the truth about the foundations of Rome,
just as we want to know the truth about the Hebrew exodus from
Egypt. The reason is of course that Jews and Romans had very definite
ideas about their own early history and attributed much importance to

them, whereas Greeks and (ancient) Germans had very confused ideas about their own past and never set much store by them. Since it was discovered that Jewish and Roman traditions cannot be accepted at their face value, attempts to put some other story in their place have never ceased. Such an interest does not necessarily lead to rational and worthwhile questions.

'Did Fabius Pictor lie?' [1965], in *Essays in Ancient and Modern Historiography*, Oxford, Basil Blackwell, 1977, p. 99.

Confucius, Buddha, Zoroaster, Isaiah, Heraclitus – or Aeschylus.   **2**

The list would probably have puzzled my grandfather and his generation. It makes sense now; it symbolizes the change in our historical perspective. We can face, more or less from the same angle, cultures which seemed wide apart; and we can find something in common among them. On a synchronous line the names stand for a more 'spiritual' life, for a better order, for a reinterpretation of the relation between gods and men, for a criticism of the traditional values in each respective society . . .

We are thus led to ask the historical questions that will interpret this relevance more precisely and consequently make it more perceptible. What conditioned the appearance of so many 'wise men' in so many different cultures within relatively narrow chronological limits? Why indeed did the cultural changes have to be brought about by 'wise men'? What is the relation between the religious stance they took and the social message they conveyed? The very nature of the questions that come spontaneously to our minds indicates that the essence of our new position towards these men is that instead of seeing *each* of them as the codifier of a new religion we now see *all* of them as reformers of the existing order. Our instinctive sympathy is for the human beings who by meditation and spiritual search freed themselves from the conventions within which they were born and reoriented the activities of other men. Though questions of truth can never be avoided entirely, we feel that it is almost indecent (and in any case too embarrassing) to ask whether what Zoroaster or Isaiah or Aeschylus had to say was true or false.

'The fault of the Greeks' [1975], in *Essays in Ancient and Modern Historiography*, pp. 9–10.

There is an old triangular culture – composed of Jewish, Greek   **3** and Latin intellectual products – which has an immediate impact on most of us that is of a quite different order from our professional or dilettante pleasure in the amenities of more distant civilizations . . . In

so far as our inheritance goes back to antiquity, it is essentially Greek-Latin-Jewish *because* it is essentially Hellenistic.
Ibid., p. 11.

4 Once again we have come up against the dilemma of Hellenistic civilization. It had all the instruments for knowing other civilizations – except command of languages. It had all the marks of a conquering and ruling upper class – except faith in its own wisdom.
Alien Wisdom: the limits of Hellenization, Cambridge, CUP, 1975, p. 149.

5 The historian is now supposed to know more facts than are compatible with the short span of an ordinary human life. He must know about statistics, technical developments, the subconscious and unconscious, savages and apes, mystical experiences and middle town facts of life: besides that he must make up his mind about progress, liberty, moral conscience, because the philosophers are chary in these matters.
'A hundred years after Ranke' [1954], in *Studies in Historiography*, London, Weidenfeld & Nicolson, 1966, p. 109.

6 History is always a choice of facts fitting into a static or dynamic situation which appears worth studying.
This characterization of historical research can be interpreted either pessimistically or optimistically. The pessimistic interpretation is that history-writing is selecting facts for a situation one envisages before having selected the facts. Consequently we shall find what we want to find because our initial hypothesis or model or idea will determine our choice of the facts . . .
I expect to modify my initial hypothesis or model as my research progresses; indeed the very selection of the facts will continuously be modified by the requirements of the research itself. Leaving aside for the moment the question of the relation between facts and evidence, historical research is controlled by the facts indicated by the evidence. In so far as evidence presents facts, facts are facts – and it is characteristic of the historian's profession to respect facts. The pessimist underrates the discipline to which the historian is submitted.
'Historicism revisited' [1974], in *Essays in Ancient and Modern Historiography*, pp. 367–8.

7 We study change *because* we are changeable. This gives us a direct experience of change: what we call memory. Because of change our

knowledge of change will never be final: the unexpected is infinite.
But our knowledge of change is real enough.
Ibid., p. 368.

Either we possess a religious or moral belief independent of history, **8**
which allows us to pronounce judgement on historical events, or we
must give up moral judging. Just because history teaches us how many
moral codes mankind has had, we cannot derive moral judgement
from history. Even the notion of transforming history by studying
history implies a meta-historical faith.
Ibid., p. 370.

MOMMSEN, THEODOR (1817–1903)

Scholarly writing is almost as corrupting a trade as play-acting. The **1**
great majority of one's colleagues are vulgar and petty and devoted to
the business of bringing those characteristics to ever fuller bloom.
Anyone who enters it with any idealistic notions will have a hard time
controlling his disgust and hatred.
Letter to Wilamovitz, May 18 1878; quoted in Ramsay MacMullen, *Changes
in the Roman Empire: essays in the ordinary*, Princeton, Princeton University
Press, 1990, p. 26. Reprinted by permission of Princeton University Press.

The distinction between ancient and modern history, therefore, is no **2**
mere accident, nor yet a mere matter of chronological convenience.
What is called modern history is in reality the formation of a new
cycle of culture, connected at several epochs of its development with
the perishing or perished civilization of the Mediterranean states . . .
It too is destined to experience in full measure vicissitudes of national
weal and woe, periods of growth, of full vigour, and of age, the
blessedness of creative effort, in religion, polity, and art, the comfort
of enjoying the material and intellectual acquisitions it has won,
perhaps also, some day, the decay of productive power in the satiety
of contentment with the goal attained. But that goal too will only be
temporary: the grandest system of civilization has its orbit, and may
complete its course; but not so the human race, to which, even when
it seems to have attained its goal, the old task is ever set anew with a
wider range and with a deeper meaning.
The History of Rome [1856], trans. W.P. Dickson, London, Richard Bentley,
1864, Vol. I. p. 4.

The story of the foundation of Rome by refugees from Alba under the **3** leadership of the sons of an Alban prince, Romulus and Remus, is nothing but a naïve attempt of primitive quasi-history to explain the singular circumstance that the place should have arisen on a site so unfavourable, and to connect at the same time the origin of Rome with the general metropolis of Latium. Such tales, which claim the name of history, but which are merely improvised explanations of no very ingenious character, it is the first duty of history to discuss.

Ibid., Vol. I p. 48.

4   In consequence of the one-sided prominence assigned to capital in the Roman economy, the evils inseparable from a pure capitalist system could not fail to appear . . . A further consequence of the one-sided power of capital was the disproportionate prominence of those branches of business which were the most sterile and least productive to the national economy as a whole. Industrial art, which ought to have held the highest place, in fact occupied the lowest. Commerce flourished; but it was universally non reciprocal.

Ibid., Vol. II pp. 386–7.

5   The system of mercantile and moneyed speculation appears to have been established in the first instance by the Greeks, and to have been simply adopted by the Romans. Yet the precision with which it was carried out and the magnitude of the scale on which its operations were conducted were so peculiarly Roman, that the spirit of the Roman economy and its grandeur whether for good or evil are pre-eminently conspicuous in its monetary transactions.

Ibid., Vol. II p. 378.

6   Thus there arose the new political economy, which desisted from the taxation of the burgesses, but regarded the body of subjects, on the other hand, as a profitable possession of the community, which it partly worked out for the public benefit, partly handed over to be worked out by the burgesses. Not only was free scope allowed with criminal indulgence to the unscrupulous greed of the Roman merchant in the provincial administration, but even the commercial rivals who were disagreeable to him were cleared away by the armies of the state, and the most glorious cities of the neighbouring lands were sacrificed, not to the barbarism of the lust of power, but to the far more horrible barbarism of speculation.

Ibid., Vol. III pp. 68–9.

If we conceive of England with its lords, its squires and above all its **7** city, but with its freeholders and farmers converted into proletarians, and its labourers and sailors converted into slaves, we shall gain an approximate image of the population of the Italian peninsula in those days.
Ibid., Vol. III p. 412.

If we try to conceive to ourselves a London with the slave-population **8** of New Orleans, with the police of Constantinople, with the non-industrial character of the modern Rome, and agitated by politics after the fashion of Paris in 1848, we shall acquire an approximate idea of the republican glory, the departure of which Cicero and his associates in their sulky letters deplore.
Ibid., Vol. IV pp. 501–2.

Riches and misery in close league drove the Italians out of Italy, and **9** filled the peninsula partly with swarms of slaves, partly with awful silence. It is a terrible picture, but not one peculiar to Italy; wherever the government of capitalists in a slave-state has fully developed itself, it has desolated God's fair world in the same way. As rivers glisten in different colours, but a common sewer everywhere looks like itself, so the Italy of the Ciceronian epoch resembles substantially the Hellas of Polybius and still more decidedly the Carthage of Hannibal's time, where in exactly similar fashion the all-powerful rule of capital ruined the middle class, raised trade and estate-farming to the highest prosperity, and ultimately led to a – hypocritically whitewashed – moral and political corruption of the nation. All the arrant sins that capital has been guilty of against nation and civilisation in the modern world, remain as far inferior to the abominations of the ancient capitalist-states as the free man, be he ever so poor, remains superior to the slave; and not until the dragon-seed of North America ripens, will the world have again similar fruits to reap.
Ibid., Vol. IV p. 521.

Such was this unique man [Caesar], whom it seems so easy and yet is **10** so infinitely difficult to describe. His whole nature is transparent clearness; and tradition preserves more copious and more vivid information regarding him than regarding any of his peers in the ancient world. Of such a person our conceptions may well vary in point of shallowness or depth, but they cannot be, strictly speaking, different; to every not utterly perverted inquirer the grand figure has exhibited the same essential features, and yet no one has succeeded in reproducing it to the life. The secret lies in its perfection. In his character as a man as well as in his place in history, Caesar occupies a place where the great contrasts of existence meet and balance each other. Of the mightiest creative powers and yet at the same time of the most penetrating judgement; no longer a youth and not yet an old man; of the highest energy of will and the highest capacity of execution; filled with republican ideals and at the same time born to be a king; a Roman in the deepest essence of his nature, and yet called to reconcile and combine in himself as well as in the outer world the Roman and the Hellenic types of culture – Caesar was the entire and perfect man. Accordingly we miss in him more than in any other historical personage what are called characteristic features, which are in reality nothing else than deviations from the natural course of human development.

History of Rome, Vol. IV.ii pp. 456–7.

11   Much might be said about the modern tone. I wanted to bring down the ancients from the fantastic pedestal on which they appear into the real world. That is why the consul had to become the burgomeister. Perhaps I have overdone it; but my intention was sound enough.

Letter to Henzen, quoted in G.P. Gooch, *History and Historians in the Nineteenth Century*, London, Longmans, Green & Co., 1920, p. 457.

NIEBUHR, B.G. (1776–1831)

1   The History of Rome was treated, during the first two centuries after the revival of letters, with the same prostration of the understanding and judgement to the written letter that had been handed down, and with the same fearfulness of going beyond it, which prevailed in all other branches of knowledge. If any one had pretended to examine into the credibility of the ancient writers, and the value of their testimony, an outcry would have been raised against such atrocious presumption. The object aimed at was, in spite of everything like internal evidence, to combine what they related. At the utmost one authority was made in some one particular instance to give way to another; and this was done as mildly as possible, and without leading to any further results.

History of Rome [1811–13], trans. J.C. Hare & C. Thirlwall, London, Walton & Maberly, 1855–60, Vol. I p. v.

2   Previous ages had been content to look at the ancient historians in the way many look at maps or landscapes, as if they were all in all; without

ever attempting to employ them as the only remaining means for producing an image of the objects they represent. But now a work on such subjects could not be esteemed satisfactory, unless its clearness and distinctness enabled it to take its stand beside the history of the present age.
Ibid., p. ix.

That we do not understand the ancients, unless we frame distinct **3** notions of such objects of their everyday life, as we have in common with them, under the forms their eyes were accustomed to; that we should go totally astray, if (as the middle ages did, and, since so many things were still unchanged, might do without being equally deceived) we too, on reading of a Roman house, a Roman ship, Roman agriculture and trade, Roman dress, or the interior of a household in ancient Rome, conceived the same notions which answer to these words in our own days – this everybody must feel.
Ibid., p. xx

The aborigines are portrayed by Sallust and Virgil as hordes of savages, **4** without manners, without laws, without agriculture, living on the produce of the chase, and on wild fruits. This probably is nothing but an ancient speculative view of the manner in which mankind advanced to civilization out of a state of animal rudeness; of the same kind with those philosophical histories, as they were called, with which we were surfeited during the latter half of the last century, more so however by the writers of other countries than those of Germany, and in which even the state of brute speechlessness was not forgotten. The pages of these observing philosophers swarm with quotations from books of travels. One point however they have overlookt, that not a single instance can be produced of a really savage people which has become civilized of its own accord, and that, where civilization has been forced upon such a people from without, the physical decay of the race has ensued . . . For every race of men has received its destination assigned to it by God, with the character which is suited to it and stamps it. The social state too, as Aristotle wisely remarks, is prior to its individual members; the whole prior to the part. The mistake of these speculators is their not perceiving that the savage is either a degenerate race, or was but half human from the first.
Ibid., pp. 82–3.

Between the purely poetical age, the relation of which to history is **5** altogether irrational, and the thoroughly historical age, there intervenes in all nations a mixt age, which, if one wishes to designate it by a single word, may be called the mythico-historical. It has no precise limits, but comes down to the point where contemporary history begins: and its character is the more strongly markt, the richer the nation has been in heroic lays, and the fewer the writers who have attempted to fill up the void in its history by the help of monuments and authentic documents, without paying attention to those lays, or trying to call up in their minds any distinct image of the past.

Ibid., p. 247.

6   Though history however rejects the incident as demonstrably false, it is well suited to the legend: and every legend which was current among the people long before the rise of literature among them, is itself a living memorial of ancient times, – even though its contents may not be so, – and deserves a place in a history of Rome written with a due love for the subject.

Ibid., Vol. II p. 530.

7   In judging of the morality of past ages, we must not form an opinion from the views familiar to ourselves, but from a knowledge of what was praiseworthy or at least allowable according to the feelings of the age in which the action took place.

Ibid., Vol. III p. 20.

8   It is a piece of philosophical ratiocination, the correctness of which is decidedly contradicted by a true knowledge of history, that the value of a conquest is never equal to the price of its cost and the loss of men calculated as national property. The former may be true in regard to the prosperity of the citizens of the conquering state, if the burthen of taxation and the corresponding diminution of property are considerable: the latter is false, if the nation remains flourishing, and the prosperous condition, which has been gained by conquests, not only of commerce but of the national power and importance gives it a life, by which the diminisht population easily raises itself even much higher than it could have attained without this transitory expenditure.

Ibid., Vol. III pp. 614–15.

NIETZSCHE, FRIEDRICH (1844–1900)

Ancient and modern

We moderns have an advantage over the Greeks in two ideas, which **1** are given as it were as a compensation to a world behaving thoroughly slavishly and yet at the same time anxiously eschewing the word 'slave': we talk of the 'dignity of man' and of the 'dignity of labour' . . . The Greeks did not require such conceptual hallucinations, for among them the idea that labour is a disgrace is expressed with startling frankness; and another piece of wisdom, more hidden and less articulate, but everywhere alive, added that the human thing was also an ignominious and piteous nothing and the 'dream of a shadow'. Labour is a disgrace, because existence has no value in itself; but even though this very existence in the alluring embellishment of artistic illusions shines forth and really seems to have a value in itself, then that proposition is still valid that labour is a disgrace – a disgrace indeed by the fact that it is impossible for man, fighting for the continuance of bare existence, to become an *artist*.

'The Greek state' [1871], in *Early Greek Philosophy and Other Essays*, trans. M.A. Mügge, London, George Allen & Unwin, 1911, pp. 3–4.

The satyr, like the idyllic shepherd of more recent times, is the **2** offspring of a longing for the primitive and the natural; but how firmly and fearlessly the Greek embraced the man of the woods, and how timorously and mawkishly modern man dallied with the faltering image of a sentimental, flute-playing, tender shepherd! Nature, as yet unchanged by knowledge, with the bolts of culture still unbroken – this is what the Greek saw in his satyr who nevertheless was not a mere ape. On the contrary, the satyr was the archetype of man, the embodiment of his highest and most intense emotions, the ecstatic reveler enraptured by the proximity of the god, the sympathetic companion in whom the suffering of the god is repeated, one who proclaims wisdom from the very heart of nature, a symbol of the sexual omnipotence of nature which the Greeks used to contemplate with reverent wonder.

The Birth of Tragedy [1872], trans. W.A. Haussman, London, George Allen & Unwin, 1909, p. 63.

On classical scholarship

I do not know what meaning classical scholarship may have for our **3** time except in its being 'unseasonable' – that is, contrary to our time,

and yet with an influence on it for the benefit, it may be hoped, of a future time.
'The use and abuse of history' [1874], in *Thoughts Out Of Season Part II*, trans. A. Collins, London, George Allen & Unwin, 1909, p. 5.

4 A historical phenomenon, completely understood and reduced to an item of knowledge, is, in relation to the man who knows it, dead: for he has found out its madness, its injustice, its blind passion, and especially the earthly and darkened horizon that was the source of its power for history. This power has now become, for him who has recognised it, powerless; not yet, perhaps, for him who is alive.
Ibid., p. 15.

5 Man must have the strength to break up the past; and apply it too, in order to live. He must bring the past to the bar of judgement, interrogate it remorselessly, and finally condemn it. Every past is worth condemning: this is the rule in mortal affairs, which always contain a large measure of human power and human weakness.
Ibid., p. 28.

6 Philology as the science of antiquity does not, of course, endure for ever; its elements are not inexhaustible. What cannot be exhausted, however, is the ever-new adaptation of one's age to antiquity; the comparison of the two. If we make it our task to understand our own age better by means of antiquity, then our task will be an everlasting one. This is the antimony of philology: people have always endeavoured to understand antiquity by means of the present – and shall the present now be understood by means of antiquity? Better: people have explained antiquity to themselves out of their own experiences; and from the amount of antiquity thus acquired they have assessed the value of their experiences.
We Philologists [1874], trans. J.M. Kennedy, in O. Levy (ed.), *Complete Works Vol. VIII: The Case of Wagner*, London, George Allen & Unwin, 1911, pp. 112–13.

7 It is difficult to justify the preference for antiquity since it has arisen from prejudices:

1. From ignorance of all non-classical antiquity.
2. From a false idealisation of humanitarianism, whilst Hindoos and Chinese are at all events more humane.
3. From the pretensions of school-teachers.

4. From the traditional admiration which emanated from antiquity itself.
5. From opposition to the Christian church; or as a support for this church.
6. From the impression created by the century-long work of the philologists, and the nature of this work: it must be a gold mine, thinks the spectator.
7. The acquirement of knowledge attained as the result of the study. The preparatory school of science.

In short, partly from ignorance, wrong impressions, and misleading conclusions; and also from the interest which philologists have in raising their science to a high level in the estimation of laymen.
Ibid., p. 127.

Education is in the first place instruction in what is necessary, and then **8** in what is changing and inconstant. The youth is introduced to nature, and the sway of laws is everywhere pointed out to him; followed by an explanation of the laws of ordinary society. Even at this early stage the question will arise: was it absolutely necessary that this should have been so? He gradually comes to need history to ascertain how these things have been brought about. He learns at the same time, however, that they may be changed into something else. What is the extent of man's power over things? This is the question in connection with all education. To show how things may become other than what they are we may, for example, point to the Greeks. We need the Romans to show how things became what they were.
Ibid., p. 185.

ROBERT, LOUIS (1904–85)

The preceding pages have already been able to show what inscriptions **1** bring to history. The main point is not what they can provide for political history, today called 'history of events'. Certainly that is not negligible . . . However, it is social history, in the broadest sense of the word, which profits the most from inscriptions and which, often, exists only through them.
'L'épigraphie' [1961], in *Opera Minora Selecta Vol. V*, Amsterdam, Hakkert, 1989, p. 78; trans. N. Morley.

Two dangers lie in wait for the historian with regard to inscriptions: **2** not to make use of them, or to do it badly.

It is not rare for historians of antiquity to have a certain attitude, well-considered or not: they feel or believe themselves to be assailed and besieged by what they call the 'auxiliary sciences', that is to say by the disciplines which study the sources which are the only means by which the historical documentation of antiquity is renewed; epigraphy, numismatics, papyrology, archaeology. They can then make a sort of passive resistance and practically ignore this flood of new documents in order to cling to the traditional historical texts, trying to renew them by paradoxes or by investigating them in excessive detail through which they are dissolved . . .

The lack of familiarity with epigraphy can be marked by another attitude, which can also be due to a lack of spirit among certain historian-epigraphists: under-interrogating the inscriptions, asking of each of them more than it can tell, generalizing unduly, interpolating. It is necessary to know when to stop in the interpretation of an inscription.

Ibid., p. 84.

ROSTOVTZEFF, M.I. (1870–1952)

1   The creation of a uniform world-wide civilization and of similar social and economic conditions is now going on before our eyes over the whole expanse of the civilized world. This process is complicated, and it is often difficult to clear up our minds about it. We ought therefore to keep in view that this condition in which we are living is not new, and that the ancient world also lived, for a series of centuries, a life which was uniform in culture and politics, in social and economic conditions. The modern development, in this sense, differs from the ancient only in quantity and not in quality.
A History of the Ancient World, trans. J.D. Duff, Oxford, OUP, 1926, Vol. I p. 10. First published in Russian.

2   In close connexion with other departments of human knowledge, history tends to become more and more a science, whose end is to define the laws under which the life of man develops, and the regular process by which one type of communal life is displaced by another. Nevertheless, history still remains a branch of literature, because the narrative of events and the lively and picturesque transmission of them, together with the truthful and artistic delineation of important historical characters, will always remain one of the historian's chief tasks, a task of a purely literary and artistic nature. While becoming

more and more a department of exact science, history cannot and must not lose its literary, and therefore individual, character.
Ibid., pp. 6–7.

The illustrations which I have added to the text are not intended to   3
amuse or to please the reader. They are an essential part of the book, as essential, in fact, as the notes and the quotations from literary or documentary sources. They are drawn from the large store of archae-ological evidence, which for a student of social and economic life is as important and as indispensable as the written evidence. Some of my inferences and conclusions are largely based on archaeological material.
The Social and Economic History of the Roman Empire, Oxford, OUP, 2nd edn 1957, p. xvii.

Never before had so considerable a part of Europe, Asia and Africa   4
presented an aspect so civilized, so modern, one may say, in its essential features.
Ibid., p. 139.

The importance of the upper class of the city bourgeoisie cannot be   5
exaggerated. It was this class that gave the empire its brilliant aspect, and it was this class that practically ruled it.
Ibid., p. 190.

The impression conveyed by our sources is that the splendour of the   6
cities was created by, and existed for, a rather small minority of their population; that the welfare even of this small minority was based on comparatively weak foundations; that the large masses of the city population had either a very moderate income or lived in extreme poverty. In a word, we must not exaggerate the wealth of the cities: their external aspect is misleading.
Ibid., p. 190.

The existence of two classes, one ever more oppressed, the other ever   7
more idle and indulging in the easy life of men of means, lay like an incubus on the Empire and arrested economic progress. All the efforts of the emperors to raise the lower classes into a working and active middle class were futile. The imperial power rested on the privileged classes, and the privileged classes were bound in a very short time to sink into sloth. The creation of new cities meant in truth the creation of new hives of drones.
Ibid., p. 380.

8 Can we be sure that representative government is the cause of the brilliant development of our civilization and not one of its aspects, as was the Greek city state? Have we the slightest reason to believe that modern democracy is a guarantee of continuous and uninterrupted progress, and is capable of preventing civil war from breaking out under the fostering influence of hatred and envy? Let us not forget that the most modern political and social theories suggest that democracy is an antiquated institution, being the offspring of capitalism, and that the only just form of government is the dictatorship of the proletariate, which means a complete destruction of civil liberty and imposes on one and all the single ideal of material welfare, and of equalitarianism founded on material welfare.
Ibid., pp. 536–7.

9 Why was the victorious advance of capitalism stopped? Why was machinery not invented? Why were the business systems not perfected? Why were the primal forces of primitive economy not overcome? They were gradually disappearing; why did they not disappear completely? To say that they were quantitatively stronger than in our own time does not help us to explain the main phenomenon.
Ibid., p. 538.

10 While appreciating the importance of the social and economic aspect of human life in general, I do not overestimate it, in the Marxian fashion . . . I have, however, kept before me as a guiding principle, in this as in the other historical works which I have written, the maxim that the complexity of life should never be forgotten and that no single feature should ever be regarded as basic and decisive.
The Social and Economic History of the Hellenistic World, Oxford, OUP, 1941, p. viii.

11 Within the great monarchical states (other than Macedonia) the rulers never succeeded in attaining stabilization and consolidation. They never found a way of escape from the great antimony in the political, social, and economic life of their dominions, to which the conquest of Alexander had given rise; the conflict between the two leading forms of civilized life, the Eastern and the Western, between Greek city-states and Oriental monarchies – between Greek 'politai' and Oriental subjects; between the Greek economic system, based on freedom and private initiative, and the State economy of the East, supervised, guided, and controlled. And finally they were faced with

the great eternal problem of human society, as acute in the ancient world as it is in the modern: the antimony between the rulers and the ruled, the 'haves' and the 'have-nots', the *bourgeoisie* and the working classes, the city and the country.
Ibid., p. 1031.

Some of my readers may feel that the description that I have given   **12**
of the urban *bourgeoisie* is too glowing and too flattering . . . They certainly were selfish, their conception of life was materialistic, their ideals somewhat distasteful, and their morality low. What they wanted was a quiet and easy life of pleasure, with the minimum of work and worry. They showed very little interest in the state or in religion. Their main endeavour was to increase their material possessions and to bequeath them to their posterity . . .

This picture is certainly a true one, though a little exaggerated. But its fundamental elements apply, to a certain extent, to the *bourgeoisie* of all times and of all countries. It does not contradict and is not irreconcilable with that which I have drawn above. No human beings are perfect, and the *bourgeoisie* of Hellenistic times was no exception to that rule. Moreover, as time went on, it deteriorated even further in respect of its failings. And yet what I have said of its ultimate role in the destinies of Greece is exact. It was in the main the Hellenistic *bourgeoisie* which preserved – for good or for evil – the leading traits of Greek city life and bequeathed them, with the sanction of their own support, to posterity.
Ibid., pp. 1125–6.

SYME, RONALD (1903–89)

The design has imposed a pessimistic and truculent tone, to the almost   **1**
complete exclusion of the gentler emotions and the domestic virtues. Δυναμις and Τυχη are the presiding divinities. The style is likewise direct and even abrupt, avoiding metaphors and abstractions. It is surely time for some reaction from the 'traditional' and conventional view of the period. Much that has recently been written about Augustus is simply panegyric, whether ingenuous or edifying. Yet it is not necessary to praise political success or to idealize the men who win wealth and honours through civil war.
The Roman Revolution, Oxford, OUP, 1939, p. viii.

The greatest of the Roman historians began his *Annals* with the   **2**
accession to the Principate of Tiberius, stepson and son by adoption

of Augustus, consort in his powers. Not until that day was the funeral of the Free State consummated in solemn and legal ceremony. The corpse had long been dead.
Ibid., p. 1.

3   But it is not enough to redeem Augustus from panegyric and revive the testimony of the vanquished cause. That would merely substitute one form of biography for another. At its worst, biography is flat and schematic: at the best, it is often baffled by the discords of human nature. Moreover, undue insistence upon the character and exploits of a single person invests history with dramatic unity at the expense of truth.
Ibid., p. 7.

4   The inquest may now begin. After a political catastrophe, why not turn round and inculpate the political system? A facile escape. It was denied to the Romans. The Republic was the very essence of Rome.
'A Roman post-mortem: an inquest on the fall of the Roman republic' [1950], in Syme, *Roman Papers Volume I*, E. Badian (ed.), Oxford, OUP, 1979, p. 206.

5   In his ordering of the Commonwealth Augustus appealed to the Republican past. No Roman could have acted otherwise. Not only were all new things detested, and tradition worshipped. Archaism, ever a highly respectable tendency, acquired new strength in the years of change – for archaism was an escape and a reaction from the present.
'History and language at Rome' [1974], in Syme, *Roman Papers Volume III*, A.R. Birley (ed.), Oxford, OUP, 1984, p. 960.

6   Diligence and accuracy (it is averred) are the only merits an historian can properly ascribe to himself. The one virtue does not always guarantee the other. The more documentation, the more chances of error. Further, time and scrutiny will reveal misconceptions as well as mistakes. The record being one of scraps and pieces, with many of the agents little better than names, and momentous transactions buried in deep obscurity, reconstruction is hazardous. But conjecture cannot be avoided, otherwise the history is not worth writing, for it does not become intelligible.
Tacitus, Oxford, OUP, 1958, p. v.

7   The ample oratorical manner which had recently been brought to perfection by Cicero was admirably designed to beguile and persuade

an audience: it dealt in generous commonplaces, facile oppositions between right and wrong, and high-minded appeals to vulgar emotion. Roman history originated in the register of bare events before eloquence was known; and, when Roman history came to its maturity in an epoch saturated and nauseated with political oratory, it fought ruthlessly to get at the facts behind the words. Smooth phrases were suspect, their authors in discredit. A plain, hard, and broken style seemed to convey a serious guarantee of incorruptible veracity.
Ibid., p. 135.

VERNANT, JEAN-PIERRE (1914–)

The advent of the *polis*, the birth of philosophy – the two sequences of **1** phenomena are so closely linked that the origin of rational thought must be seen as bound up with the social and mental structures peculiar to the Greek city.
The Origins of Greek Thought, Ithaca, Cornell University Press, 1982, p. 130. First published in French in 1962 by Presses Universitaires de France.

The writings which have come to us from Ancient Greek civilization **2** embody ideas sufficiently different from those expressed in the framework of our own intellectual universe to make us feel, not only a historical distance, but also an awareness of a fundamental change in man. At the same time, these ideas are not as alien to us as are some others. They have come down to us through an uninterrupted process of transmission. They live on in cultural traditions to which we constantly refer. The Greeks are sufficiently distant for us to be able to study them as an external subject, quite separate from ourselves, to which the psychological categories of today cannot be applied with any precision. And yet they are sufficiently close for us to be able to communicate with them without too much difficulty.
Myth and Thought amongst the Greeks, London, Boston, Melbourne and Henley, Routledge & Kegan Paul, 1983, p. x. First published in French in 1965.

In Greece, we do not find one single type of behavior, namely, work, **3** in all spheres from agriculture to commerce, but, rather, different forms of activity which seem to us to be organized in almost totally contrasting manners. Even within agriculture an opposition is drawn between the effects of the earth's natural fertility and the human efforts of the labourer. But, taken as a whole, agricultural activities are contrasted with the activities of the artisan, as natural production to technical manufacture. And, in their turn, the works of the artisans are classed with the products of the soil in the natural economy that conforms with the immutable order of men's needs. When contrasted with the making of money, which has no more than a conventional value, the work of the artisan, too, is seen as a part of nature.

Thus, in the activities of the farmers and artisans, the human aspect of work is apparent without ever quite being identified as such. On the whole, man does not feel he is transforming nature, but rather conforming to it. In this respect, commerce is, in a way, scandalous, both for intellectual and moral reasons.

Ibid., pp. 262–3.

4   For the Greeks of the fifth century acting did not mean making objects or transforming nature. It meant influencing men, overcoming them, dominating them. Within the framework of the city, speech was the instrument most necessary for action and mastery of it gave you power over others. The Sophists' reflections on human *technè*, on the means of extending one's power and perfecting one's tools, led to neither technological thinking nor to a philosophy of technology. They led to rhetoric and they established dialectic and logic.

Ibid., p. 295.

5   We may well wonder whether it is really possible today to maintain this opposition between cold societies frozen in immobility, and hot ones at grips with history. All societies, to a greater or lesser degree, experience changes which their myths reflect, integrating or digesting them in their own particular ways.

Myth and Society in Ancient Greece, trans. J. Lloyd, Sussex, Harvester, 1980, p. 238. First published in French in 1974.

6   In the historian's perspective, psychological history has been presented as part of a whole, as one element juxtaposed to others. The psychological was placed alongside the technical, the economic, the social, the political, and so forth. It had in some sense its own sphere of existence, requiring a new branch of specialized history: the history of mentalities or of collective psychology. For the psychologist, on the contrary, psychological history . . . has to be conducted from within each of the areas explored by the different specialists. The psychological no longer seems external to the works but rather is present in each and every one of them.

Mortals and Immortals: collected essays, F.I. Zeitlin (ed.), Princeton, Princeton University Press, 1991, p. 268. Copyright © 1991 by Vernant, J.-P. Reprinted by permission of Princeton University Press.

VEYNE, PAUL (1930–)

History is a true novel. A reply that at first sight seems innocuous. **1**
Writing History: essay on epistemology, trans. M. Moore-Rinvolucri, Manchester, Manchester University Press, 1984, p. x. First published in French in 1971.

History is anecdotal, it interests only by recounting, as the novel does. **2**
It differs from the novel on only one essential point. Let us suppose I am being told about a riot and that I know that the intention of this account is to tell me some history that happened at a given moment, to a given people. I shall take as a heroine the ancient nation that was unknown to me a minute before, and it will become for me the center of the story (or, rather, its indispensable support). And this is what the novel reader does. Except that here the novel is true, which does away with the need for it to be exciting. The history of the riot can afford to be boring without losing its value.
Ibid., p. 11.

There is no method of history, because history makes no demands; so **3**
long as one relates true things, it is satisfied. It seeks only truth, unlike science, which seeks exactness. It imposes no norms; no rule of the game subtends it, nothing is unacceptable to it.
Ibid., p. 12.

The historian can dwell for ten pages on one day and pass over ten **4**
years in two lines; the reader will trust him, as he trusts a good novelist, and will presume that those ten years were uneventful.
Ibid., pp. 17–18.

The gulf that separates ancient historiography, with its narrowly **5**
political point of view, from our economic and social history is enormous, but it is no greater than the one that separates history today from what it might be tomorrow.
Ibid., p. 25.

'Facts' do not exist in isolation: the historian finds them organized in **6**
wholes in which they act as causes, objectives, opportunities, risks, pretexts, and so on. Our own existence, after all, does not appear to us as a grisaille of atomic incidents; it immediately has a meaning, and we understand it. Why should the position of the historian be more Kafka-like? History is made of the same substance as the lives of each of us.

Facts thus have a natural organization that the historian finds ready-made, once he has chosen his subject.
Ibid., p. 31.

7   Then what are the facts worthy of rousing the interest of the historian? All depends on the plot chosen; in itself, a fact is not interesting or uninteresting.
Ibid., p. 33.

8   The type or the theory can thus be useful only in shortening a description; enlightened despotism or town-country conflict is spoken of in order to deal quickly with, as we say 'war' instead of 'armed conflict between powers'. Theories, types, and concepts are one and the same thing: ready-made summaries of plots. Thus, it is useless to prescribe for historians the construction or utilization of theories or of types; they have always done this, they could not do anything else, save not saying a single word, and that doesn't get them any further.
Ibid., p. 122.

9   But why would it not be possible to raise history to the height of a science, since the facts that make up history and our life are subject to the jurisdiction of science and its laws? Because there are laws *in* history (a body falling in the account of a historian obviously conforms to Galileo's law) but not laws *of* history; the course of the Fourth Crusade is not determined by a law.
Ibid., p. 236.

10   History, a few millennia ago, made a bad start. It has never completely freed itself of its social function, that of perpetuating the memory of the life of peoples or of kings.
Ibid., p. 282.

11   History is what documents make of it, history is what the conventions of the genre make of it, unknown to us.
Ibid., p. 289.

12   There is no such thing as historical method. A historical fact can be explained, and consequently described, only by applying to it sociology, political theory, anthropology, economics, and so on. It would be useless to speculate about what might be the historical explanation of an event that could differ from its 'sociological' explanation, its scientific, true explanation.

Bread and Circuses: historical sociology and political pluralism, trans. B. Pearce, Harmondsworth, Penguin/Allen Lane, 1990, p. 2. First published in French in 1976 by Editions de Seuil.

On one point, however, the difference between history and sociology **13** is considerable, and that is what endows history with its specificity. For a sociologist, historical events are only examples (or 'guinea-pigs'). He is not called upon to list all the examples, without exception, that could illustrate one of the generalities that are the true subject of his science. If he constructs the ideal type of 'monarchy by absolute right', he will quote, perhaps, two or three examples (Rome, the *ancien régime*), but not *every* possible example. He does not have to quote Ethiopia as well. For the historian, however, events are not examples, but the actual subject of his science. He cannot leave out any of them, just as a zoologist has to compile the complete inventory of all living species, and an astronomer will not overlook even the least of the galaxies. The historian therefore must talk about Ethiopia, and there have to be historians who specialize in Ethiopian history. They will talk about it in exactly the same terms as a sociologist would, *if* he were to talk about it – but *they* will definitely talk about it.
Ibid., p. 3.

The theme of this book was very simple. Merely by reading the title, **14** anyone with the slightest historical background would immediately have answered, 'But of course they believed in their myths!' We have simply wanted also to make it clear that what is true of 'them' is also true of ourselves and to bring out the implications of this primary truth.

Did the Greeks Believe in their Myths? An essay on the constitutive imagination, trans. P. Wissing, Chicago and London, University of Chicago Press, 1988, pp. 128–9. First published in French in 1983. Copyright © 1988 by The University of Chicago.

VIDAL-NAQUET, PIERRE (1930–)

The latest research, so far from making the historian's choice easier, **1** simply makes it more painful, because every historian today knows that what he studies is properly speaking neither the unique nor the universal – even if the universalism of the 'human mind' has replaced Frazer's empirical universalism. We all know as historians that the truth of the history of a Breton village is not to be found in the simple history of a Breton village; but also that the diverse metahistories which crowd us, from a more or less refurbished Marxism to psychoanalysis, from the philosophy of the price-curve to that of universal logic, will never relieve us of the obligation to get back to our village.

'Recipes for Greek adolescence', trans. R.L. Gordon, in Gordon (ed.), *Myth, Religion and Society*, Cambridge, CUP, and Paris, Editions de la Maison des Sciences de l'Homme, 1981, p. 169. First published as 'Le Cru, l'enfant grec et le cuit', in J. Le Goff & P. Nora (eds), *Faire de l'Histoire*, Paris, Gallimard, 1973.

2   The historian is condemned at every moment to define his contexts, and the contexts of his contexts; his definitions are always provisional – 'Greek culture' is a context, but a potentially illusory one if one isolates the Greek world from the Thracian world or the Illyrian, to say nothing of the Mediterranean context; he is doomed to operate simultaneously on the spatial and on the temporal axes; and if he adopts provisionally 'universal' categories like the Raw or the Cooked, it is always to make them dynamic.

Ibid., p. 170.

3   Replacing history by myth is a procedure that would hardly be dangerous if there were an absolute criterion allowing one to distinguish at first sight between the two. It is the distinguishing feature of a lie to want to pass itself off as the truth.

Assassins of Memory: essays on the denial of the Holocaust, trans. J. Mehlman, New York, Columbia University Press, 1992, pp. 50–1. First published in French in 1987.

4   I grew up with an exalted – some will say a megalomaniacal – conception of the historian's work. That is how I was raised, and it was during the war that my father had me read Chateaubriand's famous article in the *Mercure* of July 4, 1877: 'When, in the silence of abjection, all one can hear is the slave's chains and the traitor's voice, when all tremble before the tyrant, and it is as dangerous to incur his favor as to fall from his grace, the historian appears, charged with the vengeance of peoples'. I still believe in the necessity of memory and attempt, in my own way, to be a memory-man, but I no longer believe that the historian is charged with the vengeance of peoples.

Ibid., pp. 57–8.

5   Who can regret the historian's loss of innocence, the fact that he has been taken as an object or that he takes himself as an object of study?

It remains the case nonetheless that if historical discourse is not connected – by as many intermediate links as one likes – to what may be called, for lack of a better term, reality, we may still be immersed in discourse, but such discourse would no longer be historical.
Ibid., pp. 110–11.

WEBER, MAX (1864–1920)

An ideal type is achieved by the one-sided *accentuation* of one or more **1** points of view and by the synthesis of a great many diffuse, discrete, more or less present and occasionally absent *concrete individual* phenomena, which are arranged according to those one-sidedly emphasised viewpoints into a unified *analytical* construct. In its conceptual purity, this mental construct cannot be found empirically anywhere in reality. It is a *utopia*. Historical research faces the task of determining in each individual case, the extent to which this ideal construct approximates to or diverges from reality.
The Methodology of the Social Sciences [essays from 1903–17], trans. E.A. Shils & H.A. Finch, New York, The Free Press, 1949, p. 90. Copyright © 1949 by The Free Press; copyright renewed 1977 by Edward A. Shils.

The city

A genuinely analytical study comparing the stages of development of **2** the ancient polis with those of the medieval city would be welcome and productive . . . Of course I say this on the assumption that such a comparative study would not aim at finding 'analogies' and 'parallels' . . . The aim should, rather, be precisely the opposite: to identify and define the individuality of each development, the characteristics which made the one conclude in a manner so different from the other. This done, one can then determine the causes which led to those differences.
The Agrarian Sociology of Ancient Civilizations, trans. R.I. Frank, London, New Left Books, 1976, p. 385. First published in German in 1909.

Similar to the city of the prince, the inhabitants of which are eco- **3** nomically dependent upon the purchasing power of noble households, are cities in which the purchasing power of other larger consumers, such as rentiers, determines the economic opportunities of resident tradesmen and merchants . . .

It hardly needs to be mentioned that actual cities nearly always represent mixed types. Thus, if cities are to be economically classified at all, it must be in terms of their prevailing economic conditions.

The City, trans. D. Martindale & G. Neuwirth, New York, The Free Press, 1958, pp. 68, 70. First published in German in 1921. Copyright © 1958, copyright renewed 1986 by The Free Press.

4   As in the case of the medieval city, the primary orientation of ancient city politics was around the needs of city consumption. However the rigidity of policy was much greater in Antiquity since it was impossible for cities such as Athens and Rome to provide for their grain needs through private traders alone. To be sure there were also occasional traces of an ancient city production policy as when profiteering was sanctioned for some important forms of exports. However, these phenomena were incidental rather than central: ancient economic policy was not primarily concerned with industrial production nor was the polis dominated by the concerns of producers.
Ibid., p. 208.

Ancient society

5   Today the concept of 'capitalistic enterprise' is generally based on this last form, the large firm run with free wage-labour, because it is this form which is responsible for the characteristic social problems of modern capitalism. From this point of view it has been argued that capitalistic economy did not play a dominant role in Antiquity, and did not in fact exist. However, to accept this premise is to limit needlessly the concept of capitalist economy to a single form of valorization of capital – the exploitation of other people's labour on a contractual basis – and thus to introduce social factors. Instead we should take into account only economic factors. Where we find that property is an object of trade and is utilized by individuals for profit-making enterprise in a market economy, there we have capitalism. If this be accepted, then it becomes perfectly clear that capitalism shaped whole periods of Antiquity, and indeed precisely those periods we call 'golden ages'.
Agrarian Sociology, pp. 50–1.

6   To sum up, the most important hindrance to the development of capitalism in Antiquity arose from the political and economic characteristics of ancient society. The latter, to recapitulate, included: (1) the limits on market production imposed by the narrow bounds within which land transport of goods was economically feasible; (2) the inherently unstable structure and function of capital; (3) the

technical limits to the exploitation of slave labour in large enterprises and (4) the limited degree to which cost accounting was possible.
Ibid., pp. 65–6.

Ancient capitalism was suffocated because the Roman empire resorted **7** increasingly to status-liturgy and partly also to public want satisfaction . . . Conversely, during the Middle Ages and in early modern times, the trade and colonial monopolies at first facilitated the rise of capitalism, since under the given conditions only monopolies provided a sufficient profit span for capitalist enterprises.
Economy and Society, G. Roth & C. Wittich (eds), Berkeley, Los Angeles and London, University of California Press, 1968, p. 351. First published in German in 1922.

Thus the framework of ancient civilization weakened and then **8** collapsed, and the intellectual life of Western Europe sank into a long darkness. Yet its fall was like that of Antaeus, who drew new strength from Mother Earth each time he returned to it. Certainly, if one of the classic authors could have awoken from a manuscript in a monastery and looked out at the world of Carolingian times, he would have found it strange indeed. An odour of dung from the courtyard would have assailed his nostrils.

But of course no Greek or Roman authors appeared. They slept in hibernation, as did all civilization, in an economic world that had once again become rural in character. Nor were the classics remembered when the troubadours and tournaments of feudal society appeared. It was only when the mediaeval city developed out of free division of labour and commercial exchange, when the transition to a natural economy made possible the development of burgher freedoms, and when the bonds imposed by outer and inner feudal authorities were cast off, that – like Antaeus – the classical giants regained a new power, and the cultural heritage of Antiquity revived in the light of modern bourgeois civilization.
Agrarian Sociology, pp. 410–11.

Status

'Status' shall mean an effective claim to social esteem in terms of **9** positive or negative privileges; it is typically founded on (a) style of life, hence (b) formal education, which may be (α) empirical training or (β) rational instruction, and the corresponding forms of behavior, (c) hereditary or occupational prestige. In practice, status expresses

itself through (α) connubium (β) commensality, possibly (γ) monopolistic appropriation of privileged modes of acquisition or the abhorrence of certain kinds of acquisition, (δ) status conventions (traditions) of other kinds.
Economy and Society, pp. 305–6.

10   Every status society lives by conventions, which regulate the style of life, and hence creates economically irrational consumption patterns and fetters the free market through monopolistic appropriation and by curbing the individual's earning power.
Ibid., p. 307.

11   In contrast to classes, *Stände* [status groups] are normally groups. They are, however, often of an amorphous kind. In contrast to the purely economically determined 'class situation' we wish to designate as 'status situations' every typical component of the life fate of men that is determined by a specific, positive or negative, social estimation of *honour* . . . In content, status honour is normally expressed by the fact that above all else a specific *style of life* can be expected from all those who wish to belong to the circle.
Ibid., p. 932.

12   The market and its processes knows no personal distinctions: 'functional' interests dominate it. It knows nothing of honour. The status order means precisely the reverse: stratification in terms of honour and styles of life peculiar to status groups as such. The status order would be threatened at its very root if mere economic acquisition and naked economic power still bearing the stigma of its extra-status origin could bestow upon anyone who has won them the same or even greater honour as the vested interests claim for themselves.
Ibid., p. 936.

NAME INDEX

SUBJECT INDEX